CONTENTS AT A GLANCE

TABLE OF CONTENTS

OS X®
Mountain Lion
Tips and Tricks

JASON R. RICH

OS X® MOUNTAIN LION TIPS AND TRICKS

ISBN-13: 978-0-7897-4991-8
ISBN-10: 0-7897-4991-2

The Library of Congress Cataloging-in-Publication Data is on file.

Printed in the United States of America

First Printing: September 2012

TRADEMARKS

All terms mentioned in this book that are known to be trademarks or service marks have been appropriately capitalized. Que Publishing cannot attest to the accuracy of this information. Use of a term in this book should not be regarded as affecting the validity of any trademark or service mark.

WARNING AND DISCLAIMER

BULK SALES

Que Publishing offers excellent discounts on this book when ordered in quantity for bulk purchases or special sales. For more information, please contact

U.S. Corporate and Government Sales

1-800-382-3419

corpsales@pearsontechgroup.com

For sales outside of the U.S., please contact

International Sales

international@pearsoned.com

EDITOR-IN-CHIEF
Greg Wiegand

ACQUISITIONS EDITOR
Laura Norman

DEVELOPMENT AND COPY EDITOR
Keith Cline

MANAGING EDITOR
Sandra Schroeder

PROJECT EDITOR
Mandie Frank

INDEXER
Tim Wright

PROOFREADER
Leslie Joseph

TECHNICAL EDITOR
Jennifer Ackerman-Kettell

EDITORIAL ASSISTANT
Cindy Teeters

DESIGNER
Anne Jones

COMPOSITOR
Tricia Bronkella

ABOUT THE AUTHOR

Jason R. Rich (www.JasonRich.com) is the bestselling author of more than 54 books, as well as a frequent contributor to a handful of major daily newspapers, national magazines, and popular websites. He is also an accomplished photographer and an avid Apple iMac, MacBook Air, iPhone, iPad, and Apple TV user.

Some of his other recently published books include: *Your iPad At Work: 2nd Edition* (Que), *iPad and iPhone Tips and Tricks* (Que), *Your iPad At Work: 3rd Edition* (coming soon from Que), *How To Do Everything MacBook Air* (McGraw-Hill), *How To Do Everything Digital Photography* (McGraw-Hill), and *How To Do Everything Kindle Fire* (McGraw-Hill).

You can read more than 90 free feature-length "how to" articles by Jason R. Rich that cover the Apple iPhone and iPad at the Que Publishing website. Visit www. iOSArticles.com and click on the 'Articles' tab. Also, please follow Jason R. Rich on Twitter (@JasonRich7).

DEDICATION

This book is dedicated to the late Steve Jobs, as well as my baby niece Natalie, who will no doubt be part of the next generation of Apple users.

ACKNOWLEDGMENTS

Thanks to Laura Norman at Que Publishing for inviting me to work on this book, and for all of her guidance as I've worked on this project. My sincere gratitude also goes out to Romny French, Greg Wiegand, Mandie Frank, Cindy Teeters, Keith Cline, and Jennifer Ackerman-Kettell, as well as everyone else at Que Publishing and Pearson who contributed their expertise, hard work, and creativity to the creation of *OS X® Mountain Lion Tips and Tricks*.

Thanks also to my friends and family for their ongoing support. Finally, thanks to you, the reader. I hope this book helps you take full advantage of the power and capabilities of your Mac that's running the latest OS X® Mountain Lion operating system. If you're also an iPhone or iPad user, please consider reading my companion book, *iPad and iPhone Tips & Tricks*, which follows that same easy-to-read and information-packed format as this book, but covers the iOS 5.1 operating system for use with your Apple mobile device.

WE WANT TO HEAR FROM YOU!

As the reader of this book, *you* are our most important critic and commentator. We value your opinion and want to know what we're doing right, what we could do better, what areas you'd like to see us publish in, and any other words of wisdom you're willing to pass our way.

We welcome your comments. You can email or write to let us know what you did or didn't like about this book—as well as what we can do to make our books better.

Please note that we cannot help you with technical problems related to the topic of this book.

When you write, please be sure to include this book's title and author as well as your name and email address. We will carefully review your comments and share them with the author and editors who worked on the book.

Email: feedback@quepublishing.com

Mail: Que Publishing
ATTN: Reader Feedback
800 East 96th Street
Indianapolis, IN 46240 USA

READER SERVICES

Visit our website and register this book at quepublishing.com/register for convenient access to any updates, downloads, or errata that might be available for this book.

Introduction

Did you know that mountain lions are solitary animals? They go by many names, like cougar, panther, and puma, and they're considered highly efficient predators. Mountain lions have an average life span of about 12 years, and a male can grow to 8 feet in length and weigh upward of 165 pounds.

There are only about 30,000 actual mountain lions left in the western United States, and the Florida panther is considered critically endangered. This is mainly due to hunting, habitat loss, and poaching.

Oh wait! You picked up a copy of this book to learn about OS X Mountain Lion, Apple's proprietary operating system that runs on all Mac computers. Here in the United States and throughout the world, Mountain Lion users are a fast-growing population consisting of computer users from all walks of life.

When it comes to computers, Mountain Lion's biggest threat is Microsoft Windows, but Apple is making steady strides toward driving Windows users into extinction. This is because Mountain Lion is easy to use, packed with features, offers a close-to virus-free computing experience, and it provides the tools most people need to efficiently handle all their computing needs—whether they're sitting at a desk using an iMac, or they're on the go handling their computing tasks on a cutting-edge MacBook Air or MacBook Pro notebook computer.

If you've just purchased a new Mac, Mountain Lion came preinstalled on your computer. However, if you've been using a Mac for a while and it's currently running Snow Leopard or Lion, you'll need to visit the online-based App Store and spend just $19.99 to upgrade to what Apple refers to as "Our best OS [operating system] yet."

📝 **NOTE** You'll discover exactly how to upgrade your Mac to Mountain Lion within Chapter 1, "Upgrading to Mountain Lion."

What you'll discover when you begin using Mountain Lion are more than 200 new features and functions, including several new and useful apps that have been added to the extensive selection of apps that come with OS X. You'll also discover enhancements and a new look for apps you're probably already familiar with. For example, Address Book is now called Contacts, and iCal is now called Calendar. Both of these apps, as well as many of the other core apps that come with Mountain Lion, offer full integration with the operating system itself, other apps, and with Apple's iCloud service (which you'll learn more about shortly).

Many of the new features added to Mountain Lion will help you save time, become more efficient using your Mac, be able to more easily communicate and share information with other people, and better organize your data, files, documents, pictures, and multimedia content.

In fact, Mountain Lion can also change how to interact with the computer itself. Instead of just using the keyboard to enter data, as well as the mouse to navigate around, Mountain Lion allows you to take full advantage of Apple's Magic Mouse or Multi-Touch trackpad and utilize a series of finger gestures to more effectively work with your Mac.

Plus, using the new Dictation feature, instead of manually typing information into your computer, you have the option to speak directly to your Mac (using its built-in microphone) and have it translate what you say into text, and then insert that text into the app you're using. And, when it comes to sharing information, most apps now have a Share button.

Use the Share button to send app-specific content to others via email, message, Facebook, or Twitter, for example, from within the app you're currently using. Of course, you can still run multiple apps simultaneously on your Mac and easily switch between them, plus quickly locate and access specific files, folders, documents, or data using the enhanced Finder and Spotlight Search features built in to Mountain Lion.

To help quickly get you up-to-speed when it comes to upgrading your Mac to Mountain Lion, and then discover how to take full advantage of its most useful features and functions, *OS X Mountain Lion Tips and Tricks* is chock full of easy-to-understand and easy-to-implement information written specifically for non-technologically savvy people.

Each chapter of *OS X Mountain Lion Tips and Tricks* focuses on one aspect of Apple's latest operating system, or on the apps that come bundled with it. From this book, you'll learn strategies that'll help you best utilize your Mac and quickly become proficient using it.

You'll also learn how to share your data, documents, files, photos, and content with your other computers and mobile devices, including the Apple iPhone, iPad, and iPod touch, as well as with other people (even if they're using a Windows-based PC).

To draw your attention to important tidbits of information related to the specific topics you're reading about, throughout *OS X Mountain Lion Tips and Tricks* you'll notice Tip, Note, and Caution boxes. Plus, full-color screenshots are used to help more effectively explain how to use specific features and functions of the Mountain Lion operating system.

> **NOTE** Unless otherwise noted, throughout this book, the term *Mac* refers to any iMac, Mac Pro, Mac mini, MacBook Pro, or MacBook Air computer model, because all run the same operating system.

So, whether you're a first-time Mac user or someone who has been using a Mac for a while and is just now upgrading to Mountain Lion, this book will serve as an information-packed resource.

The 16 chapters that comprise this book cover just about everything you need to know to get up and running with the Mountain Lion operating system and the apps that come with it. From this book, you'll also learn how to expand your Mac with additional apps and peripherals to enhance the capabilities of what your computer is capable of.

Thanks to Mountain Lion, there's never been a better time to own and use a Mac, regardless of what you use your computer for.

UPGRADING TO MOUNTAIN LION

In July 2012, Apple introduced OS X Mountain Lion, a new version of its operating system that runs on all Mac models, including the various iMac, Mac Pro, Mac mini, MacBook Air, and MacBook Pro computers.

This latest edition of the operating system boasts more than 200 new features that are designed to make your Mac easier to use and allow the apps that come preinstalled with Mountain Lion to exchange data between each other and to integrate seamlessly with the Apple iCloud service.

The Mountain Lion operating system has been inspired by the iPad. So, many of the features and functions built in to it, and the preinstalled apps that come with it, now more fully utilize either the Mac's Magic Mouse or a multitouch trackpad, enabling you to interact with your computer using finger gestures and motions.

> **NOTE** Throughout this book, reference to a *Mac* includes any Mac model from Apple capable of running the Mountain Lion operating system, such as an iMac, Mac Pro, MacBook, MacBook Pro, MacBook Air, or Mac mini.
>
> In addition, any references to the *App Store* refer to the Mac App Store (not to the separate iOS App Store through which Apple sells iPhone, iPad, and iPod touch apps). To access the Mac App Store from your Mac, you must use the App Store app that comes preinstalled with the OS X operating system. (Unlike the App Store for iOS mobile devices [iDevices], the Mac App Store is not accessible using the iTunes app.)

The interfaces of many of the preinstalled apps, including Contacts, Calendar, Reminders, Notes, Notification Center, Messages, FaceTime, and Game Center, now look and work very much like their iPad counterparts. Plus, thanks to iCloud, data between these and other apps can automatically be synchronized between your Macs and iDevices (including your iPad and iPhone).

> **NOTE** You'll learn all about most of the preinstalled apps that come with Mountain Lion later in this book. Plus, from later chapters, you'll discover hundreds of tips and strategies to better utilize the operating system and navigate around your Mac, regardless of which apps you're running.

Especially if you've recently purchased a new Mac, you'll discover that Mountain Lion improves the overall speed and performance of your computer. In addition, the new operating system makes it easier to create, find, utilize, share, and sync your app-specific data with your other computers or devices and with other people.

> **NOTE** Using iCloud, you can easily sync app-specific data from Contacts, Calendar, Reminders, Notes, Safari, Messages, and other preinstalled apps with your other Macs/iDevices.
>
> However, a Share icon is now built in to these and other apps, which enables you to share app-specific content or data with others via email, Messages, Facebook, Twitter, and other compatible services.

WHAT'S NEW IN MOUNTAIN LION

If you've been using an older version of the OS X operating system with your Mac (such as Snow Leopard or Lion), as soon as you upgrade to Mountain Lion you'll discover a number of significant changes and improvements.

For example, the Address Book app is now called Contacts and has been totally redesigned, as shown in Figure 1.1.

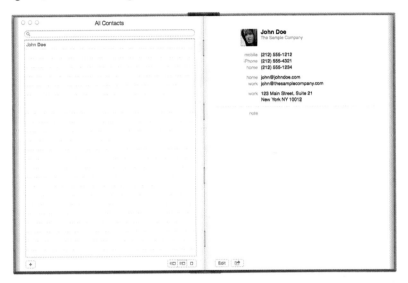

FIGURE 1.1

The Address Book app is now called Contacts, and it offers a new interface and many enhanced features, including easy-to-use iCloud integration.

Likewise, the iCal app that was used to manage your scheduling is now called Calendar, and it has also been revamped. Both apps now look and function more like their iPad counterparts and are more fully integrated with iCloud.

> **NOTE** All of your app-specific data, such as your Contacts database or schedule, that were created using Address Book / iCal are fully compatible with the Contacts and Calendar apps. However, if you have these new apps set up to sync data with iCloud, you can visit www.iCloud.com at anytime and access your app-specific databases using online versions of the apps. Just sign in to the iCloud.com website using your Apple ID and password (or iCloud account information).
>
> You'll learn more about iCloud in Chapter 11, "Navigating Around iCloud."

Just about all the apps that come preinstalled with Mountain Lion have some additional features or functionality. You'll also discover a handful of new apps that come preinstalled with the operating system that enable you to handle additional common computing tasks.

For example, the new Reminders app (shown in Figure 1.2) is a feature-packed to-do list manager. Using this app, you can create and manage a vast number of separate lists. Each list can have many separate items within it, plus each item can have a time/date-based alarm or a location-based alert associated with it. Also, all app-specific data can be synced via iCloud so that the data can automatically be shared with your other computers or iDevices.

FIGURE 1.2

The new Reminders app enables you to create and maintain multiple to-do lists simultaneously.

The new Messages app enables you to send and receive instant messages (and text messages) and easily communicate with other Mac or iDevice users using Apple's free iMessage service. This app also works with other instant messaging services, thus allowing you to connect with PC or Mac users, as well (who use AIM, Jabber, Google Talk, or Yahoo! Messenger).

If you enjoy playing single-player or multiplayer games on your Mac, the new Game Center app offers a portal to Apple's free online gaming service. From here, you can post details about your game scores, find people to play multiplayer games with, and learn about new Mac games.

Beyond offering new apps, Mountain Lion offers new features and functions that work with almost any app. For example, if you're using a MacBook Air or MacBook Pro, the new Power Nap feature lets you to conserve battery power when your computer isn't in use, even while apps and Internet connectivity still run in the background.

Because you're using many different apps with Mountain Lion, you'll find a new Share icon on the toolbar, as shown in Figure 1.3. The Share pop-up menu enables you to quickly share app-specific information with other people via a compatible online service such as email, Messages, Facebook, Twitter, or Flickr.

FIGURE 1.3

You can now find the Share icon in many apps. Use it to quickly share app-specific data with others via email, Messages, Facebook, Twitter, or another compatible service.

If you have an Apple TV device connected to your high-definition television, as well as a wireless network set up in your home or office, the AirPlay Mirroring feature enables you to stream whatever is displayed on your Mac's screen to your HD television set or monitor so that it can be shared with others. This can be done wirelessly.

Another exciting new feature that works with almost all Mac apps is called Dictation. Instead of typing text into an app using your keyboard, you can activate the Dictation feature and use your Mac's built-in microphone to speak into your computer. Mountain Lion automatically translates your speech into text and inserts it into the app you're using.

TIP To activate the Dictation feature when text needs to be entered into an app you're using, click the Dictation icon that is available within some apps, or choose Dictation from the Edit menu on the menu bar, or double-click the function (Fn) key on your keyboard.

The Dictation icon shown in Figure 1.4 will appear. Begin speaking. When you're finished, click the Done button. Your speech is then translated into text and inserted into the app you're using.

So, if you want to quickly send out a tweet to your Twitter followers from within the Notification Center panel, for example, click the Notification Center icon (on the menu bar), and then click the Twitter option that's displayed near the top of the Notification Center panel. When the Twitter window opens, activate the Dictation feature. Speak your 140-character message, click the Done button, and then click the Send button within the Twitter window to send the dictated message.

NOTE When using the Dictation feature, you can speak for up to 30 seconds at a time, have the computer translate your speech into text, and then repeat the process. As you're speaking, you can also add punctuation by saying it. To add a period at the end of a sentence, for example, say "This is a test of the Dictation feature period."

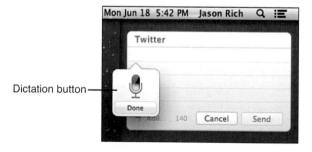

Dictation button

FIGURE 1.4

You can create and send a tweet via Twitter using the Dictation feature. This feature also works with almost any other app, such as Pages or Microsoft Word.

As you use your Mac that's running Mountain Lion, you'll also discover a broad range of new security and privacy features you can activate at your own discretion when using your computer and surfing the web. You can activate and customize many of these features within System Preferences by clicking the Security & Privacy option.

> **TIP**   Using the newly designed Parental Controls feature that's built in to Mountain Lion, you can set up a separate account for your children and thus control how they use your Mac. To set up and customize Parental Controls, launch System Preferences and select the Parental Controls option (shown in Figure 1.5).
>
> For example, you can control what apps they can use, what they can download, who they can communicate with online, and what types of content (such as apps, music, movies, TV shows, games, and so on) that they can access. You can also control how long they use the computer per day, and you can set the computer to lock your child out at bedtime.
>
> In addition, you'll also want to set up the separate Parental Controls features that are built in to the iTunes app to control what types of content your kids can purchase, download, and access via the iTunes Store. To do this, launch the iTunes app on your Mac, access the iTunes pull-down menu and select Preferences. Then, click the Parental tab near the top of the window. You can then disable certain types of content or add content restrictions for your kids.

FIGURE 1.5

If your kids will be using your Mac, consider activating and customizing the parental controls built in to Mountain Lion.

Another new Mountain Lion feature is called Notification Center. You'll learn more about it in Chapter 4, "Using Notification Center." This app continuously runs behind the scenes on your Mac and monitors a handful of other apps that you preselect. Whenever those apps or compatible online social networking sites (like Facebook or Twitter) generate an alert, alarm, or notification, they're collected and displayed within the Notification Center panel.

By customizing Notification Center, you determine which apps it monitors, how many alerts, alarms, or notifications it displays simultaneously for each app, and how the listings within the Notification Center panel are sorted and displayed. Then, as you're looking at the Notification Center panel, just click one of the listings to launch the appropriate app to view and deal with that specific alert, alarm, or notification.

> **TIP** Regardless of which app you're running, you can access the Notification Center panel by just clicking the new Notification Center icon that's continuously displayed in the upper-right corner of the screen as part of the menu bar. When you click this icon, the Notification Center panel displays along the right margin of the screen.
>
> In addition to displaying app-specific or website-specific alerts, alarms, and notifications generated by other apps, a Twitter button enables you to quickly compose and send a tweet without first launching a separate Twitter app or visiting Twitter.com.

Notification Center allows you to manage all the alerts, alarms, and notifications generated by your Mac (and the apps running on it) within one centralized location. Plus, if you need peace and quiet, you can turn on the Do Not Disturb feature. When you do this, Notification Center continues collecting the alerts, alarms, and notifications generated by your Mac, but it won't set off audible alarms or display them as alerts or banners until you turn off the Do Not Disturb feature.

> **TIP** To view a more comprehensive list of the more than 200 new features added to Mountain Lion, visit www.apple.com/osx/whats-new/features.html.

UPGRADE PREREQUISITES

Apple's latest operating system is designed to work on all currently available Mac, MacBook, and Mac mini models. If you purchased your new Mac after July 2012, it came with OS X Mountain Lion already installed, so there is no need to upgrade. (Updates to the operating system may, however, be available for download from the App Store by clicking the Updates button near the top-center of the App Store window.) When new Mountain Lion updates do become available, you will receive a notification.

> **NOTE** If you purchased a new Mac between June 11, 2012 and July 2012 (before the launch of Mountain Lion), your computer came with Lion preinstalled, but you're entitled to a free upgrade to Mountain Lion.

To upgrade your existing Mac to Mountain Lion, it must already be running Snow Leopard or Lion. To determine what version of OS X your Mac is currently running, click the Apple icon that displays in the upper-left corner of the screen (along the menu bar) and select the About This Mac option. Under the Apple logo, the OS X version number running on your Mac will be displayed.

> **TIP** To quickly determine whether you can upgrade your Mac to Mountain Lion, click the Apple icon in the upper-left of the menu bar and choose About This Mac. When the About This Mac window appears, click the More Info button. Near the top-right side of the About This Mac window, shown in Figure 1.6, the Mac model you're using will display.

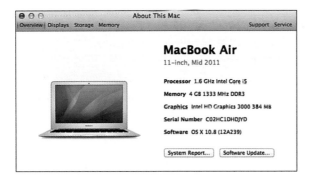

FIGURE 1.6

From the About This Mac window, you can quickly determine which model Mac you're using.

OS X 10.6.x represents Snow Leopard, and OS X 10.7.x represents Lion. If your Mac is running an even older version of the operating system (10.5.x or earlier), before upgrading to Mountain Lion you first need to upgrade to either Snow Leopard (10.6.8) or Lion.

Before purchasing, downloading, and installing Mountain Lion, be sure to create a backup of your entire computer using the Time Machine app that comes prein-stalled on your computer. See Chapter 12, "Backing Up Your Mac," for step-by-step directions for using Time Machine. Keep in mind that other third-party backup tools are available to you besides Time Machine.

CONFIRMING UPGRADE COMPATIBILITY

Unfortunately, some of the older Mac, Mac mini, and MacBook models are not compatible with Mountain Lion. Before attempting to upgrade your Mac, make sure your computer is one of the following:

- An iMac (desktop computer) purchased in mid-2007 or later
- An aluminum MacBook (notebook computer) purchased in late-2008 or later
- A MacBook (notebook computer) purchased in early-2009 or later
- A 13-inch MacBook Pro (notebook computer) purchased in 2009 or later
- A 15-inch or 17-inch MacBook Pro (notebook computer) purchased in mid-2007 or later
- A MacBook Air (notebook computer) purchased in late-2008 or later
- A Mac mini purchased in early-2009 or later
- A Mac Pro (desktop computer) purchased in early-2008 or later

You'll get the best performance from your Mac that's running Mountain Lion if it's a newer model with a fast processor, plenty of RAM, and adequate hard disk inter-nal storage space. At the bare minimum, your Mac must have at least 2GB of RAM memory and 8GB of available internal hard drive (or flash drive) storage space. Many of the operating system's new features also require access to the Internet to function properly.

Especially if you're using an older Mac, consider upgrading your computer's RAM / internal hard disk storage capacity. You can do so using third-party products. To find companies that sell Mac memory or hard drive upgrade kits, from any search engine enter the search phrase "Mac RAM Upgrade" or "Mac Hard Drive Upgrade." A Mac with 4GB or 8GB or RAM and plenty of free hard drive (flash drive) space will offer vastly better performance.

!CAUTION   If you have an older Mac that is currently incompatible with Mountain Lion, upgrading your computer's RAM or internal storage will not fix this. You'll need to purchase a newer computer to install Mountain Lion.

> **NOTE** Whereas Mac desktop computers and older MacBooks use tradi-
> tional hard drives, the newest MacBook Pro and MacBook Air models use internal
> flash drives. These flash drives give users greater flexibility when computing on
> the go. The computer autosaves your work, and you can simply close the com-
> puter to place it into Sleep (Power Nap) mode. Then, later, you can open the com-
> puter to wake it up and continue working from exactly where you left off.

PURCHASING, DOWNLOADING, AND INSTALLING

Assuming your Mac is upgradeable to Mountain Lion, connect your Mac to the
Internet, and then launch the App Store app. The App Store app comes preinstalled on your Mac and is used to access Apple's online-based store for purchasing, downloading, and installing new apps and software. You'll learn more about
the App Store in Chapter 9, "Installing New Software."

> **TIP** Just like most apps stored on your Mac, you can launch the App
> Store app from the Dock, Launchpad, or the Applications folder. You'll learn how
> to do this in Chapter 2, "Navigating Mountain Lion."

Once the App Store is running, click the listing for OS X Mountain Lion and purchase the upgrade. The one-time cost for the upgrade is $19.99. However, after the
upgrade has been purchased once, you can install it onto all of your Macs that are
linked to the same iCloud/Apple ID account.

> **TIP** To load Mountain Lion (after purchase) onto additional Macs that
> are linked to your Apple ID account without having to pay for the upgrade again,
> launch the App Store app on each of your other machines, and click the Purchases
> button that appears near the top-center of the App Store window. Look for the OS
> X Mountain Lion listing, and then click the Download button to the right of it.

After purchasing Mountain Lion from the App Store, follow the onscreen prompts
during the auto-installation process. Depending on the speed of your Internet
connection, the download process could take up 15 minutes (or longer). Then, the
auto-install process could take up to an hour, depending on the hardware configuration of your Mac and how much data is currently stored on it.

> ☑ **TIP**   If you're using a MacBook Air or MacBook Pro, be sure you have the computer plugged into an external power source when performing the operating system upgrade.

> 📝 **NOTE**   Upgrading to Mountain Lion from your home or office requires a high-speed Internet connection. If a high-speed Internet connection is not available, you can bring your computer to any Apple Store, purchase the Mountain Lion upgrade there, and have the operating system installed while you wait. Be sure to make an appointment with an Apple Genius to avoid an excessive wait time at the Apple Store. To make an appointment online, visit http://concierge. apple.com/reservation/us/en/techsupport.

CONNECTING TO THE INTERNET

Regardless of which model Mac you are using, to make full use of the many features that Mountain Lion and its preinstalled apps offer, your computer needs access to the Internet. Because many apps now integrate with iCloud (or another online-based file-sharing service, such as Dropbox or Microsoft SkyDrive), having your computer connected to the Internet is more important than ever, as is having a high-speed Internet connection.

When it comes to connecting your Mac to the web, you have a handful of options, including the following:

- Using your Mac's built-in Wi-Fi capabilities to access a wireless network in your home or office, or a public Wi-Fi hotspot (available in airports, schools, coffee shops, bookstores, libraries, hotels, and so on).

- Plugging an Ethernet cable that's also connected to an Internet router into your Mac via a built-in Ethernet port. (If you're using a MacBook Air, or another MacBook model that does not have a built-in Ethernet port, you'll need to purchase the Apple USB Ethernet adapter for $29 and plug it into your computer's USB port, and then connect the Ethernet cable to the adapter.)

- Connecting your Mac to a wireless modem so that you can connect to a 3G or 4G wireless data network offered by a company such as AT&T Wireless, Verizon Wireless, T-Mobile, or Virgin Mobile. In addition to acquiring and then plugging a wireless modem into the USB port of your computer, you'll need to subscribe to a wireless data plan from a compatible service provider. Keep in mind that wireless data networks are usually considerably slower than broadband, FiOS, and DSL Internet connections, for example.

■ Connecting your Mac to a wireless mobile hotspot created using a mobile hotspot device that grants you access to a wireless data network. A mobile hotspot device is available from a handful of different wireless data service providers and requires that you subscribe to a compatible wireless data plan. In some cases, if your smartphone allows for Internet tethering, you can create a mobile hotspot that originates from your phone that your Mac can wirelessly connect to using its built-in Wi-Fi capabilities. Again, keep in mind that wireless data networks are usually considerably slower than broadband, FiOS, and DSL Internet connections.

To connect your Mac to any type of wireless Internet connection using its built-in Wi Fi capabilities, be sure to turn on the computer's Wi-Fi functionality and select the wireless network you want to connect to. To do this, click the Wi-Fi icon on the right side of the menu bar and select Turn Wi-Fi On (shown in Figure 1.7). Then, allow your Mac to find available wireless networks. Within 5 to 30 seconds, after the available networks are displayed, click the one you wish to connect to.

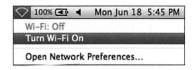

FIGURE 1.7

Turn of the Wi-Fi connectivity feature of your Mac in order to connect to a wireless network, Wi-Fi hotspot or mobile hotspot.

If the wireless network has a lock icon displayed to the immediate left of its signal-strength indicator, the wireless network is password protected. To access it, you'll need to enter the correct password.

NOTE   By connecting your Mac to an Internet connection via an Ethernet cable, your computer will automatically detect the connection and autoconfigure itself to grant you access to the Internet. However, you can also manually config-ure your Internet connection by launching System Preferences and clicking the Network option. When the Network window is visible, click the Assist Me button so that the computer walks you through the Internet connection process.

USING A MAGIC MOUSE OR MULTI-TOUCH TRACKPAD

Mountain Lion can work with any trackpad or mouse connected to your Mac, but the more recently released Macs come with either an Apple Magic Mouse or Multi-Touch trackpad, which is fully compatible with the finger-gesture interaction the operating system is capable of accepting.

> **TIP** If you want to add an optional wireless Apple Magic Mouse ($69, http://store.apple.com/us/product/MB829LL/A) or external Multi-Touch Magic Trackpad ($69, http://store.apple.com/us/product/MC380LL/A) to your Mac, you can find these devices at Apple Stores, Apple.com, and wherever Apple products are sold.

The Apple Magic Mouse is wireless and has no traditional mouse buttons. The device reacts to how it is moved around on a mouse pad, and to how you touch the top of the device with your fingers. Using this device, you can easily click, scroll, drag, zoom, or swipe. It's compatible with all Mac apps and software running Mountain Lion.

The wireless Magic Trackpad offers an external 5.17-inch by 5.17-inch touchpad surface that allows you to use finger motions and gestures to control what happens on the screen, instead of using a mouse.

Using the Magic Trackpad, you can tap to click, swipe your fingers, drag with your fingers, zoom in/out on the screen, or scroll using finger gestures. Even if your MacBook Air, for example, already has a built in Multi-Touch trackpad, this optional external trackpad offers a larger surface that can be positioned anywhere in relation to your computer.

Both devices can connect to any Mac via a Bluetooth connection, and both are powered by two AA batteries. Before you can begin using an external Apple Magic Mouse or Multi-Touch trackpad, you first need to turn on Bluetooth and "pair" the device with your computer.

PAIRING DEVICES VIA BLUETOOTH

To pair or wirelessly connect your external Multi-Touch trackpad or wireless Magic Mouse to your computer, either click the Bluetooth icon in the upper-right corner of the screen (along the menu bar) or launch System Preferences and select the Bluetooth option. Next, make sure Bluetooth functionality is turned on. Within the Bluetooth window, shown in Figure 1.8, check the On check box. You also need to check the Discoverable check box.

FIGURE 1.8

Turn on the Bluetooth feature of your Mac, and then pair the wireless mouse or trackpad to your computer.

> **NOTE** Make sure your Magic Mouse or Multi-Touch trackpad has its batteries installed and that it's powered on.

Now, to add a new Bluetooth device and pair it with your computer, while looking at the Bluetooth window on your screen click the Set Up New Device button in the center of the window. If you already have at least one device paired with your computer, to add another you just click the plus sign icon in the window.

The Bluetooth Setup Assistant will launch, and within a few seconds the new Bluetooth device (the Magic Mouse or the Multi-Touch trackpad) will be listed. Once the new device is found, click the Continue button that's displayed in the lower-right corner of the Bluetooth Setup Assistant window.

Within a few seconds, the message "Congratulations! Your computer is now set up to use your trackpad [or Magic Mouse]" will display. Click the Quit button. The mouse or trackpad will now be fully operational. This pairing process needs to be done only once per device.

> **NOTE** This same process for pairing Bluetooth devices can also be used for an external Bluetooth keyboard or wireless external speakers, for example.

CONFIGURING A MAGIC MOUSE

To quickly discover what finger gestures and motions you can use with a Magic Mouse, launch System Preferences and click the Mouse option once the Magic Mouse is paired (connected) via Bluetooth.

Then, click the Point & Click or More Gestures tabs (shown in Figure 1.9) near the top center of the Mouse window to learn about the various finger motions and gestures you can use with this device, as well as how to customize them.

FIGURE 1.9

Customize your Magic Mouse's functionality and learn how to use the various finger gestures and motions.

CONFIGURING A MULTI-TOUCH TRACKPAD

To learn about and customize the compatible finger motions and gestures you can use with any app, first launch System Preferences, and then select the Trackpad option.

Short animations that demonstrate the various finger motions and gestures are viewable by clicking the Point & Click, Scroll & Zoom, or More Gestures tabs near the top center of the Trackpad window (shown in Figure 1.10).

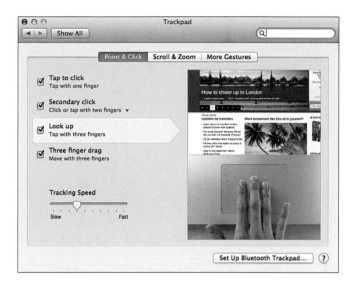

FIGURE 1.10

Customize your Multi-Touch trackpad's functionality and learn how to use the various finger gestures and motions.

> **TIP** Using either an Apple Magic Mouse or Multi-Touch trackpad with your Mac that's running Mountain Lion will provide you with an intuitive, and powerful way to easily interact with your computer and the apps you're using with it. Mountain Lion offers a handful of new ways you can interact with your computer using either of these devices.

After you have Mountain Lion installed on your computer and you're familiar with the finger gestures and motions you can use to more easily navigate your way around the computer using an Apple Magic Mouse or Multi-Touch trackpad, you're ready to begin learning all about using the operating system itself in Chapter 2.

2

NAVIGATING MOUNTAIN LION

If you're an experienced Mac user, you already know that over the years Macs have evolved a lot. Not only has the technology within the iMac and MacBook hardware advanced considerably, but the operating system and apps that come with the operating system have also undergone a tremendous metamorphosis.

The advancements you can expect from OS X Mountain Lion are no exception. It encompasses all that people love about their Macs, but incorporates hundreds of new features and functions, along with a handful of new apps, to create a more intuitive and robust computing environment.

Many of the new features added to Mountain Lion in summer 2012 have been inspired by the iPad and its user interface. This is most apparent when you use Mountain Lion with the newer MacBook Air or MacBook Pro computers that feature a Multi-Touch trackpad rather than a mouse.

> ⌇ **NOTE** Mountain Lion is designed to fully utilize a Multi-Touch trackpad or Apple Magic Mouse. If your Mac doesn't have a Multi-Touch trackpad built in, you can add an external and optional wireless Multi-Touch trackpad for $69 (http://store.apple.com/us/product/MC380LL/A) or upgrade your existing mouse to a wireless Apple Magic Mouse for $69 (http://store.apple.com/us/product/MB829LL/A).

Whether you're a first-time Mac user or someone who has used Macs for years but has recently upgraded to the Mountain Lion operating system, this chapter offers strategies to help you navigate your way around the revamped operating system.

> ⌇ **NOTE** Everything covered in this chapter applies to all Macs running Mountain Lion, including the iMac and Mac Pro computers, the Mac mini, and the MacBook Air and MacBook Pro notebook computers.

EXPLORING THE DESKTOP

Once you power up your Mac and the OS X operating system launches, you'll see the desktop displayed onscreen, as shown in Figure 2.1. This is the central hub from which you can manage files and can launch and run apps. As you'll discover, the desktop is extremely customizable.

The desktop has several main areas, and you can ultimately pick and choose what information displays on your desktop. By default, displayed along the top of the screen is the menu bar. Along the bottom of the screen is the Dock. Within the main area of the screen, you can display app, folder, and file icons, and you can display app windows (which become visible when running various apps).

WORKING WITH THE MENU BAR

The right side of the menu bar displays a series of pull-down menus, as shown in Figure 2.2. At all times when the menu bar is displayed, near the upper-left corner of the screen (along the menu bar) is the Apple icon. Clicking this icon reveals a pull-down menu with a handful of options, include the following:

Menu bar

Dock

FIGURE 2.1

By default, the OS X desktop features the Dock at the bottom and the menu bar along the top. Here, in addition to some of the preinstalled apps, the Dock shows app icons for several third-party apps that have been installed onto the Mac.

FIGURE 2.2

Clicking the Apple icon gives you access to a pull-down menu with a handful of options that remain constant, regardless of which apps are running.

■ **About This Mac**: Click this option to reveal a pop-up window that displays details about your Mac, its hardware configuration, and details about what version of the operating system you're running.

TIP To obtain your Mac's unique serial number, click the Apple icon on the menu bar, choose About This Mac, and then click the More Info button within the About This Mac window.

- **Software Update**: Determine whether you're running the most current version of Mountain Lion and its related apps by selecting this menu option. The App Store will launch with the Updates option preselected. If the message "All Apps Are Up To Date" displays, your computer is running the most current version of the operating system and related apps. If not, see Chapter 9, "Installing New Software," for details about how to download and install new apps or update existing apps (as well as OS X). Keep in mind that the Software Update feature works only with preinstalled apps and apps you've purchased from the App Store.

- **App Store**: If you're looking to add new software (apps) to your Mac, one way to do this is to visit the App Store. Select the App Store menu option to launch the App Store app. (To access the App Store, Internet access is required.)

TIP Any app can be launched in multiple ways. For example, most apps can be launched from the Applications folder, Dock, or Launchpad, as well as by creating and then clicking an alias (shortcut) icon that's placed on your desktop or within a Finder window. Some apps, like the App Store or System Preferences, can also be launched from menu options displayed as part of the menu bar.

- **System Preferences**: When it comes to customizing your Mac and controlling how it operates, much of this is done from within System Preferences, which you'll learn more about later in this chapter.

- **Dock**: The Dock is a lineup of app icons displayed on the desktop. It, too, is customizable and can display icons that represent your most frequently used or favorite apps. From this Dock menu option, you can control the appearance of the Dock and decide when it appears and whether it will be displayed along the bottom of the screen or along the left or right margin. Click the Dock Preferences option to control the appearance of the icons within the Dock.

- **Recent Items**: Gain quick access to the last files, documents, or apps you've used on your Mac. When you click the Recent Items menu option, a list of recently run applications displays, followed by recent documents or items you've worked with. Click any listing to relaunch it.

■ **Force Quit**: If a particular app you're working with freezes or crashes, you can quit the app and relaunch it, without having to reboot your entire computer. This is done using the Force Quit option. When you click the Force Quit menu option, a Force Quit window appears, as shown in Figure 2.3. It displays all the apps currently running on your computer. If the message "Not Responding" appears next to an app's listing, it's usually necessary to quit that app using the Force Quit command and then relaunch it.

FIGURE 2.3

From the Force Quit window, you can quit and restart an app that has crashed, without having to reboot the entire computer and operating system.

> **TIP**   To force quit an app from the Force Quit Applications window, click to select the app that you want to quit. Then, click the Force Quit button. Keep in mind that you can simply quit any application that's running normally by selecting the pull-down menu with the same name as the app on the menu bar and selecting the Quit option.
>
> Another way to Quit an app is by holding down the Control key while clicking an app's icon on the Dock; a menu that includes a Quit option will then appear.

■ **Sleep**: If you're using a MacBook notebook computer, simply shut the computer at anytime to place it into Sleep mode. If you're using an iMac or Mac Pro, use the Sleep command to place the computer into Sleep mode manually.

> **✓ TIP**   To configure your computer to enter Sleep mode automatically after a predetermined amount of time of inactivity, launch System Preferences and select the Energy Saver option shown in Figure 2.4.
>
> When you place your computer into Sleep mode, you can continue working on your computer and pick up exactly where you left off when the computer is later woken up. The apps that are running when you enter Sleep mode continue to run.
>
> If you're a MacBook Air or MacBook Pro user, you can adjust the Energy Saver options differently, based on whether the computer is running on battery power or is plugged in.

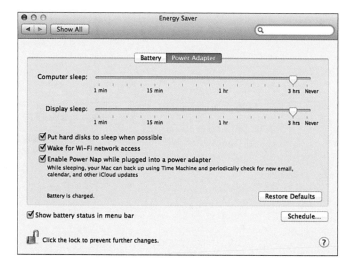

FIGURE 2.4

Determine when, after being left unattended, your Mac will automatically enter into Sleep mode. This is useful for conserving battery life when using a MacBook Air or MacBook Pro.

> **✎ NOTE**   Display Sleep mode allows your computer to keep running, even though the display is shut down. Many apps can continue functioning and can automatically wake up the computer when an alert or alarm is generated, for example. When the Mac is powered off altogether, no apps continue running in the background.

■ **Restart**: To shut your computer down and immediately restart it automatically, select the Restart option. Make sure, however, to save whatever work you are doing before restarting or powering down your computer.

■ **Shut Down**: Instead of placing your computer in Sleep mode, click the Shut Down option to power down the computer altogether. No apps will continue running in the background.

> ✓ **TIP** Before physically moving an iMac or Mac Pro (desktop computer), be sure to shut it down first.

■ **Log Out** [*Username*]: Mountain Lion enables you to set up multiple user accounts, and permits each user to customize his or her computing experience. When you log in using your account name, all of your system preferences and customized options load automatically. When you're done using the Mac, log out of your account using this command. Another user can then log in to the Mac using their account information.

> ✓ **TIP** To set up multiple accounts on your Mac, launch System Preferences and click the Users & Groups option. To create a new user, click the plus sign icon that's displayed near the lower-left corner of the Users & Groups window, shown in Figure 2.5, and follow the onscreen prompts. Before you can make changes to these settings, you must first "unlock" the Users & Groups window by clicking the lock icon and entering your computer's password.
>
> To grant someone temporary access to your Mac, without compromising your private files or data, you can set up a guest account.

Depending on what app is currently running and active on your Mac, the rest of the pull-down menu options that display along the left side of the menu bar will vary. By default, if no apps are running, Finder is active and the related Finder pull-down menu options display. You'll learn more about Finder later in this chapter.

Whatever the currently active app is on your Mac, its unique set of pull-down menu options display to the immediate right of the Apple icon.

> ✓ **TIP** Many of the commands you can access from the various pull-down menus displayed along the menu bar also have keyboard shortcuts associated with them. A keyboard shortcut allows you to press two or three specific keys on the keyboard to execute a specific command.
>
> Usually, to initiate a keyboard shortcut, you press Command or Control in conjunction with a letter or number. Some keyboard shortcuts require you to press Command or Control in conjunction with the Option key and a specific letter or number. The keyboard shortcuts available to you will vary based on the app you're using.

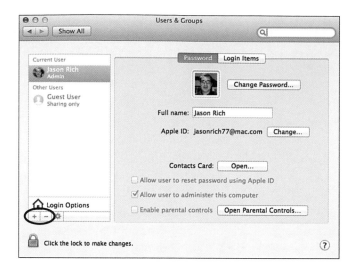

FIGURE 2.5

Create and manage user accounts on your Mac by selecting System Preferences and then click-ing the Users & Groups option. To add a user, click the plus sign icon.

> **NOTE** Most apps allow you to enter into Full Screen mode. To do this, click the full-screen icon in the upper-right corner of many app windows or select View, Enter Full Screen from the menu bar.
>
> When you do this, the menu bar for the app becomes hidden. You can always use keyboard shortcuts to utilize many of the commands available from the menu bar. To exit out of Full Screen mode and access the menu bar, press the Esc key. Some third-party apps require that you hover the mouse near the top of the screen and then select View, Exit Full Screen from the menu bar.
>
> To switch between apps (even if they're running in Full Screen mode), you can use finger gestures on the touchpad or with a Magic Mouse, or you can use Mountain Lion's Mission Control.

THE RIGHT SIDE OF THE MENU BAR

Whenever the menu bar is displayed, you'll find a collection of command icons, the time/date, the active user, and the Spotlight Search and Notification Center icons on the right side, as shown within Figure 2.6.

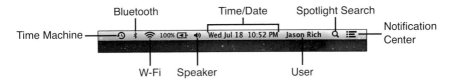

FIGURE 2.6

The right side of the menu bar offers a customizable collection of command icons used to manage various functions of your Mac. If you're using any MacBook model, a battery level indicator can also be displayed on the right side of the menu bar.

The command icons displayed along the right side of the menu bar are typically used to control specific functions of the Mac, such as finding and connecting to a Wi-Fi hotspot or wireless network, controlling the computer's speaker volume, activating Bluetooth, or manually accessing Time Machine.

> ☑ **TIP**   You can also display the current time/date in the upper-right corner of the desktop along the menu bar. From the Date & Time option within System Preferences, it's possible to customize this part of the display. If you're using a MacBook Air or MacBook Pro, for example, and you travel a lot, click the Time Zone tab at the top of the Date & Time window and set this time feature to adjust automatically based on your current location. To do this, check the Set Time Zone Automatically Using Current Location check box. By doing this, your computer will always display the current time for the location you're in, as long as it has access to the Internet.

> ✎ **NOTE**   Some of the command icons displayed along the right of the menu bar can be customized from System Preferences. For example, to control Bluetooth functionality, from System Preferences click the Bluetooth option. Near the bottom-left corner of the Bluetooth window, check the Show Bluetooth in Menu Bar check box to display the Bluetooth icon on the menu bar. Once that icon is on the menu bar, you can access Bluetooth customization options easily by clicking this icon. You can also do this with Time Machine, Sound, Battery Status (via the Energy Saver option within System preferences), Wi-Fi, and Time/Date, for example.

To access the OS X Login Window to log in to the Mac using your account name and password, or to log out of your account, click your username in upper-right corner of the screen along the menu bar. The currently active user's username is displayed there.

Located next to the active user's username is the Spotlight Search feature. Regardless of what apps are running, click this magnifying glass icon to access a blank search field. Within this field, enter any text to search for on your computer. This feature can help you find data stored in a specific app, such as Contacts, Calendar, or Reminders, or help you quickly locate a file with a specific filename.

TIP   Within the Spotlight Search field, enter any keyword, filename, or search phrase to quickly locate specific information that's stored on your Mac. To customize which apps, drives, folders, and files will be searched, launch System Preferences and select the Spotlight option. From the Spotlight window, add check marks next to the apps and folders you want the Spotlight Search feature to search whenever this feature is used.

You can also use the Spotlight Search field to look up the definition of a word or to solve math problems. To look up a definition, type the word within the Spotlight Search field, and then click the Look Up option. To solve an equation, enter it into the Spotlight Search field. The Calculator app will automatically launch.

ACCESSING THE NOTIFICATION CENTER

The to-do list-looking icon near the rightmost corner of the desktop along the menu bar is used to manually display the Notification Center panel, which is a new feature added to Mountain Lion (see Figure 2.7).

Notification Center icon

FIGURE 2.7

Notification Center panel is a new feature added to Mountain Lion.

Notification Center is a constantly running app that continuously monitors other apps running on your Mac. Within the Notification Center panel, all alerts, alarms and notifications generated by the apps that Notification Center is monitoring are displayed in one centralized place.

You can also set up Notification Center to display app-specific alerts or banners in the upper-right corner of the desktop, set up audible alarms that can be generated by apps, and for certain apps, have badges displayed within the app icon on the Dock and Launchpad.

NOTE Both alerts and banners look the same. However, a banner appears on the desktop and then automatically disappears after a few seconds. Alerts remain visible until you manually dismiss them.

From System Preferences, you can configure which apps Notification Center will monitor and determine how many notifications related to each app will show at any given time.

When you click a listing within the Notification Center panel, the appropriate app automatically launches, and the related content or information opens. For example, if the Calendar app generates an alert for an appointment, it will show within the Notification Center panel. When you click that listing, the Calendar app launches, and details about that specific appointment are shown automatically.

NOTE See Chapter 4, "Using Notification Center," to learn more about how to leverage Notification Center and customize the Notification Center panel.

To display the Notification Center panel, regardless of which apps are also running, click the Notification Center icon. To make the Notification Center panel disappear, click the circled X near the top-right corner of the panel.

NOTE When a blue dot appears to the left of a listing in the Notification Center panel, this indicates a new alert, alarm, or notification from a specific app that has not yet been viewed.

If you're working hard and concentrating on something and don't want to be disturbed by alerts, alarms, and notifications generated by your computer, temporarily turn off the Show Alerts and Banners option at the very top of the Notification Center panel. (You may need to scroll upward to see it.)

When you do this, new alerts, alarms, and notifications continue to be generated by the various apps and collected by Notification Center, but you will not hear audible alarms or see pop-up banners or alerts until the Show Alerts and Banners feature is turned back off.

> **TIP**   To turn on or off the Show Alerts and Banners feature, click the Notification Center icon and scroll to the very top of the Notification Center panel (shown in Figure 2.8). Click the virtual switch associated with the Show Alerts and Banners option to turn it on or off.

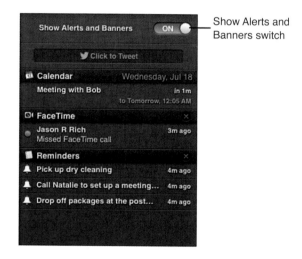

Show Alerts and Banners switch

FIGURE 2.8

The Show Alerts and Banners virtual switch is at the very top of the Notification Center panel.

LAUNCHING APPS

On a Mac, you can launch apps (software) in several ways. Keep in mind that you can have multiple apps running simultaneously, within separate app windows. Also, apps can be running in the background, but their app windows can be minimized or hidden, and thus not displayed on the desktop.

The easiest way to keep track of which apps are currently running on your Mac is to have an indicator light appear on your Dock under each running app, as shown in Figure 2.9. However, it is possible for apps that don't have icons appearing on the Dock to be running.

FIGURE 2.9

An indicator light is displayed on the Dock below icons representing apps that are currently running.

An indicator light is a small white dot that appears below the app icon. To turn on this feature, launch System Preferences, select the Dock option, and select Show Indicator Lights for Open Applications.

> ☑ **TIP**   Another way to determine which apps are running, and then quickly switch between them, is to use the OS X Mission Control feature. Or you can click the Apple icon (displayed on the menu bar) and choose the Force Quit option. The Force Quit Applications pop-up window that appears lists each application that is currently running, along with the apps that have crashed or that have stopped responding and that need to be quit and relaunched.
>
> You can also switch between running apps by pressing and holding down the Command key. When icons for the running apps appear in the center of the desktop, press the Tab key repeatedly until the app you want to switch to is highlighted. Then, release the Command and Tab keys.

> ✐ **NOTE**   Even though multiple apps can be running simultaneously, you can only work with one app at a time. The app you're currently working with, and whose menu options appear along the menu bar, is referred to as the active app.

At any given time, you have several options for launching an app, including the following:

■ Using Finder, access the Applications folder, shown in Figure 2.10, and then click the app icon or listing for the app you want to launch. If an app is stored within a different folder (besides the Applications folder), you can open that folder and click its app icon or listing to launch it.

■ View the Dock and click the app icon for the application you want to launch.

■ Click an app icon (alias) that has previously been copied onto your desktop.

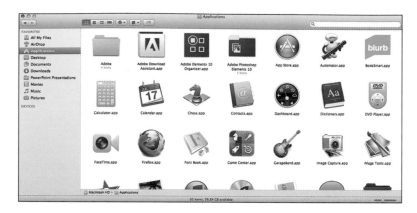

FIGURE 2.10

The Applications folder displays icons or listings representing the apps stored on your Mac that are saved within this folder, including all OS X built-in apps and the iLife and iWork apps.

■ Launch the Launchpad, shown in Figure 2.11, and then click the app icon for the application you want to launch. The Launchpad temporarily replaces whatever is displayed on the desktop with app icons that represent all core apps stored on your Mac. This includes the iLife apps (iPhoto, iMovie, and Garage Band).

FIGURE 2.11

Launchpad displays app icons for all apps stored on your Mac. Click an app icon to launch that application.

TIP To launch the Launchpad on a Mac with a Multi-Touch trackpad, such as a MacBook Air, spread out your thumb and three fingers on your hand and place them on the trackpad, and then bring your fingers together in one swift motion. An alternative is to click the Launchpad icon on the Dock. As shown in Figure 2.12, the Launchpad icon shows a rocket ship.

Launchpad app icon

FIGURE 2.12
By default, the Launchpad app icon displays on the Dock.

SWITCHING BETWEEN RUNNING APPS

If you have multiple apps running on your Mac simultaneously, you can quickly switch between them in several ways. One of the most convenient ways to do this is with Mission Control, a feature that's built in to OS X.

To launch Mission Control, shown in Figure 2.13, click the Mission Control icon that by default displays on the Dock. When you do this, the desktop screen shrinks and thumbnail-like versions of each app that is currently running on your Mac display on the desktop. Click any of these app thumbnails to switch to that app. The other apps continue running in the background.

TIP Another way to launch Mission Control is to use four fingers on the trackpad and to swipe them upward. If you're using a Magic Mouse, double-tap on the top of the mouse with two fingers simultaneously.

TIP When Mission Control is active, the Dock is also displayed. As a result, you can launch additional apps while looking at which apps are currently running.

Displayed near the top center of the Mission Control screen are two additional thumbnails. One represents the desktop, and the other represents the Dashboard. Switch between these two screens by clicking the appropriate thumbnail.

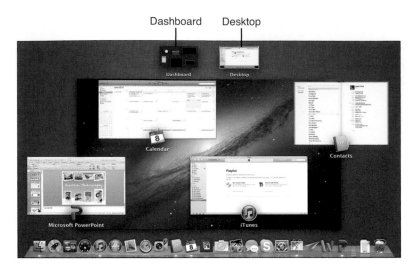

FIGURE 2.13
The main Mission Control screen temporarily replaces what's displayed on your desktop.

> ✓ **TIP** From within Mission Control, you can create multiple Desktops. To do this, move the cursor to the top-right corner of the screen and click the plus sign icon that appears.

To exit Mission Control, either click a thumbnail for an app that's running to make it the new active app or press the Esc key to return to the app you were previously using. If you want to return to the app you were previously using, click the desktop wallpaper that's visiting within Mission Control.

> ✓ **TIP** Another way to switch between apps is to click another app's icon on the Dock or press ⌘-Tab.

CUSTOMIZING THE DOCK

By default, the Dock is a collection of app icons that are displayed in a line along the bottom of the screen, from where you can launch apps with a single click. From within System Preferences, you can customize the Dock in several ways. To do this, launch System Preferences, click the Dock option, and then adjust the options within the Dock window (shown in Figure 2.14).

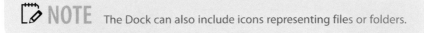

> ### NOTE The Dock can also include icons representing files or folders.

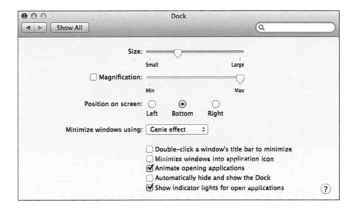

FIGURE 2.14

Customize the appearance of icons on the Dock from within System Preferences.

Ways you can customize the Dock include the following:

- You can control whether the Dock will appear on the desktop continuously or if it will appear only when you drag the cursor over it.

> ### TIP To keep the Dock hidden, except for when you hover the cursor over the bottom of the screen, select Automatically Hide and Show the Dock. This option allows you to maximize screen real estate by hiding the Dock when it's not needed.

- You can determine the size of the app icons on the Dock. To do this, from the Dock window within System Preferences, use the Size slider. Drag it to the left to make the app icons smaller or to the right to make the app icons larger. By making the app icons smaller, you can fit more of them along the Dock at any given time.

> ### TIP By selecting Magnification, and then adjusting the slider within the Dock window of System Preferences, you can make the app icons along the Dock magnify when the cursor is passed over them, as shown in Figure 2.15.

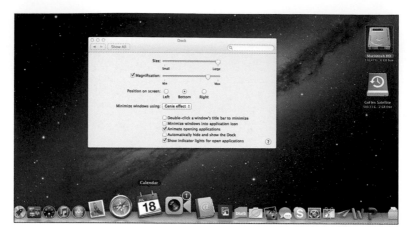

FIGURE 2.15

With the magnification feature turned on, the app icons grow when the cursor is placed over them.

■ You can choose which app icons will appear on the dock and the order in which they appear. To add an app icon to the Dock, access the Applications folder and drag one app icon at a time from the Applications folder to the Dock. To change the order of the app icons on the Dock, place the cursor over an app icon on the Dock, hold down the mouse button, and drag the icon to the desired location. To delete app icons from the Dock, drag them one at a time to the Trash icon on the right (or bottom) of the Dock.

!CAUTION When you delete an app icon from the Dock, it does not erase the app from your computer. However, when you delete an app icon from the Launchpad or from the Applications folder (or the folder in which it's stored), this does erase the app from your Mac.

■ You can select the location of the Dock. You can have it appear along the bottom of the screen or along the left or right margin of the screen. To choose a new default position for the Dock, access the Dock window from System Preferences, and from the Position On Screen option, choose Left, Bottom, or Right. Figure 2.16 shows what the Dock look like when it's displayed along the left margin of the desktop.

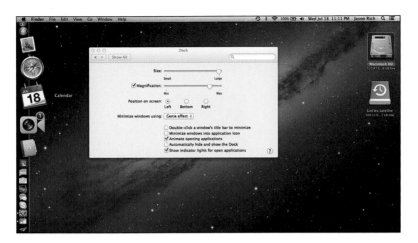

FIGURE 2.16
You can position the Dock along the left margin of the desktop (shown here), along the right margin, or along the bottom of the desktop.

■ You can animate the app icons for when an app requires your attention, for example, or when you launch or minimize an app. To do this, from the Dock window within System Preferences, check the Animated Opening Applications check box. You can also customize the icon animations by changing the pull-down menu option that's associated with the Minimize Windows Using option. It's also possible to animate app icons on the Dock to bounce when that app requires your attention. However, it will keep bouncing until you manually access the app, which some people find annoying.

> **TIP** To indicate which apps are currently running, you can display an indicator light below their icon in the Dock. Just check the Show Indicator Lights for Open Applications check box in the Dock window within System Preferences. One way to then switch between active applications is to click the appropriate app icon along the Dock for the app you want to make active.

THE FINDER ICON

Two of the icons that are permanent fixtures along the Dock are the Finder and Trash icons. Click the Finder icon (always displayed at the extreme left or top of the Dock) to open the Finder window.

> **NOTE** Shown in Figure 2.17, the Finder icon looks like a face.

FIGURE 2.17

The Finder icon is always on the Dock.

This is used to manage files and folders stored on your Mac. See the "Using Finder" section later in this chapter to learn more about using Finder.

THE TRASH ICON

The Trash icon, shown in Figure 2.18, appears on the rightmost side of the Dock (or the bottom of the Dock, if you have the Dock showing along the left or right margin of the desktop) and is used for two purposes.

FIGURE 2.18

The Trash icon is always on the Dock.

First, you can delete files or folders by dragging them from the desktop or a Finder window, for example, into the Trash. When you do this, those items are stored within a special Trash folder. You can view the Trash folder's in a Finder window by clicking the Trash icon to open it. If you use the Move to Trash option related to a file or folder, this places it into your Trash folder, too.

> **NOTE** The items in the Trash folder are not deleted until you use the Empty Trash command, which is under the Finder pull-down menu on the menu bar. Another option for emptying the Trash is to hold down the Control key, click the Trash icon, and then select the Empty Trash option.

Second, when you need to eject external storage devices from the Mac, such as an external hard drive, USB thumb drive, or digital camera memory card, you can drag the icon that represents that drive from the desktop to the Trash icon. Once ejected, it's safe to remove that storage device from the computer's USB port. This process can also be used to eject a CD/DVD from the Mac's SuperDrive, if applicable. Another way to Eject an external storage device is to hold down the Control key at the same time you click the icon for the drive on your desktop (or within the Finder window). Then, select the Eject option from the menu.

> **TIP** Once items are emptied from the Trash folder using the Erase Trash command, they cannot be retrieved unless they were previously backed up using Time Machine or another backup method.
>
> However, if you want to erase the Trash folder contents and make sure it's truly erased from your computer (as well as previous backups), use the Secure Empty Trash command that's also found under the Finder pull-down menu. When you do this, everything that was in the Trash folder gets overwritten with junk data, which makes the original content extremely difficult (if not impossible) for even the most savvy hackers to recover.
>
> Even if you use the Secure Empty Trash option, if you have a backup of the files stored elsewhere, those remain intact.

USING FINDER

When it comes to managing files and folders, as well as organizing data stored on your Mac, much of this is done using a visual interface within OS X's Finder. To launch Finder, click the Finder icon on your Dock. You can also launch Finder from the Launchpad. If no apps are currently running, by default the Finder becomes the active app when you view your desktop.

> **NOTE** If no other apps are running on your Mac, by default the Finder app will be running in the background and will be the active app. When this is the case, the Finder pull-down menus appear along the menu bar on the desktop, as shown in Figure 2.19.

FIGURE 2.19

No apps are currently running, so Finder is the default. Notice the Finder pull-down menus displayed on the menu bar.

THE MAIN FINDER WINDOW

The main Finder window has several components, as shown in Figure 2.20. From here, you can access and manage just about any file or folder stored on your Mac or on a storage drive connected to your computer.

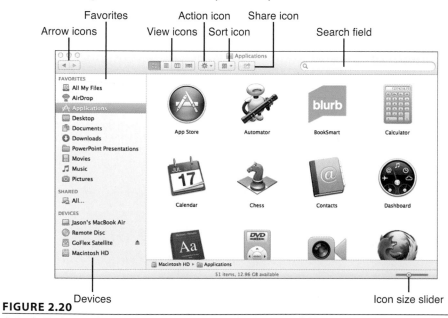

FIGURE 2.20

A single Finder window on the desktop. Here, the Applications folder is selected on the sidebar, and its contents are displayed within the main Finder window.

TIP To make moving files and folders to different locations easier, you can open two or more Finder windows on the desktop simultaneously, each with a different folder open, and then drag and drop or copy and paste app icons, files, folders, or other items between the Finder windows. Figure 2.21 shows two Finder windows open at the same time, but each is displaying the contents of different folder.

CAUTION It is not advisable to move apps out of the Applications folder. Doing this could render the app unable to function because app-specific files or folders are no longer accessible.

FIGURE 2.21
Two Finder windows open at the same time on the desktop. Both are displaying a folder's contents using the Icons view.

Along the left side of the Finder window is a list of popular folders. This area is known as the sidebar. At the top of this list is All My Files. However, as you work your way down the list, you'll discover links to quickly access your Applications, Documents, Downloads, Movies, Music, and Pictures folders. When you click any of these links, the contents of that folder display on the right side of the Finder window.

Below the Favorites heading in the sidebar is the Devices heading. In addition to your computer's main internal storage drive, if you have optional storage devices connected to your Mac via USB, Thunderbolt, or Wi-Fi, or a have CD/DVD within the computer's SuperDrive, for example, they'll be listed here. Click any of these listings to view the folder and file contents on these storage mediums, drives, or devices.

When you select a source drive or folder from the sidebar, its contents (items, folders, and files) display within the right side of the window. However, how you view this information is fully customizable using the command icons along the top of the Finder window (as well as the Icon Size slider in the lower-right corner of the window.)

NOTE The Search field in the upper-right corner of the Finder window is used to seek out files or folders, or files containing a keyword or search phrase. It works very much like the Spotlight Search option, but is limited to file searches. When you enter a keyword or search phrase within the Search field in the Finder window, the search results displays within the main area of the window.

The left-arrow and right-arrow icons near the top-left corner of the Finder window are used to move backward or forward as you navigate between folders and sub-folders using Finder.

TIP Files stored on your Mac are usually stored within folders or subfolders. To see the exact storage location of a particular file or item, select and high-light it within the Finder window by clicking it once. Then look near the bottom center of the Finder window for its hierarchical folder location. This works only if you have the Show Path Bar in Finder option activated (It's under the View pull-down menu of the Finder menu bar).

You can display folders and files within the Finder window in several ways. To change the display and sorting options, use the command icons near the top-center of the Finder window.

From left to right, as shown in Figure 2.22, the four display icons that are grouped together enable you to view the contents of a selected drive or folder. The view options include the following:

- Using thumbnail icons only (or using thumbnail icons with filenames / file sizes displayed below them)
- As a detailed text-based listing (shown in Figure 2.23)
- As a detailed, column-based listing

■ Using an animated carousel display with thumbnail icons and a text-based listing combination (shown in Figure 2.24). This is called the Cover Flow view.

FIGURE 2.22

The display icons enable you to set how files, folders, and items will display within the Finder window. Shown here is the Icons view with the filenames displayed.

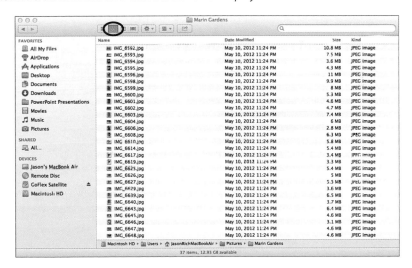

FIGURE 2.23

This is the text-based List view of the contents within a Finder window.

Cover Flow View

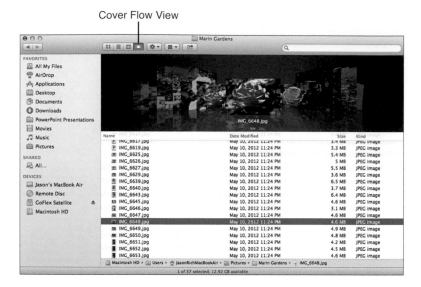

FIGURE 2.24

The Cover Flow view shows app, folder, file, and item thumbnails, plus a text-based listing.

In addition to deciding how folders and files will be displayed within the Finder window, you can choose how they're sorted by clicking the Sort icon, shown in Figure 2.25, and then selecting Name, Kind, Application, Date Last Opened, Date Added, Date Modified, Date Created, Size, Label, or None from the pull-down menu.

FIGURE 2.25

You can sort the apps, folders, files, and items within a Finder window in any of several ways, such as by name, file type (kind), application, file size, or date.

Once a file or folder is found within Finder, and then highlighted and selected by clicking it, click the Action icon shown in Figure 2.26 to reveal a pull-down menu that offers a handful of options for working with that folder or file. Depending on whether you're working with a folder or a specific file type, these pull-down menu options will vary, but most likely include the following:

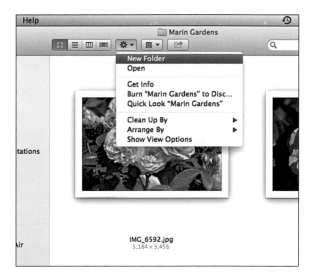

FIGURE 2.26

The Action menu offers a handful of commands and tools for managing items within a Finder window.

- **New Folder**: Create a new folder or subfolder within the Finder window.
- **Open**: Use this option to open a folder and display its contents or open a file. When you open a file, the appropriate app launches automatically. If two or more apps can be used to open a particular file type, the default app is used unless you take advantage of the Open With command to make a specific selection. This command is equivalent to double-clicking the item to open or launch it from within a Finder window.
- **Open With**: When it's possible to open an item (such as a document or photo) using multiple apps that are installed on your computer, the Open With command allows you to select which app to use to open and work with the item.
- **Move to Trash**: This erases the app, file, or folder from its current location and moves it to the Trash folder, where it will remain until you use one of the Empty Trash commands to delete the Trash folder content permanently.
- **Duplicate**: Create a copy of the file or folder within the folder the original is currently stored in. The duplicate is given a similar folder or filename, but will have the word *copy* also associated with it. Therefore, if the original filename was Sample.doc, the duplicated filename will be Sample copy.doc.

■ **Make Alias**: Instead of making a copy (duplicate) of a folder or file, creating an alias serves as a shortcut that when clicked leads to the original file or folder. For example, if you access the same Microsoft Word document often, you can create an alias for that file and display the alias on your desktop for quick and easy access (as opposed to accessing the document file from the Documents folder, for example). When you create an alias, you can then drag and drop or copy and paste it to another location, such as your desktop or another folder. When you click the alias, the appropriate app launches. In this case, Microsoft Word will launch and automatically open the specific document.

TIP When viewing files within a Finder window, you can show or hide file extensions by selecting File, Get Info, and then checking or unchecking the Hide Extension check box about halfway down on the Info window that appears.

NOTE Although they do not display an arrow icon in the lower-left corner, the app icons on the Dock are really aliases for apps stored within the Applications folder or elsewhere on your Mac.

■ **Quick Look**: Depending on the file type, the Quick Look command enables you to view or listen to a file, photo, graphic, movie, or audio file without launching a specific app. It enables you to confirm you're working with the correct file before actually opening it. This proves useful if you have several files with similar names, for example. Instead, a Quick Look window appears containing the contents of the file. You can then launch a specific (and compatible) app to work with that file. Figure 2.27 shows a PDF file being viewed using the Quick Look feature. In the upper-right corner of the window is an Open in Preview button, which you can use to launch the Preview app and then load in this file to view it properly.

■ **Copy**: This command places the folder or file on the OS X virtual clipboard. You can then open a new Finder window and paste the item into a new location, or you can paste it onto your desktop, for example. This creates a copy or duplicate of the file in the new location, but the original file also remains where it was originally stored. The copy of the file you make becomes independent of the original. So, if you later edit the copy, the original remains in its original form, while the copy will reflect the changes you make.

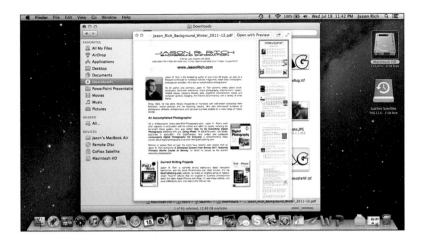

FIGURE 2.27

The Quick Look feature enables you to see the contents of a file, document, or item without launching a specific app. However, all you can do is preview that item, not work with it in any way.

- **Arrange By**: Change how files within a folder are sorted by selecting this command and choosing a sort option from the pull-down menu that appears. The Clean Up command simply reorganizes the files or folders to make them look neater within the Finder window.

- **Show View Options**: Upon choosing this command, a separate pop-up window appears in which you can customize a specific folder or file. For example, you can adjust its thumbnail icon size, decide whether the filename and file size will appear in the Finder window along with the icon, adjust the text size and location of the filename, plus make other customizable adjustments.

- **Label**: Use this command to highlight the folder or file thumbnail or filename using a selected color when it's viewed within the Finder window or the desktop. Using this tool, you can create a color-coded system for yourself and give colors specific meanings. You can associate names with the colors for your own reference by accessing the Preferences option within Finder and then clicking the Labels tab.

> **TIP** After opening the Preferences menu within Finder, click the Labels tab to assign specific meanings to the various colored labels that you can associate with folders/files. For example, you can make the red label mean Urgent. You can assign specific meanings to seven different colored labels.

- **Get Info**: Use this command when a file or folder is highlighted within a Finder window to access the Info window and see details about the file, such as its name, file size, location, and when it was last modified. There's also an Open With option you can adjust, and at the same time, view a thumbnail preview (if applicable). From this Info window, you can also adjust the permissions related to the particular file.

- **Compress**: Use this command to shrink the file size of the selected file.

- **Burn**: This command enables you to burn the selected file onto a CD or DVD if your computer has a SuperDrive connected to it.

> **NOTE** At the bottom of the Action pull-down menu, you'll probably see additional command options that specifically relate to the type of file you have highlighted and selected.

WORKING WITH FILES/FOLDERS WITHIN FINDER

In addition to the icons displayed within the Finder window itself that are used to manage files and folders, when a Finder window is open and active on your desktop, the Finder pull-down menus appear the menu bar at the top of the screen.

From the pull-down menu labeled Finder, you can access the Preferences menu, which enables you to further customize the Finder's functions and features.

To customize which files, folders, drives, and devices will be listed and displayed within the sidebar of the Finder window, from the Preferences window of Finder click the Sidebar tab, and then add check marks to the folders, folders, drives, and devices you want listed.

When you click the Finder pull-down menu, another frequently used command you'll discover is the Empty Trash option. Use it to delete the contents of the Trash folder permanently. Doing this periodically frees up storage space on your computer's hard drive.

From the File, Edit, View, and Go pull-down menus, you can further control or manage files and folders while working with Finder. For example, from the Edit pull-down menu, you can access the Select All, Copy, Cut, and Paste commands, as well as the Undo command.

TIP As you're managing files and folders within Finder, select and high-light one item at a time by clicking it. Or, you can double-click that item to open it. However, you also have the option to highlight and select multiple items, and then copy and paste, drag and drop, or use other file-management tools on them simultaneously. To do this, highlight and select one item within the Finder win-dow. Then place the cursor over a second item and press the Shift key at the same time you click the mouse. Repeat this process until you've selected all the desired items. To select all the items within a Finder window, use the Select All command that's found under the Edit pull-down window, or use the ⌘-A keyboard shortcut.

Many of the commands available from the pull-down menus associated with Finder (or any other app for that matter) have keyboard shortcuts available for them. So, instead of accessing the pull-down menu and clicking a specific com-mand (menu option), you can use the corresponding keyboard shortcut.

NOTE If you press the Option key while a Finder menu is open, addi-tional commands become available.

NOTE As you view the pull-down menu options, the keyboard shortcut for each applicable command appears to the right. The ⌘ symbol represents the Command key on the keyboard, and the [shift] key represents the Shift key. The [option] key represents the Option key. The [ctrl] symbol represents the Con-trol key.

USING THE SHARE ICON

One of the many new features of Mountain Lion is the Share icon, which you'll see when using many different apps, as well as Finder. The options found within the Share pull-down menu, which you can access by clicking the Share icon, enable you to share a specific item, file, or folder with others without exiting the app you're currently using. In this case, you can share a file or folder without leaving the active Finder window.

To use this feature, first select one or more items from within the active Finder win-dow, and then click the Share icon. Depending on the type of file you've selected, a handful of share options will display.

For example, if you've highlighted and selected a JPG (photo) file, upon clicking the Share icon shown in Figure 2.28 you'll have Email, Message, Twitter, AirDrop, and Flickr options. In the future, Mountain Lion may also integrate with other online services, such as Facebook, Tumblr, or Instagram, in which case, options for these services will be displayed under the Share menu, as well.

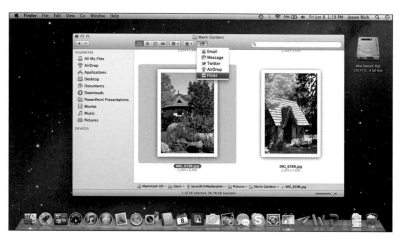

FIGURE 2.28
The Share options if you select and highlight a JPG file.

> **NOTE** AirDrop is a wireless method for transferring files or data between two Macs that are connected to the same wireless network. This AirDrop feature only works with newer Mac models. See Chapter 13, "Syncing Information with Other Macs and iDevices," for more information about using AirDrop. The Macs do not need to be linked to the same iCloud account or Apple ID account to use AirDrop. They simply need to be connected to the same Wi-Fi hotspot or wireless network.

The Share commands offer a quick and easy way to send a file, folder, or item to someone else. If you choose the Email option, for example, an outgoing message window appears with the items you selected already embedded or attached to the outgoing message. Just fill in the To and Subject fields of the email message and click Send to send the items to one or more recipients via email.

CUSTOMIZING YOUR DESKTOP AND SCREEN SAVER

You already know that you can customize the appearance of icons on your desktop. However, it's also possible to select the wallpaper graphic that shows continuously in the background. Plus, you can customize the screen saver that's displayed after a predetermined amount of time when your computer goes unused.

CHANGING THE DESKTOP WALLPAPER

The desktop wallpaper you use can be any digital image that's stored on your Mac, as shown in Figure 2.29, or you can choose from a collection of wallpaper options that come bundled with OS X. To customize your desktop's wallpaper, launch System Preferences, and then click the Desktop & Screen Saver option.

FIGURE 2.29
The desktop showcasing a custom-selected digital photo as the wallpaper.

Near the top center of the Desktop & Screen Saver window are two tabs: Desktop and Screen Saver (shown in Figure 2.30). First, click the Desktop tab to customize the desktop wallpaper. When you do this, you'll see a collection of wallpaper images you can choose from near the bottom of the Desktop & Screen Saver window. Click your selection to immediately change the appearance of your desktop.

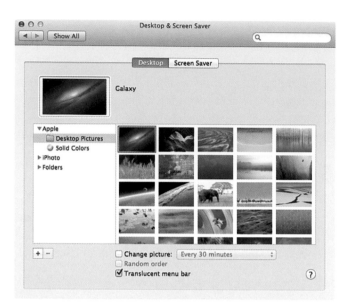

FIGURE 2.30

Customize your desktop's wallpaper from this Desktop & Screen Saver window.

To select your own digital photo, on the left side of the Desktop & Screen Saver window (the sidebar) click the location of the image that's stored on your Mac. For example, if the image is stored within the Photos folder, click the Photos listing, and then choose the appropriate album where the photo is located (see Figure 2.31). Then, click the image thumbnail when it appears on the right side of the screen. Exit System Preferences when you complete the customization.

> **TIP** If the digital image you want to use as your wallpaper is stored within the Pictures folder, click the Folders option on the left side of the Desktop & Screen Saver window (the sidebar), and then select the Pictures folder. Then, click the thumbnail image you want to use. Exit System Preferences when you complete the customization.

Near the bottom center of the Desktop & Screen Saver window, when the Desktop option is selected, are three additional options: Change Picture, Random Order, and Translucent Menu Bar.

If you want your wallpaper image to change periodically, check the Change Picture check box. You'll need to select a folder from which the desktop will access two or more photos, and then choose how often you want the image to change.

FIGURE 2.31

Choose any photo or graphic stored on your computer to serve as your desktop wallpaper.

> **TIP** If you opt to transform your desktop's wallpaper into a slide show and have the image change periodically, you can select the Random Order option, which will then cause the preselected images to display in a random order.

On some Macs, you can make the solid gray menu bar at the top of the screen translucent so that the wallpaper image you select can be seen behind it. To do this, check the Translucent Menu Bar check box.

CUSTOMIZING THE SCREEN SAVER

From System Preferences, click the Desktop & Screen Saver option, and then click the Screen Saver tab near the top center of the screen to fully customize your Mac's screen saver. If you use your computer's Sleep modes, a screen saver is not necessary to use. However, many people enjoy looking at the animations that comprise the various screen savers when they're at their desk but not using the computer.

Not only can you chose from a handful of pre-created screen saver options, you can also use your own digital images to create an animated slide show and use that as your screen saver. When you do thus, you also need to choose an image transition effect. When you choose to use the Slideshow option as your screen saver, a variety of customizable options are at your disposal. Plus, you can download additional screen savers from the Internet.

From the Screen Saver customization window shown in Figure 2.32, you can determine when the screen saver will kick in. To do this, access the Start After pull-down menu near the lower-left corner of the window.

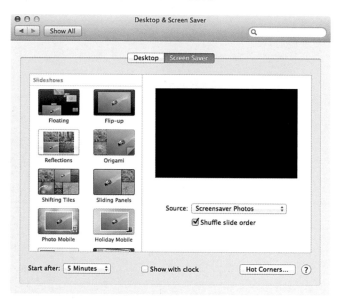

FIGURE 2.32

You can select from a handful of pre-created screen savers and then customize that screen saver from this Desktop & Screen Saver window within System Preferences.

> **TIP** By selecting the Show with Clock option, you can display the current time on the screen while any screen saver is being displayed.

Within the screen saver, you can set up the Hot Corners feature so that when you activate the screen saver at a specific time (for example, to keep someone from seeing what you're working on if someone enters the room and tries looking at your screen). From the Desktop & Screen Saver window, click the Hot Corners button. A new pop-up window appears with a pull-down menu associated with each corner of the screen.

One at a time, click a pull-down menu and then choose what function you'd like to associate with that hot corner. Your options are Start Screen Saver, Disable Screen

Saver, Mission Control, Application Windows, Desktop, Dashboard, Notification Center, Launchpad, or Put Display to Sleep. Repeat this process for each corner of the screen saver screen.

After you've selected and customized your screen saver selection, exit System Preferences. That screen saver will now be active and will appear after the pre-determined period when your Mac goes unused.

CUSTOMIZING MORE VIA SYSTEM PREFERENCES

There are many ways to customize your Mac, what you see on the screen, and how various apps respond as you're using them. When customizations are non-app specific, you usually control them with the various options found within System Preferences (shown in Figure 2.33). Throughout this chapter, and in many of the other chapters of this book that focus on specific apps, you'll discover different ways to further customize your Mac using the options within System Preferences.

FIGURE 2.33

The main System Preferences window of Mountain Lion.

To make app-specific customizations, however, after launching a specific app you'll typically discover a pull-down menu with that app's name on the menu bar. When you access this menu, you'll find a Preferences option. Click this to reveal a Preferences menu that you can use to customize this particular app.

Figure 2.34 shows the Microsoft Word app running, with the Word pull-down menu being accessed from the menu bar. As you can see, it offers a Preferences menu option for customizing the Microsoft Word app.

FIGURE 2.34

Most apps offer a Preferences menu option. Use it to customize whatever app you're running.

As you add new hardware or peripherals to your Mac, as well as some additional apps, you'll discover new options will be displayed within System Preferences that give you further control over what's been added.

Many of the commands and options available within System Preferences have been ported over from earlier versions of OS X. However, displayed within the System Preferences window, you'll also discover some new options, such as Notifications. As you open each option within System Preferences, such as for iCloud, Security & Privacy, or Parental Controls, you'll also discover new Mountain Lion features that you can customize.

IN THIS CHAPTER

- Popular apps preinstalled with Mountain Lion
- How new features impact core apps
- Sharing and syncing app-specific data

3

OPTIMIZING PREINSTALLED APPS

Apple's OS X Mountain Lion isn't just an operating system for your Mac. It also includes a collection of specialized apps that add a tremendous amount of functionality to your computer.

The more popular apps that come preinstalled with Mountain Lion include the following:

- **Calculator**: When you launch this app, a pop-up window containing an on-screen calculator is displayed. This calculator has three numeric-calculation modes: Basic, Scientific, and Programmer. The app can also serve as a currency converter and as a converter for power, pressure, speed, temperature, time, volume, weight, and mass. You'll learn more about this app later in this chapter.

- **Calendar**: Manage your schedule and easily sync your scheduling data with other computers and mobile devices using this newly redesigned and feature-packed app. You'll learn more about this app later in this chapter.

■ **Contacts**: Create and maintain a detailed personal database of your contacts, which you can fully customize and then sync with your other computers and mobile devices using iCloud. You'll learn more about this app later in this chapter.

■ **Dashboard**: Utilize mini-apps or widgets to handle a wide range of quick tasks when using your Mac.

■ **Dictionary**: Quickly look up the definition of any word with the *New Oxford American Dictionary*, *Oxford American Writer's Thesaurus*, *Apple Dictionary* or Wikipedia using this app.

■ **FaceTime**: Participate in real-time video conferences with any other Mac, iPhone, iPad, or iPod touch users, using Apple's free FaceTime service and this app. You'll learn more about this app later in this chapter.

■ **Game Center**: Play your favorite multiplayer games against people you know or total strangers by signing in to the Game Center online service that Apple operates. Game Center works with an ever-growing lineup of games compatible with the Mac, iPhone, iPad, and iPod touch. While you can play most games without connecting to Game Center, this service (in conjunction with the Game Center app) makes it easy to communicate and compete against other players. You'll learn more about Game Center in Chapter 8, "Getting the Most from iTunes and Games Center."

■ **iTunes**: The iTunes app has several functions. Use it to manage your digital music library, digital movie library, and your collection of TV show episodes. iTunes also serves as a media player for your digital content, and serves as a conduit for connecting to the iTunes Store. If you're an iOS mobile device (iDevice) user, you can use the iTunes app to sync your iPhone, iPad, or iPod touch with your Mac, plus it gives you access to the online-based App Store and iBookstore. You'll learn more about the iTunes app and iTunes in Chapter 8.

■ **Mac App Store**: From your Mac, find, purchase, download, and install a wide range of apps and software from Apple and third-party developers. From the Mac App Store, you'll also find an ever-growing selection of free apps for your Mac. You'll learn more about the Mac App Store in Chapter 9, "Installing New Software."

> **❗CAUTION** The Mac App Store is different from the App Store that's used to find, purchase, and download content for your iDevice. To access Apple's online-based Mac App Store, use the App Store app that comes preinstalled on your Mac. From your Mac, to find apps for your iDevice, use the iTunes app to access the iOS App Store (or use the App Store app that comes preinstalled on your iPhone, iPad, or iPod touch) for this purpose.

- **Mail**: Manage one or more of your preexisting email accounts from your Mac using this email management app. It enables you to read incoming emails, compose and send outgoing emails, and manage your email correspondence. Chapter 7, "Improved Web Surfing and Email Management," offers strategies for using the Mail app's newest features.

- **Messages**: Use this app to communicate with other Mac, iPhone, iPad, and iPod touch users for free using unlimited text messaging/instant messaging through Apple's own iMessage server. In addition, this app enables you to exchange text messages and instant messages with people who use other services, including AIM, Jabber, Google Talk, and Yahoo! Messenger. Starting in Fall 2012, you'll also be able to communicate via Facebook Messenger using the Messages app. Be sure to check out Chapter 5, "Communicating Effectively with Messages," to learn how to use this powerful app.

- **Notes**: At first glance, Notes is a basic text editor and can serve as a digital notebook for jotting down ideas or text-based information. However, the Notes app is fully compatible with iCloud, so your notes will automatically be synced with your other Macs and iDevices. Plus, it works with Mountain Lion's Dictation feature, so you can create text-based documents without actually typing. Discover what sets Notes apart from TextEdit and word processors like Microsoft Word or Apple's Pages, by reading Chapter 6, "Making the Most of Reminders and Notes."

- **Notification Center**: Access and manage all the alerts, alarms, and notifications that are generated by your Mac and the apps running on it within one centralized location: the Notification Center window. From Chapter 4, "Using Notification Center," you'll learn tips for easily keeping track of the information that is important to you.

- **Photo Booth**: Your Mac's built-in camera is ideal for video conferences, but you can also use it to snap photos or shoot video using the Photo Booth app. You can then add a whimsical theme to that content before viewing, saving, or sharing it. You'll find tips for snapping fun digital photos and shooting videos later in this chapter.

> **NOTE** People who record video diaries or vlogs to post online (on YouTube, for example) can use the Photo Booth app to shoot their videos, and then use an app such as iMovie to edit the footage before publishing it online.

- **Preview**: This app enables you to view and annotate documents and PDF files and to view and edit photos quickly without having to launch a specialized app. Preview offers much more functionality than the OS X Quick Look feature. You can also use it to store documents on iCloud. You'll learn more about Preview later in this chapter.

- **Reminders**: Use the Reminders app (discussed within Chapter 6) to create, manage, view, and share an unlimited number of detailed to-do lists. Your list data can easily sync with iCloud and then be shared with your other Macs and iDevices.

- **Safari**: When it comes to surfing the web, the Mac has a handful of different web browsers available. However, Safari is the web browser developed by Apple, and it fully utilizes many Mountain Lion features to make browsing the Internet easier and more efficient than ever. Find out how to make full use of Safari's newest features from Chapter 7.

- **TextEdit**: In addition to Notes, the TextEdit app offers basic text-editing functionality to your Mac. However, if you want full word processing capabilities, you'll need to use word processing software, like Microsoft Word or Pages. You'll learn more about this app and how to sync your documents with iCloud and other computers (as well as iDevices) in Chapter 13, "Syncing Information with Other Macs and iDevices."

> **☑ TIP**   Beyond just serving as a text editor, TextEdit enables you to import documents from other word processors and sync them with your iCloud account. This allows you to back up and sync Microsoft Word documents with Apple's online-based service, even though the Microsoft Word software is not directly compatible with iCloud. Using the Share button, you can also send documents to other people via email, message, or AirDrop, even if their computer is not linked to your iCloud account.

- **Time Machine**: Maintaining an ongoing, complete, and reliable backup of your entire Mac, including all your apps, data, documents, photos, videos, and files is absolutely essential. The easiest and least intrusive way to do this is by using the Time Machine app in conjunction with an external hard drive. Discover tips for backing up your Mac using Time Machine in Chapter 12, "Backing Up Your Mac."

Your Mac also came bundled with the iLife suite of apps, which includes iPhoto, iMovie, and GarageBand. Check out Chapter 10, "Getting Better Results Faster Using iPhoto," for tips and strategies on how to view, organize, edit, share, and print your digital photos using iPhoto; how to edit, view, and share videos using iMovie; and how to create (compose, record, and produce) music using GarageBand.

> **NOTE** Apple's iWork apps (Pages, Numbers, and Keynote) are sold separately and are available from the App Store ($19.99 each). These three apps are also designed to work seamlessly with the Mountain Lion operating system and to share data with the preinstalled apps. The iWork apps fully integrate with iCloud and are compatible with the versions of Pages, Numbers, and Keynote for iDevices (sold separately).

BENEFITS OF PREINSTALLED APPS

You gain several benefits by using the Mountain Lion preinstalled apps (also referred to as the core apps), as opposed to installing third-party apps or software that offers similar functionality. These benefits include the following:

- Each of the core apps (as well as most third-party apps for the Mac) is designed to fully utilize the features and functionality of the operating system itself, plus make use of features like the Share menu, the Dictation feature, and OS X functions (for example, Select All, Cut, Copy, and Paste).

- The majority of the core apps work seamlessly with Apple's iCloud service to back up and sync app-specific data. This makes it very easy to share app-specific information with other Macs and iDevices. In addition, unlike with other apps that use other cloud-based services, you can set up the backup and syncing processes to occur automatically and in the background.

- Many of the core apps can automatically share data with each other, ensuring that information you need is readily accessible when and where needed For example, the Calendar app can pull information from the Contacts app in reference to people's birthdays, and then remind you in advance so that you remember to send a card or buy a gift. Plus, any app that can generate an alert, alarm, or notification now works with Notification Center.

- App-specific data from Mac OS X apps, including Contacts, Calendar, and Reminders, are fully compatible with the Contacts, Calendar, and Reminders apps on the iPhone, iPad and iPod touch.

- Once you set up your Mac to sync data with iCloud, you can access app-specific data from the core apps from any computer (whether linked to your iCloud account or not) by visiting www.iCloud.com.

USING THE CALCULATOR APP

When it comes to performing quick numeric calculations, a powerful calculator is just a finger gesture away. If you're using a Mac with a Multi-Touch trackpad, spread out your thumb and three fingers (not your pinky) from one hand on the trackpad, and then bring them all together in one swift motion. Doing this launches the Launchpad on your Mac.

Displayed prominently on the Launchpad is the Calculator app (shown in Figure 3.1). Click the Calculator app icon to launch it. Of course, you can also launch this app from the Dock (if the Calculator app icon has been placed on the Dock), or you can launch the app from the Applications folder.

FIGURE 3.1

The Calculator app icon is on the Launchpad.

At first glance, the Calculator app, shown in Figure 3.2, offers basic calculator functions. You can add, subtract, multiply, and divide numbers. However, by accessing the menu bar for this app, you can reveal a handful of other useful features.

> **TIP** Transform the Calculator app from a basic calculator to a scientific calculator by selecting the View pull-down menu and choosing the Scientific option. Or while the app is running, press Command ⌘-2. As you can see from Figure 3.3, the look and functionality of the Calculator app can change dramatically.
>
> The Calculator app can also transform into a programmer calculator. To make this change, select Programmer from the View menu or use the ⌘-3 keyboard shortcut. To switch back to a basic calculator, select Basic from the View menu or use the Command ⌘-1 keyboard shortcut.

FIGURE 3.2

The basic Calculator app can handle straightforward numeric calculations.

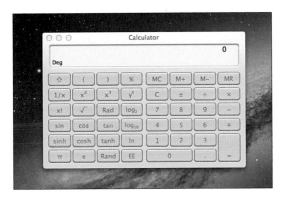

FIGURE 3.3

The Calculator app can be transformed into a scientific calculator with a few clicks.

Beyond just performing mathematical calculations that a traditional handheld calculator is capable of, the app includes a powerful conversion tool that offers a variety of options. To access the conversion calculator functionality of the app, from the Convert menu select Area, Currency, Energy or Work, Length, Power, Pressure, Speed, Temperature, Time, Volume, or Weights and Masses.

A separate pop-up window will appear, allowing you to enter raw data to be converted, as shown in Figure 3.4. For example, to quickly convert 70 degrees Fahrenheit to Celsius, launch the basic calculator and enter the number 70 using the keyboard. Then select the Temperature option from the Convert menu.

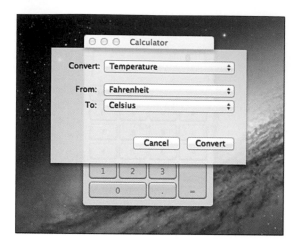

FIGURE 3.4

The Calculator app can perform a wide range of conversion-related calculations, as well, without you having to know any formulas.

Within the pop-up window that appears, in the Convert field, make sure the Temperature option is selected. Then, in the From field, select Fahrenheit. In the To field, select Celsius from the pull-down menu. Click the Convert button, and 70 degrees Fahrenheit will be converted to 21.11 degrees Celsius.

TIP To ensure accuracy as you're manually entering numeric data into the Calculator app, turn on the Speak Button Pressed option (under the Speech pull-down menu). Then, each time you enter a number or press a button on the calculator, a computer voice will say what you've pressed. Also turn on the Speak Result option from the same menu so that the app will speak the results of your calculations in addition to displaying them.

You can also transform the Calculator app into an adding machine with a virtual paper tape. This allows you to see a history of your calculators within a separate window that resembles a paper tape. To turn on this feature, from the Window menu, select Paper Tape.

Once a paper tape is displayed on the screen, you can use the Print Tape command (under the File menu) at anytime to print out that paper tape. Alternatively, just use the ⌘-P keyboard shortcut.

TIP When you are using the Calculator app, the paper tape always runs in the background, even if you choose not to display it on the screen. As a result, you can still print the paper tape, even if it's not displayed.

To save the paper tape as a file, use the Save Tape As command under the File menu. The keyboard shortcut for this command is Shift-⌘-S. When prompted, enter a filename in the Save As field, and select the destination where the file should be stored from the Where field. Click the Save button to save the file.

When using the Calculator app, you can enter numbers by positioning the cursor over the keys on the calculator and pressing the mouse button, or you can use the physical keys on your keypad to enter numbers and symbols.

TIP If you plan to use the Calculator app frequently, create an alias for it on your desktop by accessing the Applications folder and dragging the Calculator app icon from there to your desktop. Then, when you double-click the Calculator (alias) app icon on your desktop, the app will launch. This process works with any app. Of course, you can also add the app icon to your Dock by dragging the Calculator app icon from the Applications folder to the Dock.

NOTE Remember, you can always delete the alias app icon on your desktop or from the Dock by dragging it to the Trash icon on your Dock. This removes the app icon, but the app itself remains stored on your computer and is accessible from the Applications folder.

However, if you drag the app icon from the Applications folder to the Trash folder, and then use the Empty Trash command, this deletes the app from your Mac altogether.

USING THE CALENDAR APP

The newly designed Calendar app functions very much like the Calendar app for the iPad. It is also 100 percent compatible with the iCal app, which was included with earlier versions of OS X. This version of Calendar (version 6.0 or later) that comes preinstalled with Mountain Lion offers a handful of new features, however.

> **✓ TIP** When working with the Calendar app, click the Day, Week, Month, or Year tab to quickly switch calendar views. Or, to jump to a specific date and see the Day view for it, double-click that date when viewing the Month or Year view, for example. To jump to today's date, click the Today button near the upper-right corner of the Calendar app window.

CUSTOMIZING THE CALENDAR APP

The Calendar app is now more customizable than ever. To personalize this app after launching it, select Calendar, Preferences from the menu bar. Then, one at a time, click the General, Accounts, Advanced, and Alerts tabs near the top of the Preferences window to customize various aspects of the app around your personal/work schedule, as shown in Figure 3.5.

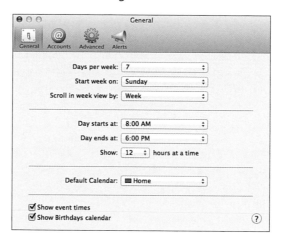

FIGURE 3.5

You can customize the Calendar app according to your personal/work schedule. The General options are shown here.

For example, after clicking the General tab, choose between a 5-day or 7-day work-week, select which day your week will begin on, decide how information within the Week view of the app will be displayed, choose the time of day your workday begins and ends, select how much of the day you want the app to display at once, and choose your default calendar.

TIP When using the Contacts app, if you filled in the Birthday field for some or all of your contact entries, this information can then be displayed within the Calendar app. To do so, choose Calendar, Preferences, and in the General window check the Show Birthdays Calendar check box. Now, whenever you fill in the Birthday field within a Contacts entry, this information will automatically display within Calendar.

To set up the Calendar app to alert you of an upcoming birthday, click the Alerts tab within the Preferences window. Using the pull-down menu next to the Birthdays option, select the alert you want: None, On Day of Event (9AM), 1 Day Before (9AM), 2 Days Before (9 AM), or 1 Week Before. Using this feature, you never have to worry about missing a birthday (and even customize extra-special birthday alerts for family and close friends).

WORKING WITH THE CALENDAR SIDEBAR

The Calendar sidebar, shown in Figure 3.6, lists all active calendars (along with their color coding). This information appears along with the left margin of the app window.

Calendar listing

At-a-glance monthly calendars

FIGURE 3.6

View a listing of separate calendars you're managing with the Calendar app and switch between them from the Calendar sidebar.

Calendar enables you to maintain separate calendars simultaneously when using the app. Maintaining multiple calendars simultaneously allows you to separate various elements of your life (and those related responsibilities) yet manage everything from a single app. You can switch between them by adding or removing a check mark next to the calendar names you want to view.

To add a new calendar (with its own color code) to the Calendar app, select File, New Calendar from the menu bar. You can then give the new calendar a custom name, such as Work, Family, Travel, or so on. You can view all events that are related to all of your calendars simultaneously, or you can pick and choose which calendars you want to view events from.

TIP When you create and maintain multiple calendars within the Calendar app, each calendar is assigned a unique color. To custom-select a color that is associated with each calendar, select and highlight the calendar within the Calendars list, but when you click the calendar listing, hold down the Control key at the same time. Then, click the Get Info option. Within the window that appears, click the color pull-down menu and choose the color you want to associate with that calendar. Your options are Red, Orange, Tallow, Green, Blue, Purple, Brown, or Other. If you choose Other, you can select any color from the Colors window that appears.

Choosing a color you relate to will help you visually associate specific calendars with specific types of appointments. For example, blue can represent work, red can represent events related to your kids, and green can represent your workout schedule.

TIP To view or hide the Calendar sidebar, select View, Show Calendar List (or Hide Calendar List) from the menu bar. You can also click on the Calendars button that's displayed above the sidebar (near the top-left corner of the app window).

NOTE Also displayed on the Calendar sidebar can be up to three at-a-glance month calendars, one for the current month and up to two more representing the next two months (refer back to Figure 3.6). To switch between one, two, or three calendars, place your mouse over the line above the top-most calendar and drag it up or down.

You can also click the small left- or right-arrow icons to the right and left of the top calendar within the sidebar to move forward or backward one month at a time. Today's date is highlighted in blue. To jump to a specific day, click any day within either of the small at-a-glace calendars.

ENTERING EVENTS INTO THE CALENDAR APP

When you enter an appointment, meeting, or another time-sensitive obligation into the Calendar app, the app itself refers to each entry as an event. There are several ways to enter new events into the Calendar app.

> **NOTE** In the past, people also used the iCal app (the predecessor to Calendar) to manage their to-do lists. Now, this is a task you can use the Reminders app for.

For example, when viewing the Day, Week, or Month view, double-click the date/time in which you want to enter a new event. You can then enter the new event name into the app. Next, add details to the event. Double-click that new event listing, and when the window appears for that new event, click the Edit button.

> **TIP** if you use multiple calendars, set your default calendar to Selected Calendar (from the Preferences option). Then, when entering new events, click the appropriate calendar in the sidebar before adding the event. By doing this, the new event will automatically be created within that calendar.
>
> However, if you set a specific calendar as the default, all new events will be created there, and you'll need to manually change the associated calendar in the Edit window if it ultimately belongs in a different calendar.

When you edit an event, you can enter details about it, including the event name, location, and date and time, as shown in Figure 3.7. You can also choose whether the event will repeat (every day, every week, every month, or every year, for example). If you're using Calendar with an Exchange Server to share your scheduling data with co-workers, for example, you can also decide how the event will be blocked out on your calendar. For example, you could have the Calendar app say you're Busy or Free.

NOTE If an event will last all day, select the All-Day option (also shown in Figure 3.7). Otherwise, you can manually enter a start date and time and an end date and time for the event.

FIGURE 3.7

When editing Calendar events, you can link various information to it, such as a location, website URL, alarms, a time/date, and notes.

TIP When you enter a location for an event (based on an address for a contact that's stored within the Contacts app), if you're syncing your Calendar data with your iPhone or iPad, this data can link with the Maps app, enabling you to map out directions to the event's location from your iDevice. (If you're using iOS 6, you can obtain turn-by-turn directions to and from the destination.)

While editing an event, you can click the Calendar option to choose which calendar the event will be added to. Then, click the Alert option to add additional alerts to that event.

Click the Add Invitees option within the event edit window to invite other people to the event. Your Mac will email them an invitation via the Mail app, and the Calendar app will keep track of their RSVP. This feature also works with Outlook, so you can invite PC users to events, as well. By clicking the Attachments option, you can link a file, such as a Word document or PDF file, with the event.

If you want to link a website to the new event (or the event you're editing), click the URL field and enter a website address. You also have the option to include text notes in the Notes field.

QUICKLY ADDING NEW EVENTS TO THE CALENDAR APP

Another way to enter a new event into the Calendar app is to select File, New Event. The keyboard shortcut is ⌘-N.

The most efficient way to enter a new event into the Calendar app is to click the plus sign icon near the upper-left corner of the app window. When you do this, a Create Quick Event window opens, as shown in Figure 3.8.

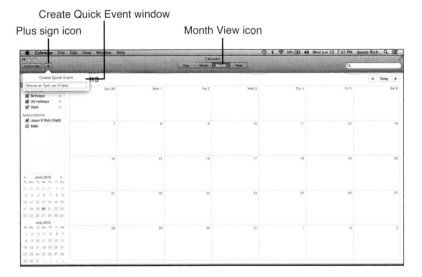

FIGURE 3.8

The Create Quick Event window. Shown here is the Month view of the Calendar app, but with no events added.

Within the Create Quick Event field, enter your new event information in your own words. For example, you can type, "Lunch meeting with Natalie at 2 p.m. tomorrow at Starbucks." When you press the Return key, the new event is created, and a New Event edit window containing the event details displays. You can then associate alerts or add additional details to the event, or click the Done button to save the information within your Calendar.

TIP To make entering a new event even easier, use the Dictation feature. To do this, click the Create Quick Event (plus sign) icon near the top-left corner of the Calendar app window. When the Create Quick Event window appears, double-click the Function (fn) key. When the Dictation icon appears, start speaking. Say something like, "Sales meeting on Thursday, December 6th at 2 p.m. in Conference Room 4." When you're done speaking, click the Done button. Once your speech has been translated to text, press the Return key to enter it into your calendar.

NOTE To delete an event from your schedule, select and highlight the event listing and press the Delete key. You can also select Edit, Delete from the menu bar.

SYNCING CALENDAR WITH ICLOUD (AND OTHER MACS AND IDEVICES)

Like many of the core apps that come with Mountain Lion, the Calendar app fully integrates with iCloud. This means that as you add, edit, or delete events from your Calendar, and as long as your computer is connected to the Internet, those updates are backed up and synced automatically with iCloud. This process happens automatically and in the background.

Any other Macs or iDevices that are linked to your iCloud account can automatically download the updated Calendar data, so your schedule is always accessible, accurate, and up-to-date on all of your computers / mobile devices.

NOTE If you add a new event on your iPhone or iPad, that new event will be synced with your Mac and visible the next time you launch the Calendar app on your Mac, assuming your iDevice and Mac are connected to the Internet and linked to the same iCloud account.

To set up iCloud functionality to work with the Calendar app, launch System Preferences and click the iCloud option. When the iCloud window appears, make sure you're signed in to your iCloud account. Then, select the Calendars & Reminders option. From this point forward, the Calendar app automatically syncs with iCloud.

> **NOTE** Once you're syncing your Calendar app data with iCloud, anytime you make a change to your schedule, that change will be reflected within the Calendar app on all of your Macs iDevices that are linked to that iCloud account. So, if you accidentally delete an important event, it will automatically be deleted from all of your computers and mobile devices that are also connected to the Internet.

Using any computer or mobile device that's connected to the Internet, you can view your schedule at anytime by visiting www.icloud.com/#calendar and signing in to the website using your Apple ID and password (or your iCloud account information).

The online-based Calendar app, which looks very similar to the one running on your Mac, will be displayed. You can access this from a PC, Mac, or any Internet-enabled mobile device (even if it's not an iPhone or iPad).

CUSTOMIZING HOW NOTIFICATION CENTER WORKS WITH THE CALENDAR APP

By default, the Calendar app works seamlessly with Notification Center. However, you can customize how Calendar displays alerts, alarms, and notifications using alerts and banners (and within the Notification Center window). You customize the app from within System Preferences.

After launching System Preferences, click the Notifications option. Then, on the right side of the Notifications window, click the Calendar listing. Then, decide whether alerts generated by the Calendar will appear on your desktop as banners or alerts or if they'll appear within the Notification Center window, as shown in Figure 3.9.

> **NOTE** On your desktop, a banner displays a pop-up window associated with an alert, alarm, or notification generated by an app (such as Calendar), but the pop-up window disappears automatically after a few seconds. An alert creates the same type of pop-up window on your desktop pertaining to an alert, alarm, or notification that's generated by an app. However, the pop-up window remains visible on your desktop until you manually dismiss it.

FIGURE 3.9

Customize how Notification Center works with the Calendar app.

To make sure that the Notification Center app monitors the Calendar app and displays alerts generated by the app within the Notification Center window, be sure to select the Show in Notification Center option. Then, from the pull-down menu, decide how many individual app-specific notifications will simultaneously be displayed within the Notification Center window at any given time. Your options include 1 Recent Item, 5 Recent Items, 10 Recent Items, or 20 Recent Items.

> **TIP** To avoid having your Notification Center window become too cluttered with app-specific notifications, it's a good strategy to limit the number of listings to five or fewer per app.

TIPS TO GET THE MOST OUT OF THE CALENDAR APP

The following seven additional tips will help you work with the Calendar app more efficiently on your Mac:

- To quickly increase (or decrease) the size of the text used to display your events, select View, Make Text Bigger (or Make Text Smaller) from the menu bar.

- If you're syncing Calendar data with iCloud, but your computer has lost its Internet connection at some point and for whatever reason, use the Refresh Calendars command when your computer is reconnected to the Internet to immediately update your Calendar data. The keyboard shortcut for this command is ⌘-R.

■ Like most core apps, you can use the Calendar app in Full Screen mode by clicking the Full Screen icon near the top-right corner of the app window. Or select View, Enter Full Screen from the menu bar. To later exit out of Full Screen mode, press Esc. Another way to exit Full Screen mode in this or any other app is to hover the mouse near the very top of the screen so that the menu bar reappears and then click the Full Screen icon again.

■ To manually create a backup of your Calendar database, select File, Export from the menu bar. This feature is also useful if you want to manually load your Calendar data into another scheduling app on a Mac or PC. If you're creating a backup for archival purposes, use the Calendar Archive feature. If the data will be exported from Calendar and then imported into another app, use the Export command.

> **NOTE** If you're not using iCloud to automatically back up your Calendar database, get into the habit of regularly using the Export command to back up your Calendar information to an external storage device, such as a USB flash drive or an external hard drive.

■ To print Calendar information, select File, Print from the menu bar. This brings up the Print window shown in Figure 3.10. From here, choose a calendar view, paper size, and time/date range. In addition, choose what Calendar data you want to print. You can also select a text size.

> **TIP** As you're using the Calendar app, you can select and copy one or more events and then paste this information into a separate text document (within Notes) or a word processing file (within Pages or Word). You can then format the event information as you see fit and print out a customized listing of specific events.
>
> You can also use the Print command within the Calendar app itself and customize what information you want printed and in what format. The available options have been greatly expanded in this Mountain Lion edition for the Calendar app.

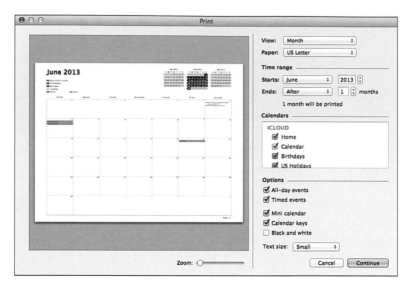

FIGURE 3.10

From Calendar, you can print out your schedule data in a variety of easy-to-read formats, and decide what information gets included within the printout.

■ In addition to automatically syncing your Calendar data with iCloud (which makes it accessible to your other Macs and iDevices that are linked to the same iCloud account), you can sync the Calendar app with Google or Yahoo! (and with Microsoft Exchange or another scheduling app that supports the CalDAV industry-standard file format). To set this up, select Calendar, Preferences from the menu bar, and then open the Accounts tab. Then, click the plus sign icon in the lower-left corner of the window and choose your account type from the pull-down menu. Based on the Account type you choose, you are prompted to enter your username and password or other information giving the Calendar app access to an online service or another scheduling application. Click the Create button to save the information and begin syncing data.

!CAUTION Keep in mind that you can set up each calendar to sync with either iCloud or another CalDAV-compatible app, but not both.

■ If you travel a lot, you can set up the Calendar app so that it automatically adjusts to whatever time zone you're in. To do this, select Calendar, Preferences, and then open the Advanced tab and check the Turn On Time Zone Support check box. When you do this, you can change the default time zone for all events, and you can select a different time zone for specific events.

USING THE CONTACTS APP

The Contacts app enables you to create and maintain a database of people and companies (your personal contacts). What's nice about the app is that it's highly customizable, based on your needs. You can create a default card format, with the specific fields you want to consistently include for all of your contacts, or you can use the default card format and then customize each new entry by picking and choosing applicable fields as you enter new information or edit card entries.

> **TIP** To create a custom card format that will be used anytime you create a new card entry within Contacts, launch the app and select Contact, Preferences from the menu bar, and then click the Template tab near the top-left corner of the screen. Then, add or delete fields within the template.
>
> When you access the Add Field menu shown in Figure 3.11, more a dozen optional fields become available. As you're creating a contact card, you can include multiple addresses, email addresses, phone numbers, and websites, but still label each of them differently.
>
> To do this, enter one address or phone number, for example, at a time. Then click the label associated with that content, and choose a label from the pull-down menu that appears. You also have the option of creating a custom label.
>
> After you've created a custom template, anytime you're using the Contacts app and choose to create a new card entry, the newly formatted card template will be available for you to fill in.

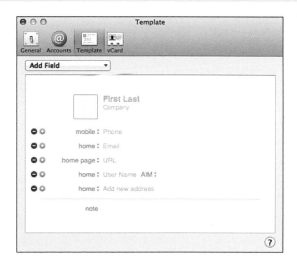

FIGURE 3.11
You can fully customize the template for creating new contact entries, or manually add custom fields as you create each new entry.

SYNCING CONTACTS DATA WITH ICLOUD (AND OTHER CONTACT MANAGEMENT APPLICATIONS)

Like the Calendar app, Contacts is fully compatible with iCloud, and it also syncs data with a handful of contact management online applications, including Yahoo! Address Book. Plus, the app is compatible with any contact management app that uses the industry-standard CardDAV or LDAP file formats. This includes Microsoft Exchange. However, you must choose just one service to sync your data with. The same calendar data cannot be synced with iCloud and Yahoo!, for example.

> ☑ **TIP** To set up applications or contact management services for Contacts to sync with, launch the Contacts app and select Contacts, Preferences from the menu bar. On the Accounts tab, click the plus sign icon in the lower-left corner of the Accounts window. Choose the type of account you want to sync your Contacts database with, and then enter your username, password, and server address (if applicable) in the appropriate fields. Contacts can sync with multiple contact management applications simultaneously, as well as with iCloud.

> ✐ **NOTE** The process for setting up the Contacts app to sync with iCloud is almost identical to the process used for the Calendar app. Launch System Preferences, select the iCloud option, make sure you're signed in to your iCloud account, and then select the Contacts app. This only needs to be done once to begin automatically syncing and backing up your Contacts database via iCloud.

Just like with the Calendar app, once your Contacts database is synced with iCloud, it becomes accessible and can be synced automatically with your other Macs and iDevices that are linked to the same iCloud account. Plus, using any computer that's connected to the Internet, you can access www.icloud.com/#contacts, sign in to the website using your Apple ID (or iCloud account information), and then access your Contacts database. Keep in mind that any changes you make to your Contacts database from the iCloud website automatically sync with your Macs and iDevices.

GROUPING YOUR CONTACTS

To help you organize your contacts and group-related contacts, the Mountain Lion version of Contacts (version 7.0 or later) offers enhanced grouping functions. It also displays your groups if you want (along the left side of the app window), as shown in Figure 3.12.

FIGURE 3.12
When the groups listing is displayed, the Contacts app contains three separate sections: the Groups listing, the All Contacts listing, and the individual card column.

> ☑ **TIP**   To display or hide the groups column, select View, Groups from the menu bar. If you select the List and Card option, the Contacts app will display only two columns. On the left will be a complete listing of the contacts in your database, and on the right will be the highlighted and selected individual card listing. If you select the Card Only option, only the currently highlighted and selected card will display within the app window. Near the bottom center of the app window, three view icons enable you to quickly switch views by clicking any one of them.

To create a new group of contacts, select File, New Group, New Group from Selection, New Smart Group (or New Smart Group from Current Search). Either option enables you to group related contact entries, but each in a slightly different way.

> ✎ **NOTE**   The keyboard shortcut to create a new card is ⌘-N. To create a new group, the keyboard shortcut is Shift-⌘-N. The keyboard shortcut to create a new Smart Group is Option-⌘-N.

For example, when you select New Group, a new group is created and listed within the groups column, but it will be empty. So, first, give a custom name to the group. Then, as you create new cards, you can place them within the newly created group. Or, as you're using the three-column Groups view, from the middle column (which lists all of your contacts) select and highlight one or more contact entries at a time and drag them to the left, into the newly created group folder.

If you select the New Group from Selection option, a new group is created (which you can custom name), but the contact entries that were already highlighted and selected from the middle column (the listing of all of your contacts) are automatically be added to the group.

The New Smart Group option enables you to search your entire contacts database for entries that contain specific content and then group together those entries. For example, if you have 10 contacts within your database for individual employees who work for the same company, you can create a new smart group and quickly group those contacts together.

> ### ☑ TIP   When you choose to create a new smart group, a Smart Group pop-up window appears in which you can define the criteria for automatically adding entries to that group. Use the pull-down menus to fine-tune the search criteria. For example, if you're looking for all contact entries that relate to employees from a specific company, from the leftmost pull-down menu select the Company option. From the middle pull-down menu, choose Contains, and then in the field on the right, enter the name of the company.

The New Smart Group from Current Search feature enables you to perform a search using the Search field at the top of the contacts list (the middle column when using the Group view). The app then creates a group based on card entries generated by the search results.

SHARING CONTACTS DATA WITH OTHERS

Near the bottom of the card column of the Contacts app window is a Share button, as shown in Figure 3.13. When you want to share the contact details from a specific Contacts entry with someone else, click this button and choose how you want to send the data. Your options include Email, Message, and AirDrop. When you send a single contact entry using one of these share options, that contact card will be sent to the recipients and can be viewed or imported into their Contacts app (or the contact management application they're using).

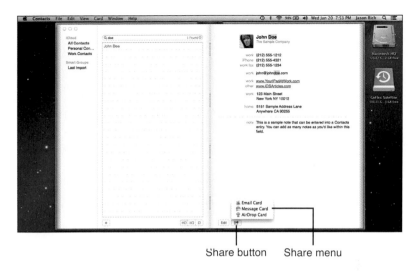

Share button   Share menu

FIGURE 3.13

From within Contacts, you can share information for one contract entry with other people via email, message, or AirDrop.

LEVERAGING FIELD LABELS WHEN CREATING NEW ENTRIES

As you're creating or editing contact entries within your database, be sure to use the specific field labels available to you. Keep in mind that other apps on your Mac (and iDevices) will access information from your Contacts database and can use specific data fields.

For example, when entering multiple physical addresses for a contact, use the Home, Work, and Other field labels. Likewise, when entering multiple email addresses or phone numbers, take advantage of the different field labels available. To choose a field label as you're creating or editing a contact entry, click the label name (as opposed to the data field next to it). A pull-down menu will display listing the available label titles for that field, as shown in Figure 3.14.

To create a custom label (that will then be accessible when creating new contacts or editing other contacts), click the Custom option on this pull-down menu. When the Add Custom Label pop-up window appears, enter the custom label you want to create. As you're creating or editing a template within Contacts (by selecting Preferences and clicking the Template tab), you can add custom fields, which will then be accessible anytime you create a new contact entry.

Field label menu

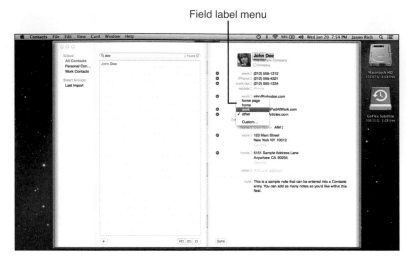

FIGURE 3.14
As you're creating or editing a contact, it's easy to customize the label associated with many of the data fields.

> **TIP** Apps like FaceTime and Messages will look for contact entries with phone numbers labeled with the iPhone label (as opposed to the Mobile label) when trying to establish connections with other people. So, if you know a contact uses an iPhone, be sure to label that person's iPhone phone number accordingly.

INTERACTIVE FIELDS IN CONTACT ENTRIES

Once contact entries are created and you're viewing them, you'll discover that many of the fields are interactive. For example, if you click someone's email address, the Mail app opens, and you can compose an email message to that person. Likewise, when you click a website URL, Safari launches and loads that website.

> **TIP** If you're syncing your Contacts database with an iPhone or iPad, the Phone Number and Address fields are also interactive. On an iPhone, if you tap on a phone number within the Contacts app, your phone will dial that number. Or if you tap on an address when using an iDevice, the Maps app will launch, enabling you to view that location on a map or obtain detailed directions to it from your current location.

CREATING A CONTACTS ENTRY FOR YOURSELF

Be sure to create an entry for yourself within your Contacts database, and then use the Make This My Card option under the Card menu. This allows your Mac to share your personal contact information with other apps (or individuals) as needed.

For example, if you're shopping online using Safari, instead of having to constantly enter your mailing address, use Safari's AutoFill option and have your address data pulled from you're My Card entry within Contacts. Or if you're communicating with someone and want to share your contact details, from within the Contacts app, use the Share My Card option (under the Card menu) to send your information to that person via email, message, or AirDrop.

> **TIP** If you'll be syncing your Contacts data with your iPhone, creating a My Card field and populating it with all of your information, including your home and work addresses, phone numbers, email address, and Related People information, is important, because Siri and your other iPhone apps will utilize this data.

> **TIP** Especially after you've synced your Contacts database with other contact management applications or online services, you'll want to weed out unwanted duplicate entries. To do so, use the Look for Duplicates feature under the Card menu.

CONTACTS IS NOW FACEBOOK COMPATIBLE

Now that Facebook functionality has been integrated into Mountain Lion (starting in Fall 2012), when you initially log in to your Facebook account from your Mac you'll be given the option to automatically add your Facebook friends to your Contacts database. When you do this, their profile photos and contact information are imported as well.

> **NOTE** To set up Facebook integration on your Mac (which only needs to be done once), launch System Preferences, select the Mail, Contacts & Calendars, and then click the Facebook logo on the right side of the window. When prompted, enter your Facebook username and password. When completed, a listing for the newly set up account will show on the left side of the Mail, Contacts & Calendars window. Facebook integration is now set up and functional. From this point forward, when applicable, a Facebook option appears within the Share menus of various apps.
>
> You can set up Twitter and Flickr integration on your Mac in the same way.

What's nice about this feature is that when your Facebook friends update their contact information or photo online, these changes are synced automatically with your Contacts database.

> **TIP**   When you set up Facebook functionality to work with Mountain Lion, your own Facebook profile photo is used within your My Card entry. This photo can then be shared (automatically) with other people whenever you communicate with them via email, message, or Facebook. Whenever you change your profile photo on Facebook, the change will be made on your Mac as well.

ENHANCING FACETIME VIDEO CONFERENCES

The FaceTime app is used for real-time video conferencing, for free, from your Mac. You can use this app (and Apple's FaceTime service) as long as your computer is connected to the Internet. FaceTime enables you to communicate with other Mac and iDevice users.

Using the FaceTime app on your Mac is pretty straightforward. The app uses your Mac's built-in camera to broadcast your video feed to the person you're video conferencing with. The built-in microphone enables you to speak to the person, and the built-in speakers enable you to hear any audio on the video feed.

The trickiest aspect of using FaceTime is establishing that initial connection. To use FaceTime, each user needs a personal FaceTime account (which is free to set up and use). When you set up an account, you must associate an email address with your account, which serves as your unique identifier (like a phone number) so that people can contact you.

To associate multiple email addresses with your FaceTime account after it's established, select FaceTime, Preferences from the menu bar, and then click the Add Another Email button.

> **NOTE**   By default, when using an iPhone to communicate via FaceTime, the iPhone's phone number is used as its unique identifier (as opposed to the user's email address).

> **TIP**   To establish a FaceTime link with someone else, you need to know the email address that person used to set up his or her FaceTime account. If that person is using an iPhone, you'll need to know the iPhone's phone number.

If you plan to communicate with someone often via FaceTime, add that person to your Favorites list. To do so, you can link a FaceTime Favorites entry with someone from your Contacts database. Alternatively, click the Recents button near the bottom-right corner of the FaceTime app window, click the > icon that's associated with a Recents listing, and then click the Add To Favorites button.

> **TIP** To avoid being disturbed by incoming FaceTime calls, you can temporarily turn off the FaceTime feature. To do so, select FaceTime, Preferences from the menu bar, and then turn off the virtual switch associated with the FaceTime option. Remember to turn it back on when you want to use the FaceTime app later to participate in video conferences.

While you're engaged in a video conference with someone else, you can do several things to improve the video and audio quality of the connection, including the following:

- Make sure you're connected to the fastest Internet connection possible. If you're using a Wi-Fi connection, choose a network with the strongest signal possible.

- If you're using a MacBook Pro or MacBook Air, place the computer on a stable surface so that the computer doesn't move around during the video conference.

- Avoid a lot of physical movement on your part during a FaceTime video conference to avoid blurs.

- To improve the sound quality, consider connecting an optional microphone and headphones or a headset (with headphones and microphone built in) to your computer. Using the same type of Bluetooth wireless headset as you'd use with your cell phone will help eliminate background noise and allow you to hear and be heard better.

- During a FaceTime conference, when your Mac's camera is on you, place a light source in front of your face. At the same time, avoid having a bright light source behind you. For example, don't sit in front of a window on a sunny day. If the primary light source (such as a lamp) is directly over your head, your face may appear dark or covered in shadow.

> **TIP** If you want to participate in video conferences with non-Apple users, you'll need to use the free Skype app (or a video conferencing app and service offered by another provider, such as Oovoo.com or GoToMeeting.com). One-to-one video conferencing with Skype, for example, is free.

If you sign up for the premium (paid) Skype service or use Oovoo.com, for example, it's possible to video conference with multiple people at the same time, even if everyone is at a different location. It will be necessary to download a separate video conferencing app, such as the free Skype app (www.skype.com), to use a service other than FaceTime for video conferencing.

USING THE PHOTO BOOTH APP

While the FaceTime app takes advantage of your Mac's built-in camera so that you can participate in real-time video conferences, the Photo Booth app enables you to use that same camera to shoot digital photos (stills) or short movies on your Mac and then share those photos or videos with others. This app offers a much slicker user interface when used in Full Screen mode.

When you launch the Photo Booth app, shown in Figure 3.15, you'll see a large red icon near the bottom center of the screen. When the app is in Photo mode, this red icon serves as your shutter button for snapping photos. When the app is in Video mode, the red icon shows a video camera within it, and it is used to start and stop the video recording.

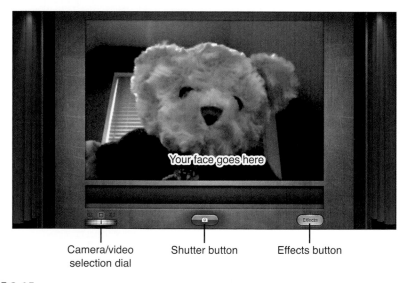

Camera/video   Shutter button   Effects button
selection dial

FIGURE 3.15

Here, the Photo Booth app is set to shoot still images (digital photos). The look of this app changes rather dramatically if you enter into Full Screen mode.

When in Full Screen mode, the dial icon near the bottom-left corner of the screen enables you to switch between Photo and Video mode. The Effects button in the lower-right corner of the window enables you to choose from up to 40 "special effects" to add to your photos or videos. These special effects include distorted lenses and custom backgrounds that can be superimposed digitally behind you. Keep in mind, if you want to add a special effect to your photo (or video), you must select the effect first.

> ### NOTE
> If you run Photo Booth in a standard app window, the command options are the same, but the look and layout of the buttons and icons are slightly different.

When you snap a photo or take a video, a thumbnail for it displays along the bottom of the Photo Booth app window. You can then select and highlight the thumbnail to export, share, or delete it.

To export a photo or video file so that it can be viewed, edited, and potentially shared with other apps, such as iPhoto or iMovie, for example, after highlighting the thumbnail select File, Export from the menu bar. When the Save pop-up window appears, enter a filename and choose where you want the file to be saved. Click the Save button. Alternatively, you can drag the thumbnail from the Photo Booth app window onto your desktop, into a Finder window, or directly into another app.

> ### NOTE
> By default, photos and videos shot using the Photo Booth app are saved in a Photo Booth Library folder that the app automatically creates within your Pictures folder. You can access this folder directly using Finder. To do this, click the Pictures option within the sidebar of a Finder window, and look for the Photo Booth Library folder. To use images or video shot with Photo Booth in other apps, you must copy or export the file out of Photo Booth first, however. Otherwise, if you just click an image within the Photo Booth Library folder, the Photo Booth app will open and display the photo.

To Share the photo or file, select and highlight the thumbnail, and then click the Share icon. The Share menu enables share the photo via email, message, AirDrop, Twitter, Facebook, and Flickr. You can also directly export the photo into iPhoto. There's also an option on the Share menu to set the photo as your default account or buddy image.

To delete a photo or video shot using Photo Booth, select and highlight the thumbnail, and then click the X in the upper-left corner of the thumbnail. Or, with the thumbnail selected, select Edit, Delete from the menu bar, or use the keyboard shortcut ⌘-Delete.

> **TIP** After a photo has been taken, to flip the image, highlight and select its thumbnail, and use the Flip Photo command from the Edit menu or use the ⌘-F keyboard shortcut. You can also set the app to auto-flip photos (using the Auto Flip New Items command under the Edit menu).
>
> Flipping images is useful if you're wearing something with text on it, for example. By default, when you snap a photo or shoot a video using Photo Booth, that text will appear backward (as if you're looking in a mirror). The Flip or Auto Flip feature will correct this.

To enhance the quality of the photos or videos you take, make sure the primary light source is in front of you. Avoid having a bright light source behind you or just over your head. To improve the audio quality when recording videos, consider connecting an external microphone to your Mac.

GETTING QUICK VIEWS VIA THE PREVIEW APP

Whether you're browsing through files stored on your Mac using Finder, you have file icons displayed on your desktop, or you receive emails with attachments, you can quickly preview the contents of compatible files using the Preview app, instead of loading a specific app compatible with the file type. Preview works with document files, text files, photos, video files and PDF files, for example.

> **NOTE** The Preview app also now enables you to easily transfer documents and files from a Finder window on your Mac to your iCloud account using iCloud's Documents in the Cloud feature.

Another new feature of Preview is the Share icon. When you have a file open within the Preview window, click the Share icon to quickly and easily share that file with others, without having to manually launch another app. Depending on the type of file you're viewing, the Share menu will include options for email, messages, AirDrop, Facebook, Twitter, and Flickr. Figure 13.16 shows the Preview app's Share button when a photo is being viewed.

Share button   Share menu

FIGURE 3.16
The options offered by the Share button within Preview change based on the type of file you're viewing.

TIP If you're viewing a PDF document within the Preview app window, you can annotate that file using inline notes, or fill in PDF-formatted forms, without launching another app. For example, if someone emails you a contract in PDF format, from within the Mail app you can open the attached PDF-formatted contract in Quick Look, select the Open in Preview option, read and digitally sign the document, and then use the Share option to send back that contract via email.

The Preview app is also compatible with external scanners that are connected to your Mac. Therefore, you can open Preview and import documents, photos, or other printed matter by scanning it into the app. Save the scanned file in one of several formats, and share it, store it on your Mac, or use the scanned files with other apps.

NOTE Need to take a screenshot of something on your Mac or within a specific window? You can do so by launching the Preview app and selecting File, Take Screen Shot from the menu bar. You can then choose to manually select an area of the screen to capture, take a screen capture of a specific window, or snap an image of the entire screen, which you can then save and use in other apps or share. You can also use the ⌘-Shift-4 keyboard shortcut or use the Grab app that's found in the Utilities subfolder of the Applications folder to take a screenshot.

Depending on the type of file you're viewing using Preview, the options available to you will vary greatly. For example, if you're viewing a graphic file or photo, click the magnifying glass icons near the top of the window to zoom in or zoom out. Use the Share button to share the image with others, or click the rotate icon to rotate the image 90 degrees at a time.

By clicking the show edit toolbar icon (near the top-right corner of the window), a handful of photo editing tools will become accessible from within the Preview app, as shown in Figure 3.17. You can, among other things, crop the image or adjust the coloring, contrast, or other elements of the image. You can also quickly resize the image from within the Preview app.

Photo-editing icons

FIGURE 3.17

When viewing a photo within Preview, you can view, edit, crop, resize, print, and share it, for example.

TIP   By resizing an image, you can dramatically reduce its file size, making it faster to upload to online services or email to other people. When you do this, the image's resolution is reduced as well, potentially preventing you from being able to make large-size prints from the smaller file. Instead of reducing your original image, make a copy of it and then reduce the size of the duplicate.

As you're working with digital images within the Preview app, in addition to the editing commands available from the icons at the top of the window, you'll discover options under the pull-down menus along the menu bar. For example, under the Tools menu, you can either rotate an image or flip it horizontally or vertically, as well as adjust its size.

> **NOTE** Use the commands found under the File menu to save, duplicate, rename, move, export, print, or close the file you're working on within Preview.
>
> The Duplicate command is somewhat similar to the now defunct Save As command, but it becomes usable only when you've made changes to a document or file. It allows you to create a duplicate of a file with the same filename as the original, but with the word *copy* added to it. Once the duplicate file is created, you must manually save it, at which time you can also manually rename it.

The command and options within Preview change if you open a PDF document, a Word or Pages document, or a different type of app-compatible file. When you are viewing a PDF file, the Tools menu includes an Annotate feature, as well as the ability to select, copy, cut, and paste text between the PDF file and other apps.

> **TIP** If you're looking at a multipage document or PDF file using Preview, click the View icon to show the contents of the document/file one page at a time or to display thumbnails or all pages along the left margin of the window. You can also view one or two full pages at a time, or choose to display a contact sheet featuring thumbnails of all pages within that document or file. You'll find the View icon near the upper-left corner of the Preview window. You can also change the view by making a selection from the View menu.

Keep in mind that although you can view or annotate a PDF file or Word/Pages document, for example, you cannot edit the document itself from within Preview. For that, you need to load the PDF file into a PDF file editor app, or load the document file into Microsoft Word, Pages, or another full-featured word processor. You can also use the TextEdit app that comes preinstalled with Mountain Lion to handle basic editing and document formatting.

While viewing a photo, graphic, PDF file, or document file within Preview, to send what you're looking at directly to your printer, use the Print command under the File menu. Alternatively, press ⌘-P as the keyboard shortcut for printing.

VIEWING IMAGES, DOCUMENTS, AND PDF FILES

When you first launch the Preview app without using it to view a specific file, the Preview app window will look somewhat similar to a Finder window, as shown in Figure 3.18. From within this window, you can find, highlight, select, and open a document, photo, or PDF file that's stored on your Mac. You can also access files stored on external hard drives (or storage devices) that are connected to your Mac, or access files stored on iCloud.

FIGURE 3.18

The Preview app window on your desktop just after the app launches. From the sidebar, you can quickly locate files/folders stored on your computer's internal storage drive or on an external drive.

Two tabs appear in the upper-left corner of the Preview app window when you first launch it: iCloud and On My Mac. To view documents, PDF files, or photos stored on iCloud, click the iCloud tab. To view something stored on your Mac, click the On My Mac tab, and then locate a file by selecting its location in the sidebar. You can then select and open a file with Preview by clicking the filename or icon on the right side of the window.

PREVIEW DIFFERS FROM QUICK LOOK

As you're using the Mail app to view incoming email with attachments, you can save the attachments on your computer. You can also click the Quick Look button to see what the file looks like (document, PDF file, or photo). What you can do with the file you're viewing within Quick Look is limited, however.

In the upper-right corner of the Quick Look window is an Open with Preview button. Use this to open the same file, document, or photo within the Preview app so that you can fully utilize all the Preview app's features and functions to work with that document, file, or photo (before you download and save it on your computer).

The Quick Look command is also accessible from within the Finder window. To use it, click a file listing or file icon and then press and hold down the Control key while clicking the mouse. The pop-up menu that appears will include a Quick Look option for opening and viewing that file, as long as it is compatible with Quick Look, as shown in Figure 3.19.

FIGURE 3.19
You can access the Quick Look feature in several ways when using Mountain Lion.

> ☑ **TIP**   You can also use the Quick Look feature from within the Finder window by clicking a file or file icon and then choosing the Quick Look option from the File menu. Yet another option is to highlight the filename or icon within the Finder window and then use the ⌘-Y keyboard shortcut.

DISCOVERING OTHER PREINSTALLED APPS

Because Mountain Lion comes with so many preinstalled apps, including a handful of new ones, subsequent chapters focus on how to best use specific apps. For example, in Chapter 4, you'll learn how to get the most out of Notification Center without becoming inundated with alerts, alarms, and notifications generated by your computer.

4

USING NOTIFICATION CENTER

The various apps you use on your Mac can generate alerts, alarms, and notifications to get your attention. In some cases, an audible alarm is generated. Other situations call for a text-based alert or banner to be displayed on the desktop.

In OS X Mountain Lion, Apple has included an app that always runs in the background and that monitors all the other compatible apps running on your Mac. It then displays all the alerts, alarms, and notifications generated by those apps (or the computer itself) in one centralized location: the Notification Center panel.

By customizing Notification Center, you can control which apps can generate audible or text alerts, alarms, and notifications, plus decide how they'll be presented to you. You can also temporarily turn off the notification process so that you can work undistributed, yet still have your computer keep track of what needs your attention.

Beyond allowing some apps to generate audible alarms, you can control how apps display text and notifications on your desktop in the form of banners or alerts. This can be in addition to or instead of what appears within the Notification Center panel.

A banner is a small information window generated by an app that pops up near the upper-right corner of the screen when an alert or notification is generated, as shown in Figure 4.1. That banner remains on the screen for several seconds and then automatically disappears. It's often accompanied by an audible alarm, but doesn't have to be.

FIGURE 4.1

A banner generated by the Calendar app. It will automatically disappear from your desktop after a few seconds.

An alert looks just like a banner, but it remains visible near the upper-right corner of the desktop until you manually dismiss it by clicking the Close or Snooze button (shown in Figure 4.2). Depending on the app, a Show or Close button may be displayed within an alert window instead. If you click a Show button, the appropriate app launches automatically and displays details related to what requires your attention. Alerts and banners are displayed regardless of which apps are currently running on your Mac.

> ✅ **TIP**   Just like the alarm clock that's probably next to your bed, if you click the Snooze button, the Alert will temporarily disappear, but automatically reappear after a few minutes.

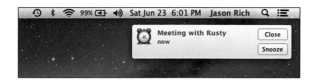

FIGURE 4.2

To make an alert window disappear from your desktop, manually click the Show, Close, or Snooze button. Otherwise, it will remain visible near the upper-right corner of the desktop. Other new alerts will be displayed below it as they're generated.

Banners and alerts can be used by specific apps to get your attention instead of, or in addition to, displaying details about the app-specific alert, alarm, or notification within the Notification Center panel, which is a comprehensive listing of notifications displayed along the right margin of the screen when you click the Notification Center icon (which you'll find on the extreme right side of the menu bar).

The various apps you use can constantly generate many different alerts, alarms, and notifications. Therefore, the trick to avoid getting inundated and overwhelmed by this information is to properly manage it. You'll definitely want to launch System Preferences and select the Notifications option so that you can fully customize how computer and app-specific notifications are generated. You want them to draw your attention only to those things you personally deem important.

NOTE   Some apps that can generate alerts, alarms, and notifications can also generate badges. This is information shown on the Dock or Launchpad screen as part of an app's icon.

For example, in relation to the Mail app, a badge can be used to display the number of new incoming email messages waiting for you to read. In conjunction with the App Store, a badge will be displayed as part of the App Store app icon to indicate how many of the apps that are installed on your Mac need to be updated. This particular badge is not user adjustable, but the rest are. The FaceTime (shown in Figure 4.3) and Messages app icons, for example, can also show badges to represent missed calls or messages.

It's possible to customize how and when badges are displayed. This, too, is done from System Preferences by selecting the Notifications option.

FaceTime icon

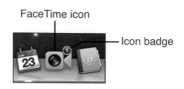

Icon badge

FIGURE 4.3

A badge associated with the FaceTime app indicates how many incoming calls you've missed.

☑ **TIP** Every app that can generate alerts, alarms, or notifications (both audible and text), as well as badges, can be customized separately. This ensures you're only alerted of information that you classify as being important, such as a new incoming email within the Mail app or an alarm associated with an upcoming appointment (event) from the Calendar app. The notification-customization process only needs to be done once, but your customizations can be updated at anytime (including, for example, when you install new apps onto your computer).

MANAGING ALL APP-SPECIFIC NOTIFICATIONS

Many of the apps that come preinstalled on your Mac with Mountain Lion, including Calendar, FaceTime, Game Center, Mail, Messages, Reminders, and Safari, can generate alerts, alarms, and notifications. Similar notifications can also be generated by Facebook and Twitter. Plus, as you install additional apps on your Mac, they may also be able to get your attention using alerts, alarms, or notifications.

Depending on how you use your Mac, you may determine that your incoming emails are extremely time sensitive (urgent), alerts associated with your schedule and to-do lists are important, and anything having to do with games you're playing on your computer, for example, have a much lower priority.

For each app that can generate notifications, you have several options, including the following:

▪ Turn off the Notification Center's ability to generate alerts, alarms, and notifications altogether. The app will still function, but it won't display information within the Notification Center panel, display banners/alerts/badges, or generate audible alarms.

▪ You can have the app only display banners when an alert, alarm, or notification is generated.

▪ You can have the app only display alerts when an alert, alarm, or notification is generated.

- You can have the app forward all alerts, alarms, and notifications to the Notification Center panel (and then decide how many items from that app will be displayed simultaneously).

- You can customize a compatible app to display a badge as part of the app's icon (on the Dock or Launchpad screen).

- You can allow the app to generate an audible alarm as a way to alert you.

- You can set up the app to generate any combination of these options for each alert, alarm, or notification so that information appears as a banner or alert, plus gets displayed within the Notification Center panel or generates an audible alarm while also displaying a badge.

To customize how each app will handle alerts, alarms, and notifications, launch System Preferences and select the Notifications option. In the Notifications window, shown in Figure 4.4, a listing of apps currently installed on your computer that can generate alerts, alarms, or notifications appears on the left side, under one of two headings: In Notification Center or Not in Notification Center.

FIGURE 4.4

The Notifications window within System Preferences is used to customize how app-specific alerts, alarms, and notifications are handled.

TIP To decide which apps will display alerts, alarms, and notifications within the Notification Center panel, highlight (one at a time) each app listing on the left side of the window. Then, on the right side of the Notifications window, select the Show in Notification Center option.

If you remove or refrain from selecting the Show in Notification Center option, that app will be moved to the Not in Notification Center listing, and information from that app will not appear within your computer's Notification Center panel.

NOTE Within the Notification Center panel, you can choose to sort the listings by the time they were generated, or select the Manual option and choose the how notifications are listed by selecting the order in which the app headings are displayed. This decision is made from within System Preferences after clicking on the Notifications option.

When a specific app is highlighted on the left side of the Notifications window within System Preferences, you can also decide whether it will be able to generate a separate banner or alert. To do this, click the None, Banners or Alerts option under the Calendar Alert Style heading.

If you click None, the app will neither display a banner nor an alert when an alert, alarm, or notification is generated. However, if you click Banners, that app will display a separate banner (near the upper-right corner of the screen) each time an alert, alarm, or notification is generated.

Finally, if you click the Alerts option with a specific app highlighted, that app will display a separate alert window each time the app generates an alert, alarm, or notification. Depending on the app and how much you rely on it, this could result in many separate alert windows being displayed along the right side of your desktop until you manually remove them by clicking their respective Show, Close, or Snooze button.

TIP If the app can generate a badge, which is displayed as part of the app's icon on the Dock or Launchpad screen, you can turn on this feature by checking the Badge App Icon check box on the right side of the Notifications window within System Preferences. If you remove the check mark from the Badge App Icon option, the app will not add badges to the app icon.

Many of the apps that can generate alerts, alarms, and notifications can also play an audible alarm. To turn on this feature, select an app from the listing on the left side of the Notifications window (within System Preferences), and then add a check the Play Sound When Receiving Notifications check box.

If you do not select this option, the app can still generate alerts and notifications that can be displayed as Banners or Alerts, or within the Notification Center panel, or as a badge, but no audible alarms will be generated.

TIP To customize the sound you hear when an audible alarm is generated on your Mac (assuming the Play Sound When Receiving Notifications option is selected for a specific app) access the Sound option within System Preferences.

When viewing the Notifications window, click the left-arrow icon in the upper-left corner of the window. From the main System Preferences window, click the Sound option.

From the Select an Alert Sound option, choose the alert sound you like from the menu. You can then select the output device (if applicable) and adjust the volume of the alert from the volume sliders displayed within the menu (shown in Figure 4.5).

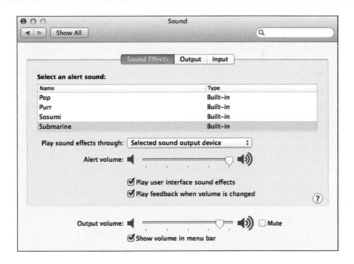

FIGURE 4.5

Customize the sound you hear when an alarm is generated by choosing the Sound option from System Preferences.

As you begin using Mountain Lion on your Mac, invest a few minutes to customize from within the Notifications window how each app will handle alerts, alarms, and notifications. As you do this, think about your work habits using your Mac and decide how you want the apps and the computer to be able to get your attention when it's needed so that you can handle something that's timely.

When you exit out of the Notifications window within System Preferences, any changes you've made are automatically saved and implemented.

NOTE If you opt to have one or more apps display alerts and notifications within the Notification Center panel, be sure to read the section "Customizing the Notification Center Panel" later in this chapter.

NOTE Prior to having Notification Center as part of the OS X operating system, many Mac users relied on a third-party app called Growl, which offered some similar functionality. In conjunction with Growl 2.0, this app is now fully compatible with Notification Center. Growl 2.0, however, offers more advanced customization options for notifications.

GETTING STARTED

Notification Center is an app that constantly runs when your computer is turned on (or in Sleep mode). It monitors all other compatible apps, and then displays any alerts or notifications generated by those apps in a centralized location (within the Notification Center panel).

TIP At anytime, regardless of what apps you're running on your Mac, to manually access and view the Notification Center panel, click the Notification Center icon near the extreme upper-right corner of the screen (shown in Figure 4.6).

When you click the Notification Center icon, whatever is being displayed on your Mac will shift slightly to the left, and the Notification Center panel will temporarily be displayed along the right margin of the desktop, as shown in Figure 4.7.

Notification
Center icon

FIGURE 4.6

The Notification Center panel icon is constantly displayed to the extreme right of the menu bar. (It does, however, get hidden if you enter into Full Screen mode when using an app.)

FIGURE 4.7

The Notification Center panel always gets displayed on the right side of the desktop.

☑ **TIP** To activate the Do Not Disturb feature and temporarily prevent alerts and banners from being displayed on the desktop while you're working, open the Notification Center panel and scroll to the top of it. Turn the virtual On/Off switch associated with the Show Alerts and Banners option to the Off position. However, don't forget to turn this feature back on when you're ready for alerts and banners to once again be displayed on your desktop.

USING THE NOTIFICATION CENTER PANEL

After opening the Notification Center panel, you will see each alert and notification generated by the apps the Notification Center app is monitoring. To determine how this information is sorted and displayed, return to System Preferences,
click the Notifications option, and then access the Sort in Notification Center pull-
down menu near the lower-left corner of the window (shown in Figure 4.8).

FIGURE 4.8

*Determine how information within the Notification Center panel will be sorted and displayed
from this pull-down menu.*

From this pull-down menu, decide whether the listing will be displayed manually (meaning you can change the order of the apps listed within the Notification
Center panel by dragging their headings up or down), or by time, which determines how the listings appear based on the date and time they are generated.

Each app that Notification Center is monitoring will display a separate heading
within the Notification Center panel. Below that heading will be the new app-
specific alerts or notifications that have been generated and that require your
attention.

The blue dot to the left of each listing (shown in Figure 4.9) indicates it's a new listing that has not been viewed or acted upon. A bell-shaped icon indicates an alarm
has been generated. Depending on the app, the information within each listing will
vary. However, each listing will always contain a heading and display the time and
date it was generated.

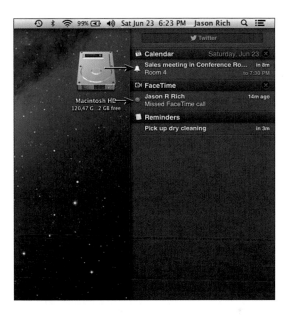

FIGURE 4.9

The blue dot displayed to the left of a Notification Center panel listing indicates it's a new item that has not been viewed or addressed by you. A bell icon indicates that an alarm has been generated.

> **TIP** As you're looking at the Notification Center panel, to clear all the alerts and notifications listed under a specific app heading, click the X icon to the left of the heading.

To immediately deal with whatever a specific alert and notification pertains to, click that listing. The appropriate app launches automatically, and whatever requires your attention appears. For example, if you click a listing for a new incoming email, the Mail app launches, and the new email displays. At the same time you click a listing within the Notification Center panel, the window itself automatically closes as the appropriate app launches.

> **TIP** To manually close the Notification Center panel and return to what you were working on without clicking any of the alerts or notifications and thus launching their relevant app, click the mouse anywhere on the desktop outside of the Notification Center panel. Or click the Close icon near the lower-right corner of the Notification Center panel. You can also click the Notification Center icon on the menu bar again.

QUICKLY SWITCHING BETWEEN RUNNING APPS

Whatever app you were working with before accessing the Notification Center panel (and potentially launching a new app) will continue to run in the background.

To quickly switch between running apps, press and hold down the ⌘ key and then press the Tab key. When you do this, app icons for each actively running app appear in the center of the screen, as shown in Figure 4.10. Keep pressing ⌘-Tab until the app icon for the app you want to switch to is highlighted, and then release the two keys. The computer will switch to the newly selected app.

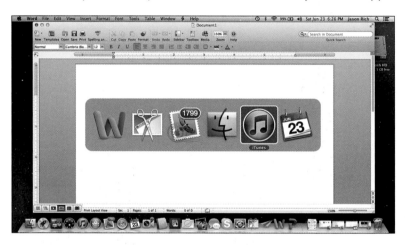

FIGURE 4.10

Press ⌘-Tab to quickly switch between apps currently running on your Mac.

You can also switch between running apps (that have windows open) by launching Mission Control. When you do this, thumbnails for each app that's running will be displayed on the screen, as shown in Figure 4.11. Click the thumbnail for the app you want to work with. All the other apps will continue running in the background.

> **NOTE** When you're viewing the Notification Center panel and then launch Mission Control, a thumbnail for the Notification Center panel will not be displayed. Only thumbnails for the actively running apps appear on the desktop. Keep in mind, Notification Center is always running in the background, but does not show up as an "open" app, because it doesn't have its own app window. Therefore, if you use the ⌘-Tab keyboard shortcut to see what apps are active and switch between them, Notification Center will not be listed.

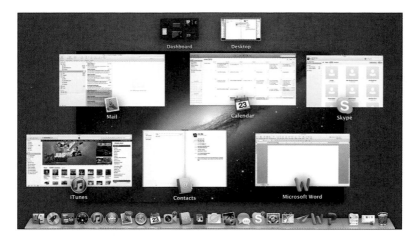

FIGURE 4.11

Switch between currently running apps by launching Mission Control. You can do so from the Dock, Launchpad, or Applications folder or by creating a shortcut icon (alias) on the desktop.

A third way to switch between actively running apps is to click the appropriate app icon in the Dock. Using this method, you can also manually launch additional apps while other apps are running.

CUSTOMIZING THE NOTIFICATION CENTER PANEL

The Notification Center panel can be fully customized in several ways, including the following:

■ Determine which apps the Notification Center app monitors.

■ Determine whether the alerts and notifications within the Notification Center panel will be displayed based on the date/time they are generated, or sorted by app in the order you choose.

■ Determine how many alerts and notifications each app can display simultaneously within your Notification Center panel. Your options include 1, 5, 10, or 20 items.

■ Determine whether a Twitter Sharing Widget will be displayed near the top of the Notification Center panel. When turned on, this feature allows you to send a tweet to your Twitter followers directly from the Notification Center panel without launching a separate Twitter app or visiting www.Twitter. com from a web browser. In late 2012, a similar feature will be available for Facebook.

■ Determine whether you want to temporarily turn off alerts and banners so that you can use your Mac without being distributed.

You already know what customizations are possible within the Notification Center panel. These customizations are done from within System Preferences, after selecting the Notifications option.

As you're looking at the Notifications window, select and highlight one app listing at a time from the left side of the screen. For that specific app, if you want it to display alerts and notifications within the Notification Center panel, select the Show in Notification Center option.

Then, click the pull-down menu displayed to the immediate left of this option and choose how many app-specific alerts or notifications you want the Notification Center panel to be able to display simultaneously. Again, your options are 1, 5, 10, or 20 items.

> **! CAUTION** Keep in mind that the number of items you select from the Show in Notification Center pull-down menu is app specific and can be changed for each app. So, for each app, if you allow for 10 items to be displayed, and Notification Center is monitoring 10 apps total, at any given time, your Notification Center panel could display up to 100 separate items.
>
> It's best to be selective and conservative when choosing how many items will be displayed within the Notification Center for each app. Otherwise, you could be inundated with alerts and notifications, which detracts from this app's ability to keep you organized and productive.
>
> For the apps you deem essential, allow 5 or 10 items to be displayed. For less-important apps, allow for just one item to be displayed, and for apps you give little importance to, refrain from having them monitored by Notification Center altogether.

Remember, at the same time you instruct Notification Center to display an app-specific alert or notification within the Notification Center panel, you can also have that app generate a banner or alert on your desktop, generate an audible alarm, or generate an app icon badge.

> **✓ TIP** When you click the Twitter button within the Notification Center panel, a tweet window opens in which you can compose and send a message (shown in Figure 4.12).
>
> If you're not active on Twitter, you can remove the Twitter button from the top of the Notification Center panel by selecting the Sharing Widget (Twitter) listing

from the left side of the Notifications window within System Preferences, and then unchecking the Show Sharing Widget in Notification Center check box (shown in Figure 4.13).

When Facebook integration is introduced into Mountain Lion in Fall 2012, an option for removing the Facebook Sharing Widget will also be displayed within the Notifications window of System Preferences.

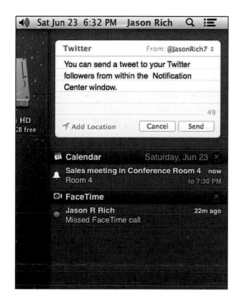

FIGURE 4.12

By default, you can send tweets from within the Notification Center panel, as long as your Mac is connected to the Internet.

NOTE If there are apps that are not important to you, and you don't care about the alerts and notifications that may be generated by them, as you're looking at the Notifications window within System Preferences highlight and select each of those apps, one at a time. Then, uncheck the Show in Notification Center check box.

As soon as you do this, the app you have selected will be moved from under the In Notification Center heading and be placed under the Not in Notification Center heading. That app will no longer be monitored by Notification Center.

FIGURE 4.13

To remove the Twitter button from the Notification Center panel, select the Sharing Widget (Twitter) option from the Notifications window and uncheck the Show Sharing Widget in Notification Center check box.

> **TIP** When looking at the listing of apps on the left side of the Notifications window within System Preferences, you can also drag and drop app listings from the In Notification Center to the Not in Notification Center list.

> **TIP** At anytime, you can have Notification Center begin monitoring a compatible app by moving the app's listing out from under the Not in Notification Center heading. To do this, when viewing the Notifications window within System Preferences, scroll down on the left side of the window to the Not in Notification Center list. Select and highlight the app that you want Notification Center to begin monitoring (shown in Figure 4.14). Then, on the right side of the Notifications window, check the Show in Notification Center check box.

FIGURE 4.14

Select and highlight an app listed under the Not in Notification Center heading that you want Notification Center to begin monitoring.

> **NOTE** Remember, even alerts and notifications generated by a specific app that are not being displayed within the Notification Center Window can still display banners, alerts, or a badge, plus have an audible alarm associated with them.

AVOIDING EXCESSIVE ALERTS, ALARMS, AND NOTIFICATIONS

Notification Center and how specific apps generate and display alerts, alarms, and notifications can be customized is several different ways. Take a few minutes to analyze your work habits on your Mac and determine which apps are the most important to you, which ones have lesser importance, and those that have no importance whatsoever.

For example, if you need to know about new incoming emails as soon as they show up in the Mail app's Inbox, you want to be alerted of an upcoming event within your Calendar app. Or maybe you want to be reminded as soon as a deadline is approaching related to a to-do list item within the Reminders app. These are apps you consider important.

Likewise, if you never play games on your Mac, or you're not active on Facebook or Twitter, any alerts, alarms, or notifications generated by Game Center or by your Facebook or Twitter online accounts will be unimportant to you.

The following are a few strategies for effectively managing the alerts, alarms, and notifications that are generated by your computer and by specific apps:

■ For the apps you classify as extremely important, make sure they're set up to display alerts and notifications within the Notification Center panel, and also set them up so that separate alerts, audible alarms, or badges are displayed by those apps.

■ Also for the apps you deem to be extremely important, allow the Notification Center panel to display up to 5 or 10 items for that app simultaneously. You can also set up those apps to be able to generate audible alarms and display banners on the desktop that will disappear automatically after a few seconds.

■ For apps that have no importance to you, keep them from being monitored by Notification Center altogether, turn off audible alarms and badges, and either just allow them to display banners (that disappear automatically) or opt for them to show no banners or alerts.

■ Based on how you set up each app to work with your Mac's notification features, if you find you're still being inundated, reduce the number of items each app can display within the Notification Center panel, turn off audible alarms for less-relevant apps, and configure (when possible) apps to display banners rather than alerts.

☑ TIP As you install new apps onto your Mac, their default options may include listing items within the Notification Center panel, displaying alerts, and having audible alarms generated. After installing a new app, launch System Preferences, select the Notifications option, and customize the notification-related options for each newly installed app.

❗CAUTION If you manually turn down the volume of your Mac's speakers or mute them altogether, you will not hear audible alarms generated by the various apps. So, if you have an app that exclusively plays audible alarms, but does not display items within the Notification Center panel, banners, alerts or badges, you could wind up missing important information.

Likewise, if you activate the Do Not Disturb feature within the Notification Center panel while you're trying to concentrate on work at hand, don't forget to turn off this feature later; otherwise, you could wind up missing important or time-sensitive information that's being conveyed to you by your various apps.

If you take a few minutes to customize the notification options for each app installed on your Mac, you'll quickly become more efficient using your computer. By doing this, you'll be alerted as soon as something important happens, whether it's a new email, text message, Facebook posting, FaceTime call, Calendar event, or to-do list item that needs your attention.

However, if you skip fine-tuning the options available that are related to notifications, you could find yourself constantly being bothered or interrupted by unimportant or irrelevant alerts, alarms, and notifications from apps you seldom use or that relate to information that is not pertinent in your life.

COMMUNICATING EFFECTIVELY WITH MESSAGES

As a method of communication using a computer, instant messaging (IMing) is nothing new. It allows you to send and receive text messages with other people in real time who are also using the same instant messaging network and who are online at the same time. Popular instant messaging services include Yahoo! Messenger, AIM, Facebook Messenger, Google Talk, and MSN Live Messenger. Instant messaging enables you to have virtual conversations using text-based dialogue via the Internet.

Apple has introduced its own instant messaging service, called iMessage, which you'll learn more about later in this chapter.

> **NOTE** Using any instant messaging service requires that your computer be connected to the Internet.

Many people enjoy text messaging and instant messaging because it allows you to communicate with people in real time but also multitask and not have to speak with individuals directly on the telephone. In fact, people in their mid-20s and younger often now rely on text messaging and instant messaging as their primary forms of communication when they're not standing face to face with someone.

> **TIP** Realistically, instead of engaging in a drawn-out messaging conversation that lasts 15 minutes or longer, you can usually get a lot more accomplished by just picking up the phone and speaking with that person. However, messaging has evolved into popular and viable forms of communication between two or more people.

INSTANT MESSAGING VERSUS TEXT MESSAGING

Communicating using an instant messaging service is always free, and it's possible to participate in several conversations at once with different people (within different windows). Many of the instant messaging services also allow you to share photos, website links, and other files with the people you're communicating with.

If you send an instant message to someone who isn't at his or her computer, the message is stored and then automatically delivered the next time the recipient signs into the instant messaging service.

> **NOTE** Due to the popularity of instant messaging, apps have been developed, including Apple's Messages, that offer compatibility with multiple instant messaging services simultaneously. This compatibility enables you to see which of your friends are online, and then be able to chat with them, using any of several services that are compatible with that app.
>
> Meanwhile, apps for popular smartphones and tablets (including the iPhone and iPad) have also been developed that offer instant messaging capabilities via the Internet. As a result, while you're on the go, you can still send and receive instant messages as long as your mobile device has Internet access and you're signed into the instant messaging service.

Traditionally, instant messaging has been something you do from your computer. For cell phone users, a separate technology was developed, called text messaging, which serves the same purpose but allows cell phone users to send and receive text-based messages from their smartphones.

Text messaging services operate using the wireless cellular network that your cell phone uses to allow for voice communication, not the Internet. Therefore, in the United States, companies such as AT&T Wireless, Verizon Wireless, Sprint PCS, and T-Mobile operate the wireless text messaging services.

> **NOTE** Text messaging is typically part of or an add-on to a cellular service plan. Most wireless service companies charge an extra fee to send/receive a pre-determined number of text messages per month, or for unlimited text messaging during a billing period. Other services include it as part of their monthly cellular plan.

While instant messaging and text messaging use two different technologies, the end result is the same. It's possible to send and receive text-based messages as well as photos, video clips, website links, and other files using these services.

COMBINING MESSAGING CAPABILITIES

With the introduction of the iMessage service and the Messages app for the Mac (as well as for the iPhone, iPad, and iPod touch), Apple has combined text messaging and instant messaging capabilities. So, Mac computer users can now send and receive text-based messages (with attachments) to other Mac users, as well as to iOS mobile device (iDevice) users, for free, via the Internet-based iMessage service.

> **NOTE** The Messages app replaces Apple's iChat app that was preinstalled with earlier editions of Mac OS X. You'll quickly discover that Messages is more robust in terms of the functionality it offers.

Along with iMessage, the Messages app is compatible with other popular instant messaging services, such as AIM, Yahoo! Messenger, and Google Talk. Using the Messages app, you can communicate with PC users or mobile device users who are not part of the iMessage network (as long as they are part of a messaging service that the Messages app supports.)

> **NOTE** While you can send messages from your Mac that's running Messages to iPhone or iPad users, or to mobile phone users who subscribe to AIM or another service that the Messages app supports, you cannot currently reach someone on their mobile phone using their cell phone number from within Messages. This functionality could, however, be added by Apple in the future.

What's great about using the Messages app is that as long as you know someone's username or cell phone number (and that they're using an iPhone), the Messages app knows how to establish the connection with the other person and does it automatically, whether that person is using AIM, iMessage, or another service.

> **TIP** Instant messaging and text messaging were originally designed for communicating one on one with other people, while allowing for multiple but separate conversations to take place simultaneously. By using the Group Messaging feature offered by the Messages app (and similar apps), however, you can invite multiple friends to participate in the same real-time chat and communicate with them at the same time, within the same chat window, so everyone who's invited can participate.

> **NOTE** Many of the popular instant messaging services now offer video/audio chatting capabilities that enable you to participate in real-time conversations with PC, Mac, or mobile device users who are part of a particular instant messaging service. Video and audio chat functionality is built in to the Messages app.

GETTING STARTED

The Messages app comes preinstalled on your Mac that's running OS X Mountain Lion. When you launch the app for the first time, you must associate your various instant messaging accounts with it. This only needs to be done once.

To set up the Messages app to work with your preexisting AIM, Yahoo! Messenger, Google Talk, Jabber, and your iMessage accounts, launch the app and select Messages, Preferences from the menu bar.

CONFIGURING TO WORK WITH BONJOUR

In the General window of Messages preferences, shown in Figure 5.1, click the Accounts tab near the top of the window. Displayed on the left side of the window will be a listing of your preexisting accounts, as shown in Figure 5.2. Right now, there are two listings: one for Bonjour and the other for iMessage. Neither is active, however.

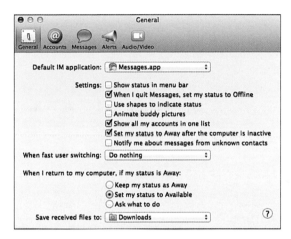

FIGURE 5.1

Add preexisting instant messaging accounts to work with the Messages app by first selecting Messages, Preferences from the menu bar. The General window will open.

FIGURE 5.2

Click the Accounts tab near the top of the window to begin adding account information to the Messages app.

> **TIP** Bonjour is a free instant messaging service that works within a local network. If your Mac is part of a local network (at work, for example), you can activate Bonjour and communicate via instant messages with other people also on that local network (including Mac or PC users).
>
> To activate Bonjour functionality on your Mac, from the Accounts window within Preferences for the Messages app, check the Enable Bonjour Instant Messaging check box (shown in Figure 5.3).

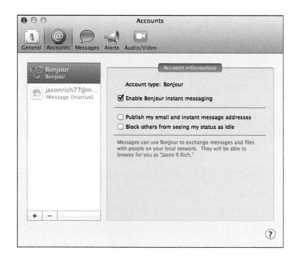

FIGURE 5.3

From the Accounts window, check the Bonjour option to activate this instant messaging service so that it can be used on your local network with the Messenger app.

CONFIGURING TO WORK WITH IMESSAGE

On the left side of the Accounts window, under the Bonjour listing, is a separate listing for Apple's iMessage service. To activate iMessage functionality with your Mac (when using the Messages app), click the iMessage listing. Then, on the right side of the window, enter your existing Apple ID and password in the appropriate fields. (Your Apple ID may already be displayed, but you will still need to provide your password.)

Upon doing this, a second iMessage account activation window will open. Within this window, shown in Figure 5.4, check the Enable This Account check box. Once the account has been verified (which happens automatically and takes just a few seconds), you're ready to use the Messages app with Apple's iMessage service.

FIGURE 5.4

After entering your Apple ID and password, add a check mark to the Enable This Account option so that you can use iMessage with the Messages app.

> ✓ **TIP**   If you need help remembering your Apple ID or the password associated with it, or you still need to create a free Apple ID account, visit https://appleid.apple.com using Safari or another web browser.

CONFIGURING TO WORK WITH OTHER IM SERVICES

To add other preexisting instant messaging accounts to the Messages app, near the lower-left corner of the Accounts window (refer back to Figure 5.4) click the plus sign icon. A separate Account Setup window will open (shown in Figure 5.5).

From the center of the Account Setup window, begin by clicking the Account Type pull-down menu and choosing which type of instant messaging account you already have established. The Messages app is currently compatible with AIM, Jabber, Google Talk, and Yahoo! Messenger. In late 2012, functionality for additional services, such as Facebook Messenger, will be added.

After selecting your account type, in the Username field enter your preexisting username for that service. Then, enter your account password within the Password field. Once this information has been entered, click the Done button. The account will automatically be verified.

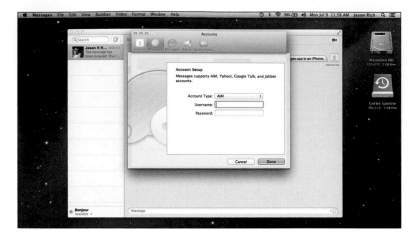

FIGURE 5.5

Click the plus sign icon near the lower-left corner of the Accounts window, and then choose the type of account you want to set up (AIM, Google Talk, Yahoo! Messenger, and so on).

You can now customize the settings that relate to that account within the Messenger app. Begin by making sure the Account Information tab near the top of the Accounts window is highlighted, that the newly created account is listed on the left side of the window, and that it's highlighted. Then, be sure to check the Enable This Account check box.

> **NOTE** Once the new account is enabled, you can customize the rest of the settings under the Account Information, Privacy, and Server Settings tabs. Depending on the type of account, these options will vary slightly. In most cases, however, the default options will work for you just fine.

Repeat this process for each of the preexisting instant messaging accounts you have that are compatible with the Messages app. When you're done, close the Accounts window to save your changes and begin using the Messages app.

> **TIP** If you don't yet have an AIM account, but you want to set one up for free, visit www.aim.com, and click the Sign Up icon on the website's home page.
>
> To set up a free Jabber instant messaging account, visit https://register.jabber.org. If you want to use the free Google Talk instant messaging service, you first need to set up a Google account. You can use the same Google account with Google's other online-based services (including Gmail); so if you already have an account

set up, use it. Otherwise, to create a new Google account, visit https://accounts.google.com/NewAccount.

To set up a free Yahoo! account that will work with the Yahoo! Messenger text messaging service, as well as Yahoo!'s other online-based services, visit https://login.yahoo.com and click the Create New Account button.

At anytime, to delete an instant messaging account from the Messages app, launch Messages, select Messages, Preferences from the menu bar, and then click the Accounts tab. Select and highlight the account you want to delete (on the left side of the window), and then click the negative sign icon near the lower-left corner of the Accounts window, or press the Delete key. Confirm your deletion decision by clicking the Delete button.

! CAUTION When you delete an account from the Messages app, in addition to erasing information about that account, all the instant messaging conversations you have saved within the app (which are related to that account) are also erased.

COMMUNICATING WITH MESSAGES

Once you've linked your preexisting accounts to the Messages app, you're ready to start communicating with other people. The main Messages app window contains two sections: a list of past and current conversations on the left, and the chat box for the conversation you're currently engaged in on the right.

When you're ready to initiate a new conversation, click the New Message icon near the top center of the Messages window (shown in Figure 5.6). Then, in the To field, enter the username or mobile phone number of the person you want to chat with.

To access your Contacts database or a list of online buddies associated with the services you're connected to through Messages, click the plus sign icon to the right of the To field to quickly locate someone. A Search field is available to help you find a particular contact.

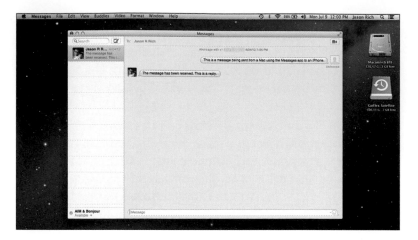

FIGURE 5.6

The main Messages app window with one conversation going. Click the New Message icon to start a new conversation.

✓ TIP If information about the person you want to chat with is already stored as an entry within the Contacts app on your Mac, just type that person's first or last name. When the search results are displayed below the To field, choose the recipient's email address or username.

To the right of each contact's listing will be a text bubble icon or dot icon that indicates that a particular phone number or email address is linked to a messaging service that you're both connected to, such as iMessage or AIM. Click that listing to initiate your conversation.

NOTE If you receive an incoming instant message, a listing for the new conversation appears on the left side of the Messages window. When you click that listing, the message is displayed on the right side of the window and you can commence with your text-based chat by responding to the message.

During a conversation, the text messages you receive from others display along the left margin of the chat window. Next to each message can be the profile photo of the person you're chatting with. (This is optional and can be set up from the View pull-down menu. Select the Messages option, followed by the Show Pictures or Show Names and Pictures option.)

To send or respond to a message, enter your text within the blank field along the bottom of the Messages window. Type your text and press the Return key to send it.

> ☑ **TIP**   Alternatively, instead of typing, it's possible to use the Dictation feature that's built in to Mountain Lion and dictate your outgoing text messages. To use this feature, click the outgoing message field. Next, quickly press the Function (Fn) key twice. When the microphone icon appears (shown in Figure 5.7), start speaking. When you finish dictating your message, click the Done button.
>
> The words you just said will be translated into text and displayed in the outgoing text message field. After proofreading the text (which is essential), press the Return key to send the message.

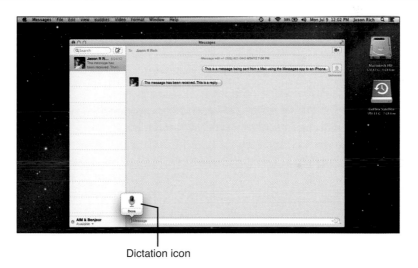

Dictation icon

FIGURE 5.7

Mountain Lion's Dictation feature works nicely with Messages. Using it, you can send text messages without actually typing.

> ☑ **NOTE**   To the extreme right of the empty message field where you type your outgoing messages, you'll see a small smiley face (emoticon) icon. Click this face to reveal a selection of emoticons and symbols you can incorporate into your messages.

> ☑ **TIP** Conversations you participate in using the Message app are automatically saved. You can view them or continue them by clicking the listing for a particular conversation that is displayed on the left side of the Messages window. To delete a conversation, place the cursor over a listing. When the X icon appears on the right side of the listing, click it. Click the Delete button to confirm your decision when the Would You Like to Delete This Conversation? pop-up window appears.

If the instant messaging service you're connected to allows for video chatting, and the person you're chatting with also has a video camera connected to his or her computer, the video camera icon in the upper-right corner of the Messages window will switch from gray to green. When it's green, click this icon to initiate a video chat.

> ☑ **TIP** Using the video chat feature within Messages enables you to communicate with a broader group of people, including Windows-based PC users who use a network that the Messages app is compatible with (such as AIM or Google Talk). Of course, you can always use FaceTime for real-time video chatting, but this service is only open to Apple Mac, iPhone, iPad, and iPod touch users.

From the main Messages window, you can bring all of your instant messaging accounts online, or pick and choose which services you want to activate once the Message app is running. To do this, access the Messages pull-down window and highlight the Accounts option. From the submenu that appears, add a check mark next to each service you want to bring online, such as Bonjour, iMessage, AIM, or Yahoo! Messenger.

EXPLOITING THE MESSAGES MENU BAR

As you're engaged in text messaging or instant messaging conversations using the Messages app, you'll discover a handful of pull-down menus along the menu bar that allow you to customize the app and make managing conversations more efficient:

■ **Messages**: Use the commands displayed as part of the Messages pull-down menu (shown in Figure 5.8) to, among other things, access the app's Preferences window and customize the app. You can also update your profile picture and online profile, view your current online status (or change it), log in to or out of specific accounts, and quit the Messages app.

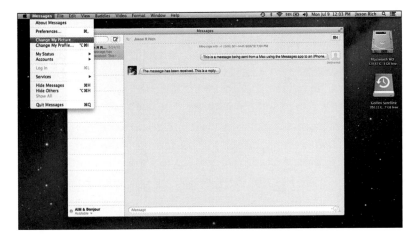

FIGURE 5.8
You can change your profile picture or edit your online profile from the Messages pull-down menu. This is public information about you your online friends can access.

- **File**: From, the File pull-down menu, you can start a new conversation by selecting the New Message option, open an existing conversation, enter into a specific chat room (if applicable), use the OS X Quick Look feature to view photos or documents being sent to you, plus close windows or conversations. You'll also find the Print command under this pull-down menu.

- **Edit**: The commands under the Edit pull-down menu are pretty consistent with other apps. From here, you can use the Undo, Redo, Cut, Copy, Paste, and Select All commands, for example, as well as the Find command and other commonly used OS X features.

> **TIP** To turn on the Messages app's Text-To-Speech option, so that a computerized voice will read aloud all incoming and outgoing text messages, select Edit, Speech from the menu bar. To turn on the feature, click the Start Speaking option. To turn off the feature, click the Stop Speaking option.

> **NOTE** You can also activate the Dictation feature from the Edit pull-down menu by selecting Start Dictation. It's easier and faster, however, to use the keyboard shortcut by quickly pressing the Function (Fn) key twice to activate this feature.

■ **View**: From the View pull-down menu, you can change the size of the text being displayed within the main Messages window, or opt to turn on or off buddy pictures or show the audio status or video status of the people you're communicating with. As you view your buddy lists (in a separate window), decide whether the full names, short names, or handles relating to each buddy or friend will be displayed, plus sort the buddy list.

Use the Messages option under the View pull-down window to change the appearance of text message bubbles or the format of the names displayed as you're participating in chats. You can also sort the conversations, or enter into Full Screen mode to make maximum use of onscreen real estate as you're chatting.

> **TIP** For each service you're connected to via the Messages app, to view a list of friends or buddies who are currently signed in to one of the services, click the Window pull-down menu and select the Buddies option. You can also use the ⌘-1 keyboard shortcut. A separate window will open and show your buddies, sorted by instant messaging service. In most cases, all buddies (whether online or not) can be displayed. However, a special icon tells you who is actively online, who is online but inactive, and who is offline.
>
> To initiate a chat with any of these buddies, double-click their listing within the Buddies window.

As you're participating in one or more chats, from the Buddies pull-down window you can view the other person's online profile and contact card, plus directly send an email or file or invite that person to switch from a text-based chat to a video or audio chat. When you choose to view a contact card, the Contacts app automatically launches and displays that person's information.

> **TIP** If a stranger harasses you on one of the instant messaging services and you want to block that person, once you receive an incoming text message from him or her, access the Buddies pull-down window and select the Block Person option. Someone who is blocked will no longer be able to send you instant messages from that account using that particular service.

■ **Video**: From the Video pull-down menu, you can activate video or audio chatting and screen sharing, if these are options supported by the instant messaging service you're connected to.

> **NOTE** Video chatting allows you to participate in real-time video confer-
> ences with other people, as long as the online service you're connected to sup-
> ports this functionality and the other person has a video camera, microphone, and
> speakers (or headphones) connected to his or her computer.
>
> Audio chatting transforms the Messages app into an Internet-based telephone
> that enables you to speak with the person you're connected to and engage in an
> online private, verbal conversations.
>
> Some instant messaging services also offer screen sharing. This allows you to share
> exactly what's displayed on your Mac's screen with the other person (and vice
> versa). This is a tool you can use to collaborate on work, for example, while run-
> ning another app, such as Microsoft Word, Excel, or PowerPoint.

Once you're engaged in a video chat, the commands available near the top
of the Video pull-down menu allow you to mute the microphone, pause your
video feed, take a snapshot of the video feed, and record the chat and then
save the file on your computer.

As you're sending your own video feed during a video chat, to add special
effects select the Show Video Effects option and choose an effect from the
menu (shown in Figure 5.9).

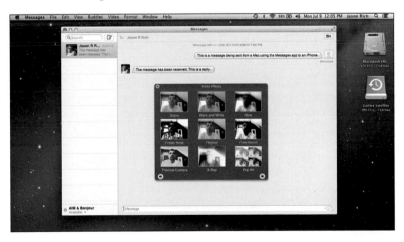

FIGURE 5.9

*Using the Messages app, you can enhance your own video feed during a video chat with special
effects, just like when you're recording videos or taking photos using the Photo Booth app.*

- **Format**: From the Format pull-down menu, it's easy to format the text you send as part of your outgoing text messages. For example, you can change the font, type style, font color, and even the writing direction.

- **Window**: The options available from the Window pull-down menu allow you to switch between and view the various windows related to the Message app, including the Messages and Buddies windows. If you open your Contacts listing while using Messages or initiate a file transfer, separate windows for these features will open, as well.

- **Help**: As with most apps, the Help pull-down menu allows you to get on-screen assistance using that app.

OTHER TEXT MESSAGING, VIDEO, AND VOICE CHAT OPTIONS

If you visit the Mac App Store (using the App Store app that comes preinstalled on your computer), or visit websites operated by third-party app developers or instant messaging services, you can find other apps besides Messages that offer text messaging, video conferencing, and audio chat capabilities.

Some of these third-party apps are designed to work exclusively with just one service. For example, the AIM for Mac app (available for free from www.aim.com/download#mac) works exclusively with the AIM service and enables you to use some of the service's features not accessible from the Messages app.

The free Skype app (www.skype.com) allows for text messaging, but is primarily used for video conferencing or voice chats and Voice over IP telephone calls.

Oovoo.com (www.oovoo.com) is another online video chatting service. What sets this free service apart is that you can video conference with up to 12 friends simultaneously, for free. The service also offers instant messaging. A free Mac app for using this service is downloadable from the company's website.

To use Google Talk without the Messages app, download a free web browser plug-in for Safari (or other popular web browsers, including Google Chrome). The plug-is is available at www.google.com/talk.

> **NOTE** You can also use other third-party apps, such as Adium and Trillian (which are available from the App Store), with a broader range of services, including Twitter and Facebook, in addition to AIM, Microsoft Messenger, GTalk, Windows Live, and Yahoo!, for example.

TIP To video conference with other Mac and iDevice users, another solution is to use the free FaceTime app that also comes preinstalled on your Mac. To learn more about FaceTime, see Chapter 3, "Optimizing Preinstalled Apps."

NOTE Starting in late 2012, the Messages app will most likely integrate seamlessly with Facebook Messenger, allowing you to communicate with your online Facebook friends without having to first access the Facebook website.

SENDING TEXT MESSAGES FROM A MAC TO A MOBILE PHONE

If you want to send text messages from your Mac to a cell phone user (not just iPhone users via iMessage), you can purchase and download an app such as SMS Mac (www.smsmac.com). This app charges a low initial $15 fee (which includes 50 messages). Additional packets available for $10 include 100 messages. There's also an annual access fee of $10.

NOTE Using the Messages app, you can send text messages for free, but only to iPhone or iPad users.

You can download a free Dashboard wizard for sending text messages to cell phones from your Mac from www.keakaj.com. It's called SMS Widget. This Dashboard widget integrates with the Contacts app, so you can easily look up mobile phone numbers of your contacts.

TIP Another option for sending text messages from you Mac to any cellular phone user, for free, is to visit the TXTDrop.com website (www.textdrop.com). Simply enter your email address, the recipient's mobile phone number and your outgoing text message, and then click the Send button. You can download a free Dashboard widget for this service from the company's website (www.txtdrop.com/widget.php).

If you have the need to send outgoing text messages to mobile phones from your Mac in bulk (to more than one user at a time), consider the Bulk SMS Software offered by TextMagic.

The Bulk SMS app is ideal for SMS text message marketing for your business (assuming you have a list of people who agree to receive text messages from you on their mobile phone). In most places, it's illegal to send unsolicited text messages for advertising or marketing purposes to people who have not requested it.

With a few clicks, you can send a single text message to between 2 and 50,000 recipients. Although the Mac version of the Bulk SMS software is free, a fee applies to sending text messages. For example, you'll need to pre-purchase at least 200 messages for $27.

Whether you use the Messages app or a third-party app, you'll quickly discover a vast selection of instant messaging and text messaging tools that enable you to inexpensively communicate with other people directly from your Mac.

IN THIS CHAPTER

- Setting Up Reminders and Notes
- Syncing app-specific data with other Macs and iDevices
- Optimizing the use of Reminders and Notes

6

MAKING THE MOST OF REMINDERS AND NOTES

The Reminders and Notes apps that come preinstalled with OS X Mountain Lion are faithfully adapted from their iOS mobile device (iDevice) counterparts, and both fully integrate with iCloud. These apps are extremely versatile and are used for managing information.

ADVANTAGES OF REMINDERS

You'll quickly discover that Reminders is a versatile and powerful list management app. Advantages to using this app (or one like it) include the following:

■ Reminders enables you to create as many separate lists as you want or need.

■ Each list can have an unlimited number of items or entries.

■ Each entry or item on a list can have a time/date-based alarm, a location-based alarm, a priority, and text-based notes associated with it.

■ All information stored within Reminders can be automatically backed up and synced with iCloud. This is something that happens in the background, as long as your Mac is connected to the Internet.

■ Once Reminders data is synced with iCloud, your lists can automatically be synced with other Macs, as well as with your iPhone, iPad, and iPod touch. Therefore, if you create or edit a list or modify an existing list on your iDevice, those changes will almost immediately be updated on your Macs that are linked to the same iCloud account.

■ Reminders is compatible with Mountain Lion's Dictation feature, so you can create to-do list items by speaking into your Mac, as opposed to typing the information.

■ Reminders keeps track of which items on your lists have been completed (as well as the time and date of their completion).

ADVANTAGES OF NOTES

Whenever you need to take notes and write down important ideas or information, you'll find the Notes app helpful. You can use it as a note-taking, organizational, and brainstorming tool. The Notes app window simulates the familiar yellow note-pad. On the surface, the app is a basic text editor. For example, you can use the computer keyboard to enter text-based information. However, you can also create bulleted and numbered lists.

As you're entering text, you can format it; the app enables you to choose a font, type style, and font size. In addition, you can left-, right-, or center-justify the text on the page as you're typing. If you don't need a full-featured word processor, Notes offers a simple way to manage text-based information.

The Notes app offers a handful of advantages, including the following:

■ Each note you create can be stored on a virtual page of the notepad. A listing for each note is displayed on the left side of the app window (within the sidebar), along with the date it was created. You can then search through your various notes using the app's Search field to quickly find exactly what you're looking for.

■ You can store groups of notes in separate and custom-labeled folders.

TIP   As you create each note, the app automatically keeps track of the time and date it was created or last updated. This information displays in the upper-right corner of each note page.

■ You can store an unlimited number of separate notes within the Notes app. Each can be as long as you desire and have a separate title associated.

■ The Notes app works seamlessly with iCloud to automatically back up and sync your notes as long as the computer is connected to the Internet.

■ Once your Notes data is synced with iCloud, it can automatically be shared with your iPhone, iPad, and iPod touch (which also has the Notes app preinstalled).

TIP   Using the Select, Copy, Cut, and Paste commands or the drag-and-drop process, you can insert photos or graphics into the Notes app (shown in Figure 6.1). However, once a photo is imported into a note, you cannot resize or position text to the right or left of it. You can, however, placed text above or below an imported photo or graphic.

FIGURE 6.1

You can drag a photo (for example, from iPhoto or your Pictures folder) into a note within the Notes app.

- The Notes app utilizes the OS X Share feature, enabling you to share individual notes with anyone via email or message.

- Instead of manually typing notes, you can use the OS X Dictation feature. Then, when you're ready to read back the text, you can activate the app's Speech feature and have the text read aloud to you by a computerized voice.

- You can print notes using any printer connected to your computer or transformed them into PDF files from within the app.

> **TIP** To create a PDF file from a note, select File, Print from the menu bar. Alternatively, press the ⌘-P keyboard short, and then from the Print window click the PDF button in the lower-left corner. Choose Save as PDF (or one of the other options from the menu that enable you to create and share a PDF).

OPTIMIZING YOUR USE OF REMINDERS

As soon as you begin using the Reminders app, you'll discover it has a wide range of potential uses in your personal and professional life, including the following:

- Keeping track of things you want to accomplish
- Creating detailed to-do lists
- Tracking goals
- Maintaining various types of shopping lists
- Jotting down ideas or brainstorming
- Documenting meeting agendas
- Creating a list of phone calls you need to make
- Managing any other type of information that can use a list format

When you launch the Reminders app, by default its app window has two main sections, as shown in Figure 6.2. The left side of the app window comprises the sidebar, which consists of a Search field, a list of your lists stored within the app, and an at-a-glance monthly calendar. On the right side of the app window, the currently selected and active list appears.

Search Field

Sidebar

At A Glance
Calendar

View icon
buttons

Main List

FIGURE 6.2

The main Reminders app window.

> ☑ **TIP** Using the options from the View pull-down menu, you can hide the
> sidebar or calendar. You can also do so by using the View icons in the lower-left
> corner of the app window. Also near the lower-left corner of the app window,
> you'll find a Hide Sidebar icon (which looks like a square containing an upward-
> pointing arrow) and, to the right of it, a Hide Calendar icon (which looks like a
> grid).

When using the Reminders app for the first time, you must create a new list. Each
list can have its own label and an unlimited number of items within it. There are
three ways to create a new list:

■ Select File, New List from the menu bar.

■ Use the ⌘-L keyboard shortcut.

■ Click the plus sign icon at the bottom of the sidebar, to the right of the Hide
Sidebar and Hide Calendar icons.

When you create a new list, a listing for it is added to the sidebar with the default
label New List. Enter the custom label you want to create for the list, such as

Grocery List, Today's Phone Calls, Meeting Agenda, Today's To-Do List, Packing List, and so on.

> 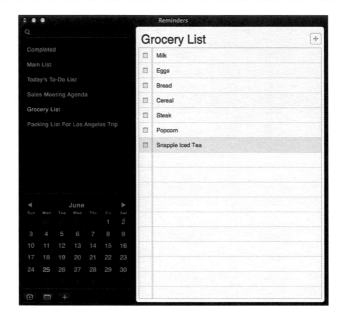 **NOTE** When you custom name a list, that name shows in the sidebar of the app window and at the top of the main list page (shown in Figure 6.3). Later, if you want to rename a list, highlight and select it in the sidebar, and then click it. You can then enter the new name. (You can also press the Control key as you click the list name to access the context menu, which includes a Rename command.

FIGURE 6.3

Each list within Reminders can have its own name, which you can create or change at any time.

After the list itself has been created, begin filling it in. To do so, move over to the right side of the app window. You can then add new items to a list in several ways, including the following:

- Select File, New Reminder from the menu bar.
- Use the ⌘-N keyboard shortcut.
- Press the plus sign icon near the top-right corner of the app window.
- Click the next open line within a list.

As soon as you add a new Reminder item, an empty check box appears on the first line of the page, under the list's heading. Enter the item title. For example, if you're creating a grocery list, type the first item on your list (for example, Milk).

When you begin entering an item title, to the right of that item, an Inspector (i) icon appears, as shown in Figure 6.4. At this point, either press the Return key to store that item and immediately enter a second item, such as Eggs, or click the Inspector (i) icon and further customize the first item listing.

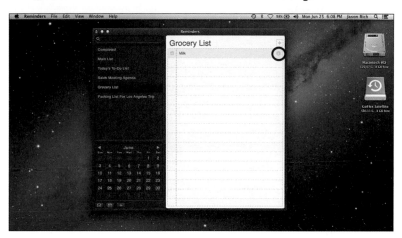

FIGURE 6.4

Customize each item within a list by clicking the Inspector icon to the right of it.

> **TIP** Even after you've added multiple items to a list, or at any time later as you're viewing or editing a list on any Mac, you can go back and click a specific item to make the Inspector icon appear.

Upon clicking the Inspector icon, you're given a handful of options that enable you to associate a time/date or location-based alarm with the item itself, as well as priority/notes. From the pop-up window that appears, as shown in Figure 6.5, check the On a Day or At a Location check box to associate an alarm with your listed Item.

By adding a check mark to the On a Day check box, you associate an alarm to this item for a specific date and time of your choosing. Click the Date option to choose a month and day (shown in Figure 6.6). By default, the current date appears. Then click the Hour, Minute, and AM or PM fields, one at a time, to customize the alarm time.

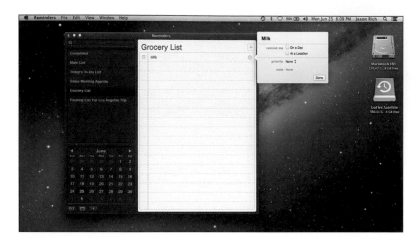

FIGURE 6.5

After clicking the Inspector icon, customize a listing by associating an alarm, priority, or notes with it.

FIGURE 6.6

Associate a date and time with each alarm you create for a list item.

If you're using Reminders on a MacBook Pro or MacBook Air, or if you sync your Reminders data with an iPhone, you can also associate an alarm with a specific location by checking the At a Location check box.

! CAUTION If you're using Reminders to create a grocery or shopping list for a specific store, you only need to set one location-based alarm and associate it with one item on the list. Otherwise, if you set a location-based alarm for every item on the list, when you get to that location, multiple alarms will be generated.

Upon doing this, you can select any address that's listed within the Contacts app for yourself or any contact, such as your Home or Work, or the address of your grocery store (shown in Figure 6.7). By default, your current location is used. For this feature to work on your Mac, the computer must be connected to the Internet. Then, you can choose between either the Leaving or Arriving option. Once set, Reminders generates an alarm for the item on your list when you arrive at or leave a specific location.

TIP If you plan to use location-based alarms in conjunction with multiple commonly visited locations, within the Contacts app create a group of contacts that contain these frequented destinations, such as the grocery store, dry cleaner, salon, post office, bank, and so on. Also, within your own contact entry, be sure to include your home and work addresses.

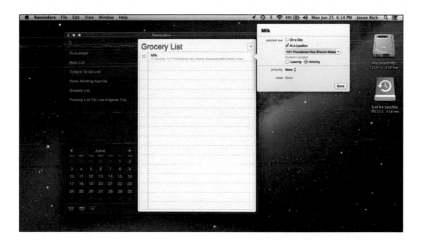

FIGURE 6.7

In addition to associating an alarm with a date and time, you can create a location-based alarm for each item so that you're reminded when you arrive at or leave a specific geographic location.

NOTE   You can set both a date/time and a location-based alarm for a specific item, or choose just one option, or neither, depending on the type of list you're creating and whether specific deadlines are associated with each list item.

TIP   You can also set up an auto-recurring alarm for a list item. To do this, click the Repeat option's pull down menu and choose between None (meaning the item's alarm in nonrecurring), Every Day, Every Week, Every 2 Weeks, Every Month, or Every Year. The default is None.

Each item on each of your lists can have a separate priority associated with it, as well. To set a priority, click the Priority option's pull down menu (after clicking the Inspector icon associated with a list item) and choose between None, Low, Medium, or High.

One red exclamation point will appear to the left of a low-priority item on your list. Two red exclamation points will appear to the left of a medium-priority item, and three red exclamation points will appear to the left of a high-priority item, as shown in Figure 6.8.

FIGURE 6.8

Set a low, medium, or high priority for each list item to help you stay organized and efficiently juggle and manage your most important responsibilities, or to highlight your best ideas.

Finally, by clicking the Note option, you can type as many text-based notes as you want to be associated with each item on your list. Instead of typing notes, use the OS X Dictation feature to speak into your Mac and have what you say translated into text and inserted into the Note field.

> ☑ **TIP**   After customizing an item within your list with an alarm, priority, or notes, be sure to click the Done button in the lower-right corner of the pop-up window. Details related to your customizations, such as the time, date, and location of an alarm, will appear, if applicable, within the main list.

At anytime, it's easy to create another list and begin adding as many items to it as you want, or switch between existing lists to view/modify them. To delete an individual item from a specific list, click that item (on the right side of the app window) and press the Delete key. To delete an entire list from the Reminders app, select and highlight a list in the sidebar and press the Delete key. A confirmation pop-up window will display, as shown in Figure 6.9. Click the Delete button to confirm your decision.

FIGURE 6.9

Select and highlight a list you want to delete, press the Delete key, and then click the Delete button shown here to confirm your decision.

> **TIP** As you complete items on your various lists, check each finished item's check box. When you do this, the item will disappear from its current list and be moved to the master Completed list, which you can access from the sidebar.

If you opt to keep the at-a-glance calendar displayed near the bottom of the sidebar, you can jump to a specific day by clicking it. Or, you can use the left- and right-arrow icons to the right and left of the Month and Year heading to move forward or backward one month at a time. Clicking the dot icon that appears when you stray from the current day and month enables you to instantly jump back to it.

> **NOTE** You can adjust the size of the Reminders app window by positioning the cursor at one of the app window's corners, holding down the mouse button (or trackpad button) and dragging it outward or inward. This app does not have a Full Screen mode. To make the app fully utilize the main desktop area (but still display the menu bar and potentially the Dock), click the green dot icon in the upper-left corner of the app window.

> **TIP** By clicking a specific date using the at-a-glance calendar within the sidebar, it's possible to automatically create a new list related to that date, as shown in Figure 6.10. This is a quick way to create a to-do or call list, for example, related to a specific date. Keep in mind that a list you create related to a specific date will include items from all your lists that have that date associated with it.

As you're viewing one list on the right side of the app window, and can see a listing of your lists within the sidebar, you have the option to drag an item from the active list (on the right side of the window) and move it to any other list within the sidebar. To do this, click an item within a list you're viewing on the right side of the window, hold down the mouse button (or trackpad button), and drag the item to the left, onto another list's label within the sidebar.

You can also use the Select, Copy, and Paste commands (under Edit on the menu bar), or their related keyboard shortcuts, to copy items between lists or move items around within a specific list.

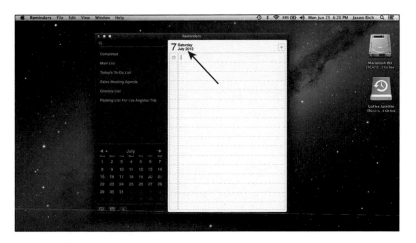

FIGURE 6.10

By clicking a date within the at-a-glance monthly calendar, you can create a new list that contains to-do items, goals, or tasks that need to be accomplished on a specific date. Notice that the label on the list is the date you selected from the calendar.

> **TIP**   If you're using Reminders with your iPhone (or a new iPad running iOS 6), use Siri to create new Reminder items that will automatically sync via iCloud with the Reminders app on your Mac. To do this, from your iDevice, activate Siri by holding down the Home button. Begin your command by saying, "Remind me to…." Your reminder can include a date, time, and location. For example, say, "Remind me to pick up my dry cleaning on Saturday, July 7th at 4 p.m."

> **NOTE**   Keep in mind that the Reminders app also works seamlessly with Notification Center. You can customize Notification Center to generate banners or alerts related to Reminder alarms, and display them on your desktop, as well as within the Notification Center panel. Refer back to Chapter 4, "Using Notification Center," for information about how to set up Reminders to work with Notification Center.

OPTIMIZING YOUR USE OF NOTES

The Notes app can be used as a virtual notepad. Each page of the notepad can contain lengthy notes and be stored within the app as a separate, custom-labeled file. Although your formatting options are limited, you can cut and paste or drag and drop content from other apps, including photos, into your notes.

The Notes app is not meant to be a full-featured word processor. For that, use Pages or Microsoft Word, for example. Instead, Notes enables you to quickly jot down information and ideas and to create lists, which you can then view, share with others (via email or message), sync with your other Macs or iDevice, or print.

Depending on how you customize the Notes app, the app window can consist of one, two, or three separate columns. Figure 6.11 shows the app with all three columns visible.

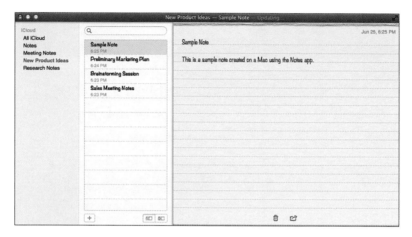

FIGURE 6.11

The Notes app with its three columns showing. If you don't choose to create and use folders with this app, you can hide the folders column (the leftmost column).

The main (rightmost column) serves as your virtual yellow notepad. The leftmost column displays a list of custom-labeled folders within which you can store and organize your individual notes. The middle column offers a complete list of notes that have been created and saved using the app.

> **TIP**   To decide whether the folders column will be displayed or hidden, select View, Hide Folders List or Show Folders List from the menu bar, or click one of the two View icons near the bottom-right corner of the middle column.

NOTE Within the middle column, a Search field is always visible. Use this field to quickly find notes based on any keyword or search phrase, including a date.

Begin using this app by either creating a new note or clicking a listing within the middle column to view, edit, print, share, or delete an existing note. The following are the three ways to create a new note using the Notes app:

- Select File, New Note from the menu bar.
- Use the ⌘-N keyboard shortcut.
- Click the plus sign icon near the bottom-left corner of the middle column within the app window.

After you create a new note, a blank page appears on the virtual notepad. Displayed in the upper-right corner of the page is the time and date. Within the middle column, the default label New Note appears. What you type into the very first line at the top of the virtual notepad becomes that note's name.

As you're creating a note, manually type text in a freeform format. For example, you can use full sentences and paragraphs, short phrases, or create a list of key-words. You can also copy and paste or drag and drop content from other apps onto the page, or use the OS X Dictation feature to speak into the app and have your words translated into text.

TIP To use the Dictate command, create a new note and place the cursor where you want the text to be placed. Next, press the Function (Fn) key twice to activate the Dictation feature. When the microphone appears and you hear a tone, begin speaking. When you're done, click the Done button. Your words will be translated into text and be displayed on the page.

If you opt to manually type your notes, use the commands under Format on the menu bar to select a font, type style, and font color. You can also right-, left-, or center-justify your text, select a writing direction, adjust indentation, and create numbered or bulleted lists.

TIP At anytime, it's possible to go back and modify, add, or delete text. In addition, you can select and highlight text, and then use any of the formatting options available from the Format menu to customize its appearance.

Once a note is created, view it on the right side of the app window to read its contents, or turn on the Speech feature from the Edit menu and have the text read aloud to you by a computer-generated voice. Also from the Edit menu, you can check the spelling and grammar within your document and take advantage of other popular OS X commands.

It's also possible to use the Select, Select All, Copy, Cut, and Paste commands within the Notes app (found under the Edit menu) to move content from a specific note into another app, such as an outgoing email, or a Microsoft Word (or Pages) document or into another note (within the Notes app).

To quickly switch between notes that have been created, click their listing within the middle column. To delete a specific note, select and highlight the note's listing from the middle column and press the Delete key. Or to delete the note you're currently viewing within the right column of the app window, click the Trash Can icon near the bottom center of the right column.

Just like the Reminders app, your Notes data can be set up to automatically back up and sync with iCloud (as well as with your other Macs and iDevices), and networks or online services such as Microsoft Exchange, Yahoo!, and Google.

By turning on the iCloud backup and syncing functionality, all of your notes you create will automatically be synced with iCloud as they're created or modified. However, if you want to share one note with someone else, use the app's Share button.

You'll find the Share icon near the bottom center of the rightmost column of the Notes app window. The Share menu for this app enables you to email one note at a time to one or more recipients or to send it to other people via a message, as shown in Figure 6.12.

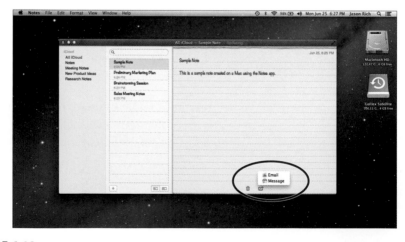

FIGURE 6.12

The Notes app has its own Share icon, like many preinstalled Mountain Lion apps. Use it to send individual notes via email or messages.

As you're viewing a particular note, to print it select File, Print from the menu bar, or press the ⌘-P keyboard shortcut. From the Print window that appears, you also have the option to create a PDF file from the note. To do this, click the PDF button in the lower-left corner of the Print window (shown in Figure 6.13).

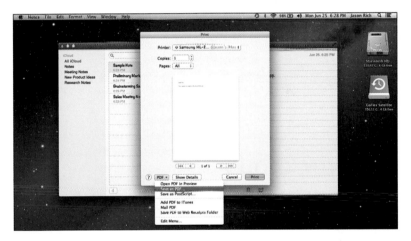

FIGURE 6.13

From your note, you can create separate PDF documents that can then be shared with others or viewed with other apps (including Preview). PDF files can be viewed on PCs, Macs, and most smartphones and tablets.

TIP   To enter into Full Screen mode when using the Notes app, click the Full Screen icon near the upper-right corner of the app window, or select View, Enter Full Screen from the menu bar. To then exit Full Screen mode, press the Esc key.

The Notes app offers a quick and easy way to store information, notes, ideas, and other content in a way that's accessible, easy to search, and in a format that can be synced with your other computers or shared with other people. Its functionality does overlap a bit with the Reminders app (in that Notes can be used to create lists), plus it offers some basic features of a word processor. Even so, you'll probably find a number of uses for this app in your personal and professional life.

TIP   To quit the Reminders or Notes app, click Reminders or Notes on the menu bar and select Quit. You can also use the ⌘-Q keyboard shortcut. For these two apps, clicking the red dot icon near the upper-left corner of the app window will also quit the app (as opposed to hide the app window).

SYNCING WITH ICLOUD

Reminders and Notes can be used as standalone apps on your Mac. However, activating iCloud functionality in conjunction with these apps serves two main purposes. A backup of all your data is automatically stored (safely) in the cloud. Plus, your app-specific data can then be automatically synced with the other Macs and iDevices linked to the same iCloud account.

TIP   Using any computer (such as a PC or Mac) or any Internet-enabled mobile device, once your Reminders/Notes data is being synced with iCloud, you can also access it by visiting the iCloud.com website. To do this using any web browser, visit www.iCloud.com and log in using your Apple ID and password. Then, click the Reminders or Notes icon to use an online-based version of the Reminders or Notes app, which will be populated with all of your up-to-date data.

To set up Reminders/Notes to sync with iCloud, launch System Preferences and select iCloud. From the iCloud window, make sure your Mac is currently linked with your iCloud account, and then select the Calendars and Reminders option on the right side of the window to turn on iCloud functionality in conjunction with the

Reminders app. (In the future, Reminders may be given its own check box within the iCloud window.)

To activate iCloud functionality for Notes, check the Notes check box on the right side of the iCloud window (shown in Figure 6.14).

FIGURE 6.14

Set up the Notes app to sync app-specific data with iCloud from within System Preferences.

Once you exit out of System Preferences, the Reminders/Notes apps will sync your app-specific data with iCloud automatically and in the background, as long as your computer is connected to the Internet. As you make changes to any list or items within a list when using Reminders or alter any notes using the Notes app, those updates are reflected online (and synced with your other Macs and iDevices) almost instantly.

> **TIP** You can also set up Reminders/Notes to sync with other compatible accounts online or on a network, such as Microsoft Exchange, Yahoo!, or Google. To do this, launch System Preferences and select the Mail, Contacts & Calendars. Click an account type and provide your account information as prompted.
>
> Next, click the Calendars & Reminders or Notes option as you're setting up that account. For example, if you set up a Yahoo! account, as shown in Figure 6.15, from within the Mail, Contacts & Calendars window, be sure to check the Calendars and Reminders check box to sync Reminders data. Check the Notes check box to sync your notes with your Yahoo! account. Also check the Contacts check box to sync your contacts.

FIGURE 6.15

From System Preferences, you can set up Reminders and Notes to sync your app-specific data with Microsoft Exchange, Yahoo!, or your Google accounts.

Because your Reminders app-specific data syncs and updates in real-time with other Macs and iDevices via iCloud, your spouse can create or update a list on your Mac at home, and the updated information will appear on your iPhone or iPad almost instantly, wherever you happen to be.

So, if you're working from a shopping list created using Reminders, and you're at the grocery store, your spouse at home can add items to the list in real time, as long as the computer or mobile device he or she is using is linked to your iCloud account. On your iOS device, items will be displayed in the order they're added.

IN THIS CHAPTER

- Streamlining Safari to enhance your web surfing
- Reading web content offline
- Managing your email accounts
- Sending very large files via email

7

IMPROVED WEB SURFING AND EMAIL MANAGEMENT

Chances are, as a Mac user, you already know how to surf the Internet using a web browser, such as Safari. However, in its ongoing effort to enhance what's possible on a Mac, and in conjunction with the release of OS X Mountain Lion, Apple has added some new features to its web browser that can make surfing the web more efficient.

> ☐ **NOTE** You don't have to rely on the Safari web browser that comes pre-installed with Mountain Lion. Several other popular third-party web browsers can be downloaded and used for free, including Google Chrome (www.google.com/chrome), Opera (www.opera.com), and Mozilla Foxfire (www.mozilla.org/en-US/firefox/new). Each offers a different collection of features and a unique user interface that some people may prefer.

Likewise, when it comes to managing one or more of your preexisting email accounts using your Mac, the Mail app that comes preinstalled with Mountain Lion has also benefitted from a few enhancements that make managing and organizing incoming and outgoing emails easier.

> ☐ **NOTE** Depending on the types of email accounts you already have, from the App Store you may also discover third-party apps that can be used to manage your email. For example, if you exclusively use a Google Gmail account, the Email Pro for Gmail app ($1.99) or MailTab for Gmail app (free) can be useful.
>
> If you use an IMAP, POP3, or SMTP in Exchange-compatible email account the Mail Access app ($7.99) is a useful email management tool. Sparrow ($9.99) is also a feature-packed email management app for the Mac that offers an alternative to the Mail app.

While third-party options are available for surfing the web and managing email accounts, there are several advantages to using Apple's own Safari web browser and Mail email app. Most notably, these apps work seamlessly with other Mountain Lion apps, as well as incorporate OS X features and functionality, like the Share icon. You can also use iCloud with Safari to sync your bookmarks, Reading List, and active browser tabs, for example.

STREAMLINING SAFARI

As you probably know, the Safari web browser for the Mac is chock full of features that offers a robust and customizable web surfing experience. For example, you can fully customize the appearance and functionality of the app's toolbar so that only your favorite or most frequently used features display as command icons. (Of course, the other features remain accessible from Safari's various pull-down menus and via keyboard shortcuts.)

NOTE When using many apps on your Mac, it's possible to customize the toolbar. This doesn't just apply to Safari, although this is one app where being able to customize the toolbar comes in handy, because everyone has his or her own preferences when it comes to surfing the Web.

TABBED BROWSING

When using Safari, you have the option to take advantage of tabbed web browsing, which enables you to have multiple browser windows open at the same time and then quickly switch between them by clicking a tab along the top of the app window (shown in Figure 7.1). This is more efficient than having several independent web browser windows open simultaneously that will overlap one another (shown in Figure 7.2).

FIGURE 7.1
Safari (version 6.0 or later) offers tabbed web browsing as an option.

TIP To use Safari's tabbed web browser feature, and to open new browser windows, select File, New Tab from the menu bar, or use the ⌘-T keyboard shortcut. Another option is to click the New Tab icon on the toolbar, or the plus sign icon to the right of the bookmark bar. A dozen tabs can be displayed at once within the Safari app's window. More tabs can be open, but you'll need to scroll to the left or right to view them.

FIGURE 7.2

Without using tabbed browsing, multiple browser windows can be open simultaneously, but the windows will overlap each other.

Once multiple tabs are open within Safari, to switch between them just click the tab below the toolbar and bookmarks bar.

To close a tab, hover the cursor over it and then click the Close button (X) that appears to the left of the tab's label.

> **TIP** If your computer is connected to iCloud, as you open up new browser tabs that information can be synced with iCloud, as well. When the iCloud Tabs feature is used, the same tabs you open on your Mac browser can be opened (or closed) on all other computers and iOS mobile devices (iDevices) that are linked to your iCloud account.
>
> To view these tabs, click the iCloud Tabs icon on the toolbar (shown in Figure 7.3). You can then switch between devices while web surfing, yet be able to pick up exactly where you left off almost instantly.
>
> To set up this feature, launch System Preferences and click the iCloud option. Then, add a check mark to Safari check box.

> **NOTE** To customize the Tabs feature of Safari, select Safari, Preferences from the menu bar, and then click the Tabs tab along the top of the window.

FIGURE 7.3

Shown here are the browser tabs currently open on an iPad. They are being viewed from Safari running on a MacBook Air linked to the same iCloud account.

SMARTER SEARCH FIELD

In older versions of Safari, near the top of the app window was an Address field and a separate Search field. Now, the web browser features just one field that can be used to manually enter the website's address (URL) that you want to visit, or it can be used to enter keywords or search phrases to use with the browser's default Search Engine (Google, Yahoo!, or Bing).

Plus, as you enter information into the Smart Search field (shown in Figure 7.4), the browser offers suggestions, based on your past browsing history, for possible matches to what you're looking for.

FIGURE 7.4

Safari now uses a single Smart Search field instead of a separate Address field and Search field.

> **☑ TIP** To select the default search engine that Safari will rely on when you use the Smart Search field, select Safari, Preferences from the menu bar. When the Preferences window appears, click the General tab (shown in Figure 7.5), and then display the Default Search Engine pull-down menu.
>
> Choose between Google, Yahoo!, and Bing as Safari's default search engine. You can manually use any search engine, however, by first surfing to that search engine's website (for example, www.google.com, www.yahoo.com, or www.bing.com).

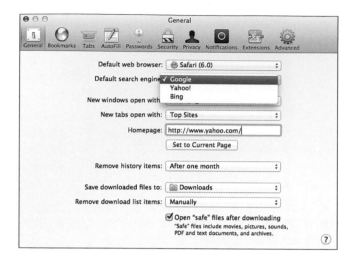

FIGURE 7.5

Choose the default search engine that Safari will use when you enter a keyword or search phrase into the Smart Search field.

As you enter website addresses manually into the Smart Search field, the browser is lenient about the format you use. If the website's address is http://www. jasonrich.com, for example, you could enter the full address, or simply enter www. jasonrich.com or jasonrich.com, and Safari will lead you to the right place.

SHARING

Anytime you're browsing the Internet and come across a website you want to share with other people, you can do so directly from within Safari. Just click the Share button on the toolbar (or select File, Share from the menu bar).

The Share menu (shown in Figure 7.6) enables you to email the website address (URL) of the site you're currently viewing to someone else via email, message, or tweet. From the Share menu, you can also add a bookmark to the page and add the page to your Reading List.

READING WEBSITE CONTENT OFFLINE

Thanks to the Reading List feature of Safari, anytime you come across a web page or an article of interest but you don't have time to read it right away, you can just add it to your Reading List.

To do this, click the Share icon and select the Add to Reading List option, or select Bookmarks, Add to Reading List from the menu bar. You can also use the Shift-⌘-D keyboard shortcut.

FIGURE 7.6

The Share icon gives you access to the Share menu from within Safari. Use it to send details about a website to someone else via email, message, or tweet.

> **TIP** If you have Safari set up to sync your bookmarks and Reading List with iCloud, that information will automatically sync with your other Macs and iDevices linked to the same iCloud account. Therefore, if you stumble upon an interesting website while using your Mac, you can add a bookmark, and within a few seconds, it will be synced with the Bookmarks menu on all your linked computers and devices. As a result, all your favorite websites are accessible to you, and your Bookmarks menu and the websites stored on the bookmark bar will be consistent.

The content will then be saved within Safari and become accessible to you, whether you're online or offline. To access your saved Reading List, click the Reading List icon on the toolbar; select View, Show Reading List from the menu bar; or press the Shift-⌘-L keyboard shortcut. Figure 7.7 shows the Reading List column.

When you view your Reading List, a new column appears along the left side of the browser window. It lists each of the web pages or articles you've previously saved. Click any of these listings to view the web content within.

FIGURE 7.7
Internet content stored in your Reading List can be read while your computer is online or offline.

> **☑ TIP**   To help you manage your Reading List, several command tabs are displayed at the top of the Reading List column. The Clear All tab will erase all the articles currently stored within your Reading List. The All tab allows you to view all the items currently stored, and the Unread tab allows you to view only the items stored within your Reading List that you have not yet read. There's also an Add Page tab that allows you to add the page you're currently viewing in your open browser window to the Reading List. However, while you're surfing the Web, you can better utilize your onscreen real estate by hiding the Reading List column when it's not being used.

> **! CAUTION**   When reading web content from your Reading List offline (so that you're Mac is not connected to the web), certain animations, hyperlinks, and video that may be embedded into the web pages you've saved may not be visible. If you attempt to click the Play icon for an embedded video or access a link within the saved page, a message that says "You are not connected to the Internet" will appear.

USING THE READER FEATURE

Keep in mind that the Reading List feature of Safari is different from the Reader feature. As you're viewing certain compatible websites, to the immediate right of the Smart Search field you may notice the Reader button turns blue (shown in Figure 7.8).

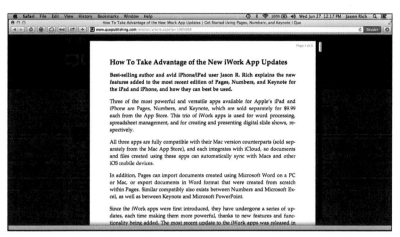

FIGURE 7.8

The Reader feature enables you to remove onscreen clutter from a web page or article you're reading online and view only the relevant text and photos.

When you click this Reader button, all the clutter associated with the web page or article you're reading online will be removed, and a new window that displays only the Internet content you want to view will appear. This feature works only with some websites, not all.

AVOIDING REPETITIVE DATA ENTRY WITH AUTOFILL

If you include an entry for yourself within the Contacts app, and that entry contains your email address, mailing address, and other details that you often need to type into a website when shopping online, Safari's AutoFill feature will access the Contacts app and automatically fill in the appropriate data fields within a website form when you use the AutoFill feature.

AutoFill also works with website usernames and passwords, so you don't have to retype this information each time you visit a website.

> **☑ TIP** To use the AutoFill feature, select Edit, AutoFill Form from the menu bar. You can also click the AutoFill icon on the toolbar, or use the Shift-⌘-A keyboard shortcut.

> **❗CAUTION** If other people will be using your Mac (without using their own account on your Mac), they could also use the AutoFill feature to log in (using your username and password) to websites you've visited in the past. When you visit a website for the first time and enter your username and password, by default Safari will remember this information in the future. To prevent other people from signing into websites as you, do not use AutoFill in conjunction with website usernames and passwords.
>
> Another way to prevent people from using your AutoFill settings is to add a password on your computer for your user account. Then, when you're not using your computer, be sure to log out of your account. You can then create a guest account or separate accounts for other people who want to use your Mac, without giving them access to your settings and confidential information. This will also prevent people from accessing your History folder, Reading List, or other saved information.

Safari automatically keeps track of the usernames and password you use to access websites. If you forget a particular username or password, select Safari, Preferences from the menu bar. In Preferences window that opens, click the Password tab. A window displaying all the websites and their respective usernames stored in Safari will appear.

To view the passwords that go along with each website username, select the Show Passwords option near the bottom center of the Passwords window. When prompted, enter your master computer password (or your Mac's account password). The passwords associated with each website will then display.

PREVENTING WEBSITE TRACKING

An ever-growing number of websites now track and remember your actions while visiting the site. To prevent this from happening, turn on Safari's Do Not Track feature. To activate this feature, select Safari, Preferences. When the Preferences window appears, click the Privacy tab. From the Privacy window (shown in Figure 7.9), select Website Tracking - Ask Websites Not to Track Me.

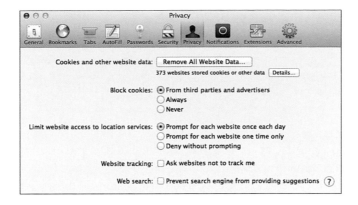

FIGURE 7.9

In the Privacy window, you can turn on or off the Do Not Track feature.

> **TIP** Another thing you can to do protect your privacy while surfing the Web is to block cookies. Doing so prevents websites you visit from storing information about your actions on your computer (which can potentially be accessed by other people using your computer). The Block Cookies option is also available from the Privacy window.

One other strategy for keeping your web surfing habits private is to use the Private Browsing feature found under the Safari pull-down menu. When you turn on this feature, Safari will *not* store details about what web pages you visit, maintain a search history, or store AutoFill information.

CUSTOMIZING YOUR TOOLBAR

There are several ways to customize the look of the Safari web browser while surfing the Web. You can opt to display or hide various elements of the browser window, including the toolbar, bookmark bar, status bar, tabs, and Reading List. To do so, just select view from the menu bar and then one or more of the following options:

- Show/Hide Toolbar
- Show/Hide Status Bar
- Show/Hide All Tabs
- Show/Hide Reading List

> **TIP** To view a listing of recently downloaded files (acquired while surfing the Web), select View, Show Downloads from the menu bar, or click the Show Downloads icon to the extreme right of the toolbar (just below the Full Screen icon). The keyboard shortcut for this is Option-⌘-L.

The toolbar is a menu of command icons that can be displayed along the top of the Safari app window as you're surfing the Web to give you quick access to commonly used commands and features. One nice aspect of Safari, as well as many apps that run on your Mac, is that you can fully customize the layout of the toolbar.

To do this, select View, Customize Toolbar. A window that showcases all the available command icons will appear, as shown in Figure 7.10. Your options include the following:

FIGURE 7.10

Drag the icons you want to appear on your toolbar from the Customize Toolbar window onto the toolbar within Safari. Here, the Top Sites tab is being moved between the iCloud Tabs and Reading List icons.

- **Back/Forward**: Move back and forth between previously viewed web pages that were opened within the same browser window.

- **Reading List**: Open the Reading List window and access your saved articles or webpages to read.

- **iCloud Tabs**: Access the tabs currently open on web browsers being used on the other Macs and iDevices linked to your iCloud account and that have the Safari feature of iCloud turned on.

- **Share**: Access Safari's Share menu, which enables you to share the web page you're currently viewing with others via email, message, or tweet, as well as add the page to your Reading List or Bookmarks menu.
- **Top Sites**: Access the Top Sites view offered within Safari.

> **✓ TIP**   To quickly view updated thumbnails of your favorite or most fre-
> quented websites, and be able to switch between them, use Safari's Top Sites fea-
> ture (shown in Figure 7.11). Or select History, Show Top Sites from the menu bar.
> You can also access it by clicking the Top Sites icon on the toolbar.
>
> To edit which web pages appear on your personalized Top Sites display, when
> viewing Top Sites click the Edit button in the lower-left corner of the window.
>
> From the Top Sites display, click the History tab to switch to thumbnails of web-
> sites you've previously visited. This is a graphical display that offers the same
> information as accessing the History pull-down menu (which shows a text-based
> listing of web pages you've visited in reverse chronological order).

FIGURE 7.11
Safari's Top Sites view is customizable by clicking the Edit button.

- **Home**: Quickly return to the website you designate as your home page within Safari. To set your home page, select Safari, Preferences from the menu bar, and then click the General tab. Then, within the Homepage field, enter the website address you want to designate as your home page. Just below the Homepage field is a Set to Current Page button. Click this if you want the currently open web page to be your new home page. By doing this, you don't have to retype the site's URL.

- **New Tab**: Open a new tab within Safari so that you can open multiple web pages simultaneously and then quickly switch between them.

- **History**: View a comprehensive listing of websites you've previously visited, displayed in reverse chronological order. You can also access your history by clicking the History pull-down menu. Use the Clear History option (displayed at the bottom of your History list) to erase the contents of this listing.

- **Bookmarks**: View your currently stored bookmarks.

- **Add Bookmark**: Add a bookmark for the web page you're currently viewing to your personal bookmarks list.

- **Bookmarks Bar**: In addition to the Bookmarks menu, you can save frequently visited websites on Safari's bookmarks bar, which can be displayed horizontally across the app window, directly below the toolbar.

- **AutoFill**: When visiting a website with a form that needs to be filled in use this feature so that you don't have to manually type the requested information. If you use this feature often, be sure to add an icon for it onto your toolbar.

- **Zoom**: Zoom in on a web page to get a closer look at various aspects of it.

- **Open in Dashboard**: Open and display the contents of a website on your Mac's Dashboard.

- **Mail:** Quickly launch the Mail app from within Safari.

- **Print**: Print the web page you're currently viewing.

- **Smart Search Field**: Perform a keyword search or manually enter the website address (URL) for the website you want to visit.

One at a time, drag the icons you want to appear on your toolbar from the Customize Toolbar window to the toolbar in Safari. Keep in mind that you can also determine the location of the icons, not just which icons appear.

> **TIP** To return your toolbar to its default appearance, drag the Toolbar layout at the bottom of the Customize Toolbar window to the toolbar within Safari.

MANAGING EMAIL USING THE MAIL APP

The Mail app that comes preinstalled with Mountain Lion enables you to efficiently manage one or more preexisting email accounts from a single app. While Mail always keeps the individual emails sent and received from each account separate, you can view all your incoming or outgoing emails from a single screen, so you can save time having to constantly switch between accounts.

Another nice feature of the Mail app is that you can customize how you view your messages and how they're grouped together.

> **TIP** To customize the toolbar within the Mail app, select View, Customize Toolbar from the menu bar. A window will appear with a number of options, as shown in Figure 7.12. Then drag the individual command icons from the window that appears up to the actual Mail Toolbar, and place them in the order you want them.

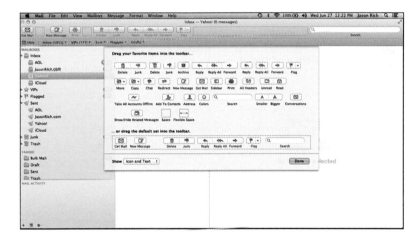

FIGURE 7.12
You can customize the toolbar within the Mail app. Drag the command icons and buttons from the Customize Toolbar window onto the Mail app's toolbar.

By default, the Mail app displays three columns (shown in Figure 7.13). On the left is a Mailboxes list. Each item on the list represents one of your email accounts and the folders available within that account (such as your Inbox, Sent, Junk, and Trash folders). The middle column displays your Inbox (either for one account or all of your accounts), and the column on the right displays the individual email that's selected and highlighted from your Inbox.

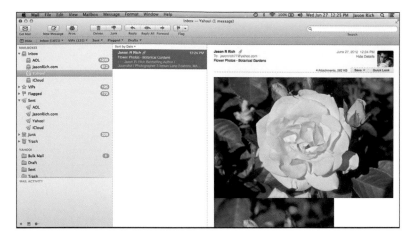

FIGURE 7.13

The app window for Mail has three main columns.

From the View pull-down menu, you can opt to show or hide the toolbar, Mailboxes list (left column), and the Favorites bar. If you're managing only one email account using Mail, you might opt to hide the Mailboxes list to conserve onscreen real estate. However, the Mailboxes list might also display folders or Smart Folders you've associated with the email account, so you might not want them hidden.

> **✓ TIP**   Located just above the Mailboxes list on the left side of the app window, you can also click the Show/Hide button to make the Mailboxes list appear or disappear.

> **✎ NOTE**   The Favorites bar can be displayed below the toolbar and offers quick access to your Inbox, VIPs, Send, Flagged, and Draft email folders. You can also add custom folders to this bar.

CONFERRING VIP STATUS

If you regularly receive emails from certain people who are important to you, you can add them to the Mail app's VIP list feature. By doing this, all incoming emails from your VIPs will display a star next to them. Plus, incoming emails from your VIPs automatically get sorted and placed into a separate VIPs mailbox folder for quick access.

NOTE The VIPs folder combines incoming emails from VIPs related to all of your accounts. While they become viewable within this centralized folder, they are kept separate based on which email account they were received from. So, when you respond to the email, your response will come from the email address the original email was sent to.

TIP When looking at an incoming email from someone you want to add to your VIPs list, look at the top of the email's heading information, and wave your mouse over the From field (to the left of the person's name). A hollow star icon will appear, as shown in Figure 7.14.

Click this star icon to add that person to your VIPs list. From this point forward, all new and unread emails from that person within your Inbox will display a solid blue star (instead of a blue dot), and emails you've read from that person will display a hollow gray star icon to the left of the listing's Subject line within the Inbox listing.

To remove someone from your VIPs list, view one of his or her incoming emails and again click the star icon to the left of the From field.

FIGURE 7.14

Click the star icon to the left of a sender's name when looking at the From field of an incoming email to make that sender a VIP. Wave your mouse over the From field to make the star icon appear.

As soon as you add the first person to your VIPs list, this results in a VIPs Smart Folder being created automatically. Therefore, a new VIPs mailbox folder appears on the mailbox list (on the left side of the app window) and within the favorites bar. Click either of these to view a comprehensive list of all incoming emails from your VIPs.

FLAGGING INDIVIDUAL EMAILS TO SIGNIFY IMPORTANCE

In addition to adding someone to your VIPs list to identify important emails, you can flag individual emails to signify their importance. To flag an email, click the Flag icon on the toolbar, select the Flag option from the Messages pull-down menu, or use the Shift-⌘-L keyboard shortcut.

When you flag an email, the default flag color is red. However, you can manually choose between red, orange, yellow, green, blue, purple, or gray. Each color can represent a different level of importance, or represent a particular sender or category of email, based on your own preference and work habits.

> **NOTE** When you flag an email, a small flag icon appears within the email message's listing as you look at your Inbox, as well as to the left of the Subject line within the actual email. Displayed within the Mailboxes list on the left side of the app window, you'll also see a listing for Flagged emails. Click this to view only emails that you have flagged.

WORKING SEAMLESSLY WITH NOTIFICATION CENTER

Based on how you set up Notifications Center to work with the Mail app, your Mac can display an alert or banner near the top-right corner of the desktop anytime a new incoming email arrives. Plus, you can set up the Mail app icon (displayed on your desktop or the Launchpad screen) to display a badge that indicates how many new, unread emails are waiting in your Inboxes. Or, you can set up the badge to display the number of new messages in your Inbox, as opposed to those that have been placed into other folders.

In conjunction with displaying a banner, alert, or badge or displaying incoming email alerts within the Notification Center panel, you can also customize the Mail app to play an audible alarm when new email messages arrive in your Inbox.

> **NOTE** See Chapter 4, "Using Notification Center," for more information about how to set up Notification Center to work with the Mail app.

Up to 20 alerts about new incoming emails can also be displayed within the Notification Center panel at any given time. Each alert displays the incoming email's sender, subject line, when it was received, and the first few lines of the email's body text.

To set up the various notification options in conjunction with the Mail app, launch System Preferences and select the Notifications option. When the Notifications window appears, select and highlight the Mail app listing on the left side of the window (shown in Figure 7.15). Then, adjust the app-specific banner, alert, notification center, badge and play sound options that are displayed on the right side of the Notifications window.

> **NOTE** You will be alerted of new incoming emails through Notification Center, even if the Mail app isn't currently running. This also works while the Mac is in Power Nap mode.

FIGURE 7.15

You can customize the Notification Center options related specifically to the Mail app and determine how you'll be notified by your Mac when new emails arrive, even if the Mail app isn't currently running.

> **TIP** To access the email alerts within the Notification Center panel, click the Notification Center panel icon that's continuously displayed near the top-right corner of the desktop screen (along the menu bar). When viewing the Notification Center panel, look under the Mail heading to see app-specific alerts.
>
> Then, click any of the email alerts within the Notification Center panel to launch the Mail app and view that particular email in its entirety. After which time you can reply to the email or manage it (delete, print, share, save it, and so on) from within the Mail app.

CUSTOM SIGNING YOUR OUTGOING EMAILS

The Mail app enables you to automatically attach text to the end of every outgoing email you send from any or all of your separate email accounts. This text is called a signature. Within the Mail app, you can create and store an unlimited number of separate signatures, and then choose which one to attach to a particular outgoing email, or you can create a default signature that will be attached to all outgoing emails automatically.

> **TIP** A signature can also include an image (such as a company logo). To attach an image when creating a signature, drag it from Finder into the right column of the Signature window and place it where you want it to appear in conjunction with your Signature-related text. When you do this, however, the image will be displayed within the message itself, but will also be sent as a separate email attachment.

To create individual signatures for specific email accounts, or that are accessible from all the email accounts being managed by the Mail app, select Mail, Preferences from the menu bar. Then, from the Preferences window, click the Signatures tab.

On the left side of the Signatures window (shown in Figure 7.16), you'll see a listing for each of your separate email accounts. As you create new signatures, you can associate them with a specific account, or store them within the All Signatures listing, so that they are accessible from all of your email accounts as you compose new emails.

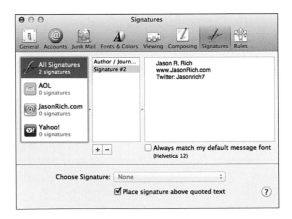

FIGURE 7.16

Create signatures that you can display at the end of your outgoing emails.

To create a new signature, click the plus sign icon below the middle column of the Signatures window. It's within this column that each of your Signatures will be listed, based on the label you assign to each of them.

After clicking the plus sign icon, within the middle column enter a custom label for the signature. This is how you'll identify and select it later. Then, within the right column of the Signature window, compose your custom signature.

> **TIP** Some people opt to include their name, company, address, phone number, email address, Facebook/Twitter username, website URL, and other contact information within their signature. Others include an inspirational quote or their company's marketing slogan. What you include within your signatures is entirely up to you, but it is text that will be displayed at the end of the email you send out from within the Mail app.

Once a signature has been created, you can set it up so it automatically gets displayed at the bottom of every outgoing message you compose within the Mail app.

You can also opt to add a signature manually to only the messages you choose. To do this, or if you have multiple signatures stored within the Mail app, as you're composing an email click the pull-down menu that's associated with the Signature option and choose which signature you want to use.

SEARCHING YOUR INBOX AND ALL MAIL FOLDERS

If you're looking for a particular email, you can enter any keyword or search phrase into the Search field in the upper-right corner of the Mail app window to find email messages stored in any of your Inboxes, Sent folders, or any other mailbox folders associated with any of your email accounts.

> **TIP** You can perform a search by entering someone's name, a keyword, date or a search phrase relevant to what you're looking for. As you enter information into the Search field, related results appear almost instantly within the center column of the Mail app.
>
> Within the Search field, you can include multiple search terms, separated by a comma, to help you narrow down the search results. You can also use Boolean searches that include the commands AND, OR, and NOT. For example, if you want to find an email from John Doe that includes the word *iPhone*, you can enter the search phrase "John Doe AND iPhone" (with the word *AND* in capital letters.

To exit out of the Search and return to viewing the regular Inbox column, delete the contents within the Search field using the Delete key or by clicking the Close button (X) to the right.

Another way to perform a search within the Mail app is select Edit, Find from the menu bar.

DICTATING YOUR OUTGOING EMAILS

The Mail app is fully compatible with Mountain Lion's Dictation feature. As you're composing an outgoing email, place the cursor where you want to insert text, and then press the Function (fn) key twice on the keyboard. When the Dictation icon appears and you hear a tone, start speaking into your Mac.

When you finish dictating your outgoing email, click the Done button within the Dictation icon. The words you spoke will be translated into text by the computer and inserted into your outgoing email.

! CAUTION The Dictation feature is pretty accurate, but not foolproof. Be sure to proofread your outgoing email before sending it to make sure that the computer accurately converted your dictation into text.

☑ TIP When dictating text, you can speak the punctuation that should appear. Here's a sample sentence that includes punctuation:

This is a sample sentence entered into the mail app! "I love speaking into my computer, instead of typing."

Using the Dictation feature, you'd say the following:

This is a sample sentence entered into the mail app exclamation point open quote I love speaking into my computer comma instead of typing period close quote

It is not yet possible to tell the Dictation feature to capitalize specific words within a sentence, such as the word Mail. However, you can say most punctuation symbols and numbers and use commands like new line or new paragraph.

MANAGING YOUR EMAILS BETTER

Depending on your email account, it probably includes an Inbox as well as a Drafts, Sent, Saved, Junk, and Trash mailbox folder. After you've read an incoming email, you have a handful of options as to what to do with it. For example, you can do the following:

- Delete the email by clicking the Delete icon or by selecting Edit, Delete from the menu bar. You can also use the Delete key keyboard shortcut. When you delete an email, it gets placed in your Trash folder.

> **✓ TIP** Deleted emails within the Mail app remain in the Trash folder until you manually delete them using the Erase Deleted Items command from the Mailbox pull-down menu. To save storage space on your computer, you'll want to empty the Trash folder periodically while using the Mail app. This will erase the messages permanently from your computer.

- Print the email using the Print command under the File pull-down menu. You can also print by clicking the Print icon on the toolbar (if you have placed it there when customizing the toolbar) or by using the ⌘-P keyboard shortcut.
- Reply to the email and send a message back to the sender. To do this, click the Reply button on the toolbar, choose the Reply option from the Message pull-down menu, or use the ⌘-R keyboard shortcut. (You also have the Reply All command at your disposal.)
- Forward the email to someone else using the Forward command. To do this, click the Forward button on the toolbar, choose the Forward option from the Message pull-down menu, or use the Shift-⌘-F keyboard shortcut.
- Move or copy the email message from your Inbox into another mailbox folder. When you move the message, it does not remain in your Inbox. However, when you copy the message, a copy of it remains in your Inbox. You can also drag messages from one location to another within the Mail app.
- Categorize the incoming email as spam or junk. This moves the email message from your Inbox into the Mail app's Junk folder. Once you categorize a message from a particular sender as junk, any further incoming emails from that sender are automatically classified as junk and are placed in your Junk folder, as opposed to your Inbox.

> **TIP** When you categorize an email message as spam or junk, it will be placed within the Mail app's Junk folder. It remains there until you manually erase the Junk folder, which is something you should get into the habit of doing periodically. To do this, select Mailbox, Erase Junk Mail from the menu bar.

Depending on the type of email account you're managing using the Mail app, you may also have the option to create custom folders (mailboxes), and then manually or automatically sort emails into those folders.

To create a new mailbox and potentially associate it with a particular email account (although this isn't necessary), click the small plus sign icon near the bottom-left corner of the Mail app window (within the mailbox list column), or select Mailbox, New Mailbox from the menu bar. You can then give that mailbox a custom label. Once the new mailbox is created, you can drag and drop or copy and paste messages from your Inbox or other mailbox folders into it.

The Mail app also enables you to create and manage Smart Mailboxes. When you choose this option, you are presented with a series of pull-down menus and empty fields with which you can set the criteria for what will automatically be placed within the Smart Mailbox. For example, you can choose emails from a specific sender, with a specific subject, or that contain a specific keyword.

WORKING WITH ICLOUD

In addition to automatically syncing all aspects of your iCloud email account (which was set up for you, for free, when you established your iCloud account), you can set up iCloud so that it automatically syncs your Mail app customizations and preferences with your other Macs and iDevices as they're related to your iCloud account. This includes your VIPs list, signatures, email account information, and the customized mail rules you set up.

To set up the Mail app to work with iCloud, launch System Preferences and select the iCloud option. Make sure your Mac is logged in to your iCloud account, and then add a check mark to the Mail check box.

> **NOTE** iCloud will automatically sync your iCloud-specific email account, but not your other email accounts. Plus, when you access the iCloud website (www.icloud.com), only your iCloud email account-specific emails will be accessible.
>
> It is, however, possible to manage your Yahoo! Mail, Microsoft Hotmail, Google Gmail, AOL Mail, or many other types of email accounts from the websites operated by those email services and to thus circumvent using the Mail app altogether.

> ☑ **TIP**   To further customize the Mail app, select Mail, Preferences from the menu bar. Then, one at a time, click the command tabs at the top of the window. Under the General, Accounts, Junk Mail, Fonts & Colors, Viewing, Composing, Signatures, and Rules tabs, you'll discover submenus that enable you to customize various features and functions of the Mail app. This is something you only need to do once; however, you can update your customizations at anytime.

SENDING LARGE FILES VIA EMAIL

When composing an email, you can include one or more attachments (such as a document, photo, or file). However, you're limited somewhat by the maximum file size that a email message can be.

To include an email attachment, click the paperclip-shaped icon near the upper-right corner of the New Message window. Then, when the Finder-like window appears, select the items you want to include as attachments to the email message. Click the Choose File button to continue.

As soon as you add an attachment to an email, displayed directly below the From field within the New Message window is the message size. If you've included images as part of your attachment (such as digital photos), to the extreme right of the message size information you'll see a pull-down menu associated with image size. From this menu, you can reduce the image size and resolution of the image attachments, making them more efficient to send via email.

Keep in mind that most email accounts limit the file size of attachments to 5MB per email. If you need to transfer large files (such as high-resolution digital photos or video files) to other people, you have several solutions for doing this.

First, you can set up a free Dropbox account (www.dropbox.com), which is a cloud-based file-sharing service. Unlike iCloud, when you upload a file to Dropbox, you can grant permission for other people to access and download it. A number of services like Dropbox offer this functionality, including Microsoft SkyDrive and Box.com.

Another solution for sending large files to other people is to use the YouSendIt.com service. You can either access this service from the company's website (www.yousendit.com) or download the free Mac app (shown in Figure 7.17) which makes sending large files or entire folders containing multiple files an easy process.

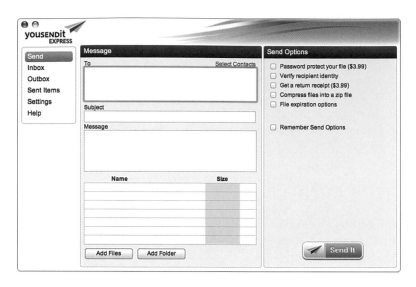

FIGURE 7.17

The YouSendIt app enables you to send large files online to other people as long as you know their email address.

YouSendIt offers a free file-sharing service, which has some limitations, and a more feature-packed premium service for a flat monthly fee. The premium service has no file-size limitations or limits related to how many times you can use it. Some of the service's premium options can also be purchased as needed on an à la carte basis.

8

GETTING THE MOST FROM ITUNES AND GAME CENTER

One of the great things about owning and using a Mac is all the incredible forms of digital entertainment that are available for it. Although this certainly isn't exclusive to the Mac, Apple has done a remarkable job making it easy to acquire, manage, experience, and in some cases share (with your iDevices) many forms of digital entertainment using the iTunes and Game Center apps.

In this chapter, you'll discover all that the iTunes app is capable of, plus take a look at the Game Center app and how it makes it easy to enjoy a wide range of multiplayer games while your computer is connected to the Internet.

So, whether you want to experience music, TV show episodes, movies, eBooks, podcasts, iTunes U content, music videos, download apps and sync content with your iDevices, or play games on your Mac, this chapter will be helpful.

EXPLORING ITUNES

Although not actually considered part of OS X Mountain Lion, Apple's iTunes app, like the iLife apps, comes bundled on all Macs. You can use it for a handful of separate but related tasks.

To fully utilize the iTunes app with Mountain Lion, your iOS mobile devices (iDevices), and iCloud, you must download and install the most current version of the free app.

> **NOTE** Each time Apple updates OS X, the iTunes Store, or apps that use iTunes-related content, the iTunes app gets updated, as well. Therefore, it becomes necessary to download and install the free updates onto your Mac. This is done from within the App Store, or by selecting the Check for Updates option found under iTunes on the menu bar when the app is running. A significant iTunes app update (to iTunes version 10) was released in conjunction with the release of Mountain Lion.
>
> However, in connection with this update, rumors were circulating that by late 2012, Apple would release a totally redesigned iTunes app that would more seamlessly integrate with iCloud, plus offer a collection of new features. At the same time, rumors suggested that Apple would discontinue its online-based Ping social networking service, which has been accessible exclusively through the iTunes app.
>
> So, by the time you read this chapter, a redesigned iTunes app may be available. Although the specific functions of the app that are described within this chapter will most likely remain the same, how you access each feature or function, as well as the overall look of the app itself, may be vastly different.

Currently, the iTunes app (version 10) serves as a conduit for accessing Apple's online-based content stores and libraries, including the following:

- Apple's iTunes Store, shown in Figure 8.1, from which you can purchase and download digital content from one of the Internet's largest digital music, movie, music video, audiobook, and TV show episode (and full season) selections. In addition to selling digital content, the iTunes Store offers some free content.

- Apple's iBookstore, which offers one of the Internet's largest selections of eBooks and digital publications (including newspapers and magazines) that can then be read on an iDevice using the iBooks or Newsstand apps.

FIGURE 8.1

From Apple's online iTunes Store, you can purchase a vast selection of multimedia content that can be enjoyed on your Mac and your iDevices, as well as on your Apple TV.

- Apple's iOS App Store, from which apps for the iPhone, iPad, and iPod touch can be acquired, downloaded, and organized. Those apps can then be transferred to your iDevice using the iTunes Sync or Wireless iTunes Sync process. (This App Store, which offers a vast selection of iDevice apps, is separate from the Mac App Store, which offers apps for the Mac and is accessible using the App Store app on the Mac.)

- Podcasts allows you to access and experience a vast and ever-growing selection of free audio and video podcasts from the iTunes app on the Mac.

- iTunes U, shown in Figure 8.2, offers an ever-expanding collection of educational content created and offered by some of the world's leading academic institutions, libraries, museums, and philanthropic organizations. Using video, audio, digital texts, and other multimedia content, courses covering thousands of subjects allow you to enhance your knowledge, expand your skill set, or engage in some type of personal enrichment.

FIGURE 8.2

iTunes U offers a vast selection of free educational and personal-enrichment content that covers literally thousands of different subjects and areas of interest.

> **TIP** The iTunes app also grants you free access to iTunes U, a massive and ever-growing collection of free online courses, seminars, and lectures produced by some of the world's leading academic institutions, libraries, museums, and educational organizations. This multimedia content includes texts, video, and audio-based programming and covers literally thousands of subjects.
>
> To access iTunes U and participate in online courses, launch the iTunes app and click the iTunes U command tab near the top center of the app window. You can then browse through the course catalog and register to participate in the free educational and personal-enrichment programs.
>
> You'll find iTunes U content designed for all ages, from elementary school through college, as well as advanced graduate-level courses and personal-enrichment programs for adults. Whether you're looking to expand your professional skill set, broaden your general knowledge, or learn about a highly specific topic, you'll find iTunes U programs that are easily accessible and suitable.
>
> One of the great things about iTunes U is that the courses are prepared and taught by leading professors, educators, and experts from top-notch institutions, such as Harvard University, Stanford, Duke University, MIT, MoMA (Museum of Modern Art), Oxford University, UC Berkeley, UCLA, Yale University, the Smithsonian, and National Geographic.

> **✐ NOTE** To shop for or acquire free content from the iTunes Store, iBookstore, Newsstand, App Store, Podcast library, or iTunes U, your Mac must be connected to the Internet, and you'll need an active Apple ID account.

> **✐ NOTE** The iTunes app can also be used to manage and experience your own digital music, even if it wasn't purchased or acquired from the iTunes Store. You can use iTunes to import, manage and play digital music from other sources, including your own audio CDs that you "rip" to create digital files.

Beyond granting you access to online stores owned and operated by Apple, through which you can acquire various types of multimedia content, the iTunes app also serves as a tool for managing and experiencing much of that content. Plus, it offers two methods for syncing information with an iDevice.

> **☑ TIP** The first time you use iTunes on a particular Mac, you must authorize the computer to work with iTunes and give you access to the iTunes Store. To do this, select Store, Authorize This Computer from the menu bar. You have to do this only one time.

As you begin using the iTunes app to connect to any of the online stores that Apple operates, you need to sign in using your Apple ID and password. To do this, click the iTunes Store in the sidebar, and then click the Sign In option near the top-right corner of the app window. You can also select Store, Sign In from the menu bar.

Once you sign in, your Apple ID username appears in the upper-right corner of the iTunes app window. Plus, if you have an iTunes credit available (as a result of redeeming an iTunes Gift Card, for example), the available balance displays near your username.

MANAGING YOUR DIGITAL MUSIC LIBRARY

If you acquire your digital music from the iTunes Store, you can manage and experience your entire personal digital music library using the iTunes app on your Mac.

Digital music files acquired from other sources can be imported into iTunes, so you can manage, organize, and experience the music through this app. iTunes also enables you to "rip" your music CDs and create digital music files from them. These files can also be stored, managed, and played using the app.

> **✓ TIP** To import music into iTunes, select File, Add to Library from the menu bar. Select the drive and folder where the music (or compatible content) is stored from within the Finder window that appears. Select and highlight the content you want to import, and then click the Open button in Add to Library window.
>
> To rip an audio CD and convert its contents to digital audio files, insert the CD into your Mac's optical drive while iTunes is running. Follow the onscreen prompts. The process is almost entirely automated.

Once your music is being stored on your Mac and has been imported into iTunes, the app serves as a feature-packed digital music player (shown in Figure 8.3). You can sort and listen to individual songs, entire albums, or create and listen to your own custom playlists.

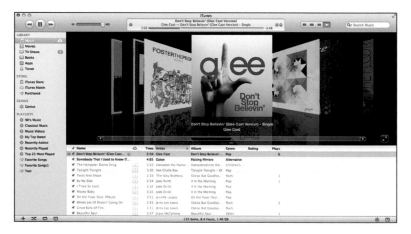

FIGURE 8.3

One capability of the iTunes app is to serve as a feature-packed digital music player.

The music you purchase using your Mac through the iTunes Store is automatically downloaded and accessible from your Mac. However, all of your music purchases from iTunes are also automatically stored within your iCloud account. So, if you purchase songs or albums on our iPhone or iPad, for example, you can set up the iTunes app on your Mac to access iCloud and automatically sync all of your purchases on your computers and iDevices that are linked to the same iCloud account.

So, regardless of which computer or iDevice you acquire music from, your personal digital music library that's acquired through iTunes can remain synced, and you won't have to purchase the same music multiple times to experience it on your various computers and iDevices.

Meanwhile, if you want to keep your entire digital music library synced, including music that's acquired from other sources besides iTunes, you can subscribe to the iTunes Match service.

> **NOTE**   You'll learn more about how iTunes can work with iCloud and the iTunes Match service from Chapter 11, "Navigating Around iCloud."

CREATING PLAYLISTS

A custom playlist is like a "mix tape" that you create using the songs in your personal digital music library (shown in Figure 8.4). Using iTunes, you can create as many different playlists as you desire, and each can have as many songs (from any music genre or from different albums) included within them. Each playlist is given a unique title. When listening to a playlist, you can hear songs in the order you preselect, or have iTunes randomize the song order using the Shuffle command.

FIGURE 8.4

A custom playlist, called Favorite Songs, is shown here using the Cover Flow view. As you can see, it contains seven personally selected songs from a variety of different artists and albums.

To create a playlist, launch the iTunes app. Then, select File, New Playlist from the menu bar, or use the ⌘-N keyboard shortcut.

A new Unnamed Playlist will be created and displayed in the iTunes app window. Enter a custom name for the playlist, such as Workout Music, Driving Music, Relaxation Mix, or Favorite Songs.

> **TIP** After you create a playlist , you can burn that collection of songs onto a CD, so you can play it on your car stereo, for example. You can also sync your playlists with your iDevices and enjoy your favorite music anytime and wherever you happen to be.

After the playlist file has been created within iTunes, click the Music option within the sidebar. Doing so will display a complete listing of songs you own and that are stored on your Mac. You also have the option to list songs that you own that are stored online (within your iCloud account) but that have not yet been downloaded to your Mac.

Select and highlight the songs you want to add to your playlist and drag them to the playlist's listing (which is now displayed on the left side of the iTunes app window, within the sidebar).

> **TIP** To view a playlist, click its listing under the Playlists heading on the left side of the sidebar. You can then rearrange the song order by dragging song listings up or down within the playlist listing. To delete a song from a playlist, highlight and select the song listing and press the Delete key. (When you delete a song from your playlist, it remains stored on your Mac and accessible within the iTunes app within your Music library.) You can also opt to delete a song from iTunes or from your computer altogether, however, if that song was purchased from the iTunes Store or you subscribe to iTunes Match, you can always redownload the music for free later.
>
> To delete an entire playlist, select and highlight the playlist's listing within the sidebar and press the Delete key. Your playlists can automatically be set up to sync with your other Macs and iDevices linked to your iCloud account.

> **NOTE** You'll notice that the iTunes app pre-creates a handful of Smart Playlists for you, all of which are listed under the Playlists heading within the sidebar. These playlists include My Top Rated, Recently Added, Recently Played, and Top 25 Most Played. Based on the genres of music that are already part of your digital music library, other pre-created playlists might include 90's Music or Classical Music, for example. Any of these playlists can be edited or deleted.

After creating a custom playlist, use the commands found under File on the menu bar to burn the playlist to a CD (using the Burn Playlist to Disc option). Use the commands displayed under View to determine how the songs in your digital music library and playlists will be displayed within the iTunes app window, and use the commands found under Controls to listen to your digital music.

It's also possible to create folders within iTunes to help you organize your playlists. To create a playlist folder, select File, New Playlist Folder from the menu bar.

> **TIP**   In addition to utilizing the Play, Next, Previous, Increase/Decrease Volume, Shuffle, or Repeat commands found under the Controls pull-down menu to listen to your music, you can use the icon-based control panel that appears along the top of the iTunes app window when the Music option or any playlist listing is selected.

When playing your music from iTunes, use your Mac's built-in speakers, connect wireless Bluetooth speakers to the computer, plug in stereo headphones, or use wireless Bluetooth headphones to hear the audio content.

> **TIP**   As you're using iTunes to play audio content , you can easily adjust the volume in a number of ways:
>
> ■ From the Speaker Volume slider icon on the right side of the menu bar
>
> ■ From the Speaker Volume slider near the top-left corner of the iTunes app window
>
> ■ By selecting Controls, Increase/Decrease from the menu bar
>
> ■ You can use the Function keys on your keyboard. F10 is used to mute the music, F11 decreases the volume, and F12 increases the volume.
>
> ■ By using the ⌘ - up arrow (volume up) or ⌘ - down arrow (volume down) keyboard shortcuts. If you're using headsets that connect via a cable to your Mac, along the cable a volume switch or dial may also be available.

As you're viewing a listing of specific content within iTunes, if you select anything but the Icons view, separate user-selectable columns are used to display details about the content. For example, if you select to view your Music using the List view, the name of each song, its time, artist, album title, genre, rating, and number of plays, for example, can be displayed in separate columns.

To re-sort the listing based on one of these headings, click the heading at the top of a column. Thus, if you click the Name heading, your music display alphabetically by song title. If you click the Artist heading, the music listing is sorted alphabetically by artist name. The same is true for each other column heading.

> **TIP** To determine what columns will be displayed, select View, View Options from the menu bar. A pop-up window displays more than 40 possible column headings and allows you to add columns for things like Composer, Date Added, Purchase Date, Time, or Track Number.

> **NOTE** To add a star-based rating to any content that's acquired from iTunes, select and highlight a particular song, movie, or TV show episode, and then select File, Rating from the menu bar. From the submenu that's displayed, choose between zero (none) and five stars. You can later sort or search for content based on the star rating you've assigned to specific content. The star-based ratings offer yet another way to personalize how you organize your content within the iTunes app.
>
> Depending on which view your using, you can also simply select a song and then click on the Rating option to choose a rating for that song. This works in the List view, Album List view, or Cover Flow view, for example.

WATCHING MOVIES, TV SHOWS, AND MUSIC VIDEOS

Any video-based content that was purchased (or rented) from the iTunes Store or videos that you've imported into iTunes (including non-copy protected or non-copyrighted movies, or movies you've edited using iMovie) can be experienced using the iTunes app on your Mac.

For example, if you've purchased or rented movies from the iTunes Store, click the Movies option within the iTunes sidebar to view the movies stored on your Mac, and then double-click a movie selection to watch it.

Figure 8.5 shows a sample listing for a movie that can be purchased or rented from the iTunes Store in both Standard and HD format. If you click the Buy HD Movie or Buy Movie buttons, the movie will download and be accessible by clicking the Movies option in the sidebar under the Library heading.

FIGURE 8.5
Star Trek *is one of thousands of movies that you can either purchase or rent from the iTunes Store and then view on your Mac using the iTunes app.*

! CAUTION If you have rented a movie from the iTunes Store, that movie will be downloaded to your Mac and remain there for up to 30 days before it automatically erases itself. However, once you begin watching that movie, you can view it as often as you want within a 24-hour period before the movie file automatically erases itself from your computer.

NOTE Movies rented from iTunes can be stored and viewed on your Mac, or transferred to your Apple TV or an iDevices, but they can only be stored on one computer or device at a time.

Movies that you've purchased from the iTunes Store or that you've imported into your iTunes digital library can be played as often as you want. Purchased content also gets stored automatically within your iCloud account, so it can be downloaded and experienced on the other Macs, Apple TV devices, or iDevices linked to the same iCloud account.

NOTE To play traditional DVDs on your Mac, use the DVD Player app that comes preinstalled with Mountain Lion. Using Finder, you'll find it listed within your Mac's Applications folder. It's also accessible from the Launchpad within the Other folder. To play DVDs on your Mac, the computer must be equipped with an optical drive (or have an optical drive connected to it). The MacBook Air, for example, does not have a built-in optical drive, but an external one can be connected, or you can use the Share feature built into Mountain Lion to share an optical drive wirelessly with another computer that's on the same network.

By clicking the TV Shows option under the Library heading of iTunes (within the sidebar), you can view a listing of individual TV show episodes or complete TV series seasons you've acquired and that are stored on your Mac. Double-click a listing to begin watching that content.

TIP To watch music videos stored on your Mac, click the Music option below the Library option within the sidebar. From this listing, click the music video you want to watch. Listings that are music videos, as opposed to songs, have a video monitor icon associated with them.

To use iTunes to watch video content on your Mac, double-click the contents listing to begin playing it. Onscreen controls display along the top of the app window, as well as near the bottom center of the app window. After a few seconds, these controls disappear while your video content is playing. To make the controls reappear, move the mouse around on the screen.

Click the Esc key to exit out of the video-watching mode of iTunes and return to the previous menu or screen you were viewing.

TIP As you're watching video content on your Mac, to fully utilize the screen, click the Full Screen mode icon on the right side of the control panel near the bottom center of the app window, or select View, Enter Full Screen from the menu bar. The keyboard shortcut to enter into or exit out of Full Screen mode is Control-⌘-F.

Depending on the video content you're watching, an icon to switch between a Normal or Widescreen viewing mode may also become available.

ACCESSING ITUNES COMMANDS AND FEATURES

Just about all the commands and features that iTunes offers are accessible in several ways. For example, you can click on or otherwise utilize command buttons, icons, and sliders that are displayed within the iTunes app window itself. Or, you can access commands from the various pull-down menus on the menu bar at the top of the screen.

Many commands and features offered within the iTunes app also have a keyboard shortcut associated with them.

To quickly find any content you have stored within iTunes, use the Search field near the top-right corner of the screen. (Again, the location of this and other fields and command options may change in future versions of iTunes released after Version 10.)

> ☑ **TIP**   If your Mac came with an Apple Remote, or you purchase an optional Apple Remote ($19.99, http://store.apple.com/us/product/MC377LL/A), it's possible to wirelessly control audio and video playback of content, plus adjust the volume of your computer's speakers.
>
> Similar wireless remote control functionality when using the iTunes app on your Mac is available using your iPhone, iPad, or iPod touch if you download the free Remote app for your iDevice from the App Store. This same app can also be used with the AirPlay feature built in to Mountain Lion and with your Apple TV device.

> ✎ **NOTE**   In addition to the command buttons and icons displayed within the app window, you'll discover four command icons near the bottom-left corner of the iTunes app window (below the sidebar).
>
> From left to right, these icons are used to as follows:
>
> ■ Create a Playlist
>
> ■ Turn Shuffle On/Off (which determines whether songs will be played in order or randomized)
>
> ■ Turn Repeat On/Off (which determines whether a currently playing playlist will play once and stop, or if it'll continuously repeat until you click the Pause or Stop button. It can also be set to repeat a single song repeatedly.
>
> ■ Item Artwork, which allows you to decide whether you want iTunes to display item artwork (such as album covers) when you are viewing or playing content stored within iTunes

BUILT-IN GENIUS

Built in to iTunes are several "genius" features. For example, based on the music in your personal digital music library and your music purchase history through the iTunes Store, the iTunes Genius feature can recommend similar music that it believes you might enjoy. You can then purchase and download those recommendations. This feature also works for other types of iTunes content, such as TV shows, movies, and iOS apps.

From the Music library, use the Genius Mixes feature to allow iTunes to create customized playlists just for you. To use this feature, select one song from your music library, and then click the Genius icon near the lower-right corner of the app window. Based on your initial song selection, this feature will create playlists containing similar music.

> ☑ TIP   When a Genius playlist is being displayed, look to the upper-right corner of the window to find a Limit To option (accompanied by the pull-down menu), along with a Refresh and Save Playlist button. Use the Limit To option to determine the maximum number of songs the Genius Playlist feature will add to each playlist. The Refresh button updates the playlist, and the Save Playlist option allows you to save the playlist using a title you provide.

MANAGING EBOOKS, AUDIOBOOKS, IDEVICE APPS, AND RINGTONES

You can use iTunes to purchase, download, and manage your library of eBooks acquired from Apple's iBookstore. You can then sync the eBook files with your iPhone, iPad, or iPod touch to read them using the free iBooks app.

Figure 8.6 shows what it looks like when you access Apple's online-based iBookstore to purchase eBooks that can later be transferred to and read on your iDevice.

Likewise, you can use the iTunes app on your Mac to find, purchase (or acquire), and download apps for your iDevice, and then store and organize those apps on your Mac before transferring them to your iDevice using one of the iTunes sync processes.

Ringtones for your iPhone can also be acquired, downloaded, organized, and stored on your Mac (within the iTunes app), and then be transferred to your iPhone using the iTunes sync process.

To manage eBooks, iOS apps, and ringtones, click the Books, Apps, or Tones option under the Library heading within the iTunes sidebar.

FIGURE 8.6
From the iTunes app, you can access Apple's iBookstore by clicking the Books option near the top center of the screen once you have iTunes Store selected in the sidebar.

> **TIP** Audiobooks purchased (or acquired), downloaded, and stored on your Mac via iTunes can be managed, stored, or played on your Mac using the iTunes app, or you can transfer them to you iDevice. Another source for audiobooks for your Mac is Audible.com.
>
> Using the Open Stream option under the Advanced pull-down menu within the iTunes app, you can stream radio stations that broadcast via the Internet. You'll need to know the website address (URL) used by the radio station to stream its content.

PURCHASING CONTENT FROM THE ITUNES STORE

Everything you purchase from the iTunes Store (music, music videos, TV show episodes, entire TV seasons, movies, audiobooks, eBooks, iDevice apps) and movies you rent and content you acquire for free from the iTunes Store automatically get downloaded to the computer or mobile device it is purchased from.

However, that same content also gets stored automatically within your iCloud account, so you can access it from any other Mac or compatible iDevice (or Apple TV) that's linked to the same account, without having to repurchase that content.

To make purchases from the iTunes Store, your Apple ID needs to be linked to a major credit card or a debit card. However, you also have the option of pre-purchasing iTunes Gift Cards and redeeming them from your Apple ID account, so you can make purchases on iTunes via iTunes.

> **TIP**   If you initially purchase one or more songs from a single album, but not the whole album, and you later choose to go back and acquire the entire album, use the Complete My Album feature of iTunes. This allows you to purchase the remaining songs from a specific album at a discounted (prorated) price, without having to repurchase the songs you already own.
>
> Likewise, the Complete My Season feature works when you've acquired one or more episodes from a particular TV series season and then want to go back and acquire all the remaining episodes from that season. This, too, can be done at a discounted (prorated) price.

When you acquire free content from the iTunes Store, you still need to supply your Apple ID to download that content; however, you are not charged for it. The free content then becomes part of your personal digital library and also gets stored within your iCloud account, as if it were purchased content.

> **TIP**   To find free content downloadable from iTunes, access the iTunes Store from the iTunes app, and click the Free on iTunes option on the Quick Links menu.
>
> From the Free on iTunes screen, you'll find a constantly changing selection of music, movie featurettes, movie trailers, TV show episodes, TV show "sneak peaks" and featurettes, iDevice apps, eBooks, and podcasts.

To quickly find any content that's available from the iTunes Store, launch iTunes, click the iTunes Store option, and then use the Search field near the upper-right corner of the app window. Any keyword or search phrase associated with a song, album, artist, TV show, movie, or actor, for example, can be entered into the Search field. The related search results appear within the iTunes app window, sorted by content type.

After you've purchased content from iTunes, if that content is not yet stored on your Mac, click the Purchased option to display a complete listing of past purchases available for download.

> **NOTE**   If you have iTunes set up to automatically download new purchases, regardless of from which computer or device the content is acquired, it's not necessary to use the Purchased feature, because all content you own from the iTunes Store will automatically be transferred to the Mac you're using. To set up this option, just select iTunes, Preferences from the menu bar, and then click the Store tab.

THE ITUNES MATCH SERVICE

The free iTunes app that comes preinstalled on your Mac is designed to manage your entire personal digital music library stored on your Mac. However, as an added feature, any digital music you purchase from the iTunes Store automatically becomes part of your iCloud account. As a result, those digital music purchases can also be downloaded by all the other Macs, Apple TV, and iDevices linked to the same iCloud account, without you having to repurchase that content.

This iCloud functionality does not work with digital music you import into iTunes from other sources, such as music you compose using GarageBand, music you acquire from Amazon.com (or another online music store or service), or audio CDs you convert (rip) into digital music files.

To add iCloud music syncing functionality to your entire personal digital music library, so that all your music, regardless of how It was acquired, becomes accessible on all of the Macs, Apple TV, and iDevices linked to your iCloud account, you'll need to upgrade to Apple's premium iTunes Match service for $24.95 per year.

When you subscribe to this service, iTunes analyzes your personal digital music library on each of your computers and devices linked to the same account, and then syncs that content. Depending on how you then customize the app, iTunes can automatically download all your music on all your computers or devices or simply make the music selections you own available for download (for free) on each computer or device.

> **TIP**   To customize the functionality of the iTunes Match feature after you subscribe to it, select iTunes, Preferences from the menu bar. Then, click the Store near the top-center of the Store Preferences window. Select the Music option if you want iTunes to automatically download all music from your iCloud account, as well as new music purchases (regardless of how or where they're acquired on your other computers or devices) to the Mac you're currently using. Also, select the Always Check for Available Downloads option.

CUSTOMIZING ITUNES

There are many ways to customize the features and functions built in to the iTunes. For example, you can set up parental controls to ensure your kids cannot download, access, or experience inappropriate audio or video content. You can also determine where on your computer your digital content will be stored, and which options are displayed within the app's sidebar.

Another thing you can do is set up iTunes content sharing on your local network, so the content that is stored on your computer (music, movies, TV shows, and so on) can be experienced on other computers also connected to that network, even if they're not linked to the same iCloud or Apple ID account.

All of these options, plus dozens of others, can be customized via iTunes, Preferences within the General, Playback, Sharing, Store, Parental, Devices, and Advanced tabs (shown in Figure 8.7).

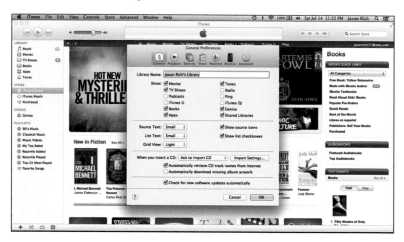

FIGURE 8.7

To access the Preferences window within iTunes, access the iTunes pull-down menu and choose the Preferences option. Then click the tabs along the top of the window to access and customize the various options.

SYNCING AND BACKING UP IDEVICE CONTENT

Whether you have an iPhone, iPad, or any model iPod, you can transfer, sync, and share your music, video, or other iTunes content with the device using the iTunes sync process or the wireless iTunes sync process.

The iTunes sync process involves connecting your iDevice to your Mac using the white USB cable that came with the mobile device. One end of this cable connects to the USB port on your Mac, while the other gets plugged into the dock connector at the bottom of your mobile device.

Once the connection is established, the iTunes app on your Mac automatically launches, and content (music, movies, TV shows, music videos, eBooks, audiobooks, ringtones, and so on) can be transferred or synced. At the same time, your iDevice can be backed up, so the backup files get stored on your Mac.

The wireless iTunes sync process works exactly like the traditional iTunes sync process, except that a wireless connection between your Mac and iDevice is established via your wireless network. For this feature to work, the Wi-Fi feature of your Mac and iDevice needs to be turned on, and both the computer and mobile device must be connected to the same wireless network. However, no cables are required to establish the connection.

> **TIP** Your iDevice can now obtain iTunes content and back itself up to your iCloud account, without using the iTunes sync process at all. When you use this iCloud functionality, your backup files are stored online. So, if you need to restore your iDevice, you can do so from wherever a Wi-Fi Internet connection is available. Otherwise, if you use the iTunes sync process, your backup files are stored on your Mac. Therefore, you need to reconnect with that Mac to restore your iDevice if this becomes necessary.

MAKING THE MOST OF GAME CENTER

Thousands of individual games can be acquired from the Mac App Store (using the App Store app), downloaded from other online sources, or installed from a CD/DVD-ROM. Some games are single player. Others are multiplayer games that allow multiple people to sit in front of the same computer to complete. Yet another category of multiplayer games allows you to compete against one or more opponents via the Internet.

To play an online multiplayer game, all players need to have Internet access and have the same game installed on their computer (and be connected to the same online game's website).

Apple's Game Center, shown in Figure 8.8, is a free online service that enables you to experience compatible online multiplayer games and compete against friends or total strangers. The service allows you to set up an account and then safely interact with or play against other people via the Internet.

To access Game Center, you just use the Game Center app that comes preinstalled with Mountain Lion.

FIGURE 8.8

Apple's Game Center app enables you to connect to the online Game Center service to play multiplayer games via the Internet.

! CAUTION   Although Game Center does not automatically share personal information about you with other people, except for information you add to your online profile, to protect yourself and your identity, refrain from disclosing personal information when communicating with the people you're playing games against online. During this game-related communication, what information you reveal and to whom is at your discretion.

☑ TIP   As a parent, you can set up parental controls and determine whether your kids will be able to participate in online multiplayer games, and if so, with whom. To adjust these settings, launch System Preferences and click the Parental Controls option. Follow the onscreen prompts to set up applicable controls and limitations related to Game Center.

Game Center is compatible with Macs running Mountain Lion, as well as with iPhone, iPad, and iPod touch devices connected to the Internet. Therefore, you can play a game on your Mac and compete against other people who are located anywhere in the world and who are using a Mac or iDevice.

Or, if you have the same game app installed on your Mac and iDevice, you can switch between playing a specific game on your Mac and iPhone, iPad, or iPod touch.

> **TIP** When you first begin using Game Center, you must create a profile for yourself, which will include your unique username (which you create), your Apple ID (or the email address you use to set up your free account), as well as a photo you upload (which is optional). Click the Me tab near the top of the Game Center app window to customize your profile.

To find and add friends to your Game Center account, click the Friends tab near the top center of Game Center. On the left of the Friends screen, click the Add Friends banner. You can then send an email request to specific people, asking them to become your Game Center friend.

After you become friends with someone online, you can compete against that person in games that you both have installed on your Mac (or iDevice), plus you can view details about their gaming achievements, including their high scores. It's also possible to see which games your friends are playing, so you can then choose to acquire those games from the App Store and play them as well.

> **TIP** To "unfriend" someone who is your online friend within Game Center, click the Friends tab near the top center of Game Center, select and highlight a specific friend from the list that appears on the left side of the screen, and then scroll down to the bottom of the app window and click the Unfriend banner.

By clicking the Games tab, you can view a list of the games currently installed on your Mac and compatible with Game Center.

Each listing includes details about your current progress within the game and your high scores. Click any listed game to launch and begin playing it. Keep in mind that the games are sorted based on whether they're installed on your Mac (under the OS X Games heading) or on one of your iDevices (under the IOS Games heading).

> **TIP** To find new games compatible with Game Center to download and play on your Mac, click the Find Games on the App Store option under the OS X Games heading. The App Store app will launch, and a list of compatible games will display.
>
> Some games for the Mac that are Game Center compatible are available for free. Others are free, but require or have in-app purchases available. Some games you purchase outright. Some purchased games also have in-app purchase options available.

> **NOTE** When manually searching the App Store's Games category for Game Center-compatible games, look for the Game Center logo or a mention of Game Center compatibility within the game's description or under the Information box related to a game when viewing its description page.

To respond to friend requests and challenges from your online friends, click the Requests tab. It, too, is displayed near the top center of the Game Center app window, to the right of the Me, Friends, and Games tabs.

OTHER GAMING OPTIONS

Without accessing Game Center, there are several ways to experience online-based multiplayer games on your Mac. Some games have their own Internet-based servers and player match-up services (operated by the game developer) and allow you to connect to those servers from within the game.

There are also online-based games you can access and play from within Facebook and other popular online social networking sites that do not require you to download additional apps or content to your Mac to play them. Facebook, for example, offers access to hundreds of free (advertiser supported) games in a wide range of game genres that can be experienced against other players (either your Facebook friends or strangers).

On the Internet, you'll also discover a handful of other online gaming sites that enable you to compete against other players, typically for free. For example, there's Addicting Games (www.addictinggames.com), FreeOnlineGames (www.freeonlinegames.com), PlayFish (www.Playfish.com), PoGo (www.www.pogo.com), and Yahoo! Games (http://games.yahoo.com).

Available on these online gaming sites, you'll find computerized adaptations of popular board games, card games, and casino games, plus simulation and strategy-based games, puzzle games, shooters, action/adventure games, and even adaptations of classic coin-op arcade games.

INSTALLING NEW SOFTWARE

OS X Mountain Lion comes with a nice selection of preinstalled apps that can handle a wide range of popular computing tasks. These core apps, such as Contacts, Calendar, Reminders, Safari, FaceTime, and Notification Center, to name just a few, integrate and exchange information with each other, as well as with Apple's iCloud file-sharing service.

> **NOTE** Every Mac also comes with the iLife apps (iPhoto, iMovie, and GarageBand) preinstalled, plus you can purchase the optional iWork apps (Pages, Numbers, and Keynote) separately from the App Store.

Because Apple core apps work seamlessly with iCloud, app-related data gets backed up to the cloud-based service and syncs wirelessly with your other Macs and iDevices as long as an Internet connection is present.

iCloud data syncing happens automatically and in the background, so all of your most current data and files related to the core apps, iLife apps, and iWork apps are always up-to-date and accessible when and where needed, including directly from the Internet when you visit www.iCloud.com and log in to your iCloud account using your Apple ID and password. This is a feature that most third-party apps do not offer, at least not with iCloud. Some third-party apps offer similar data syncing functionality, but work with services such as Dropbox or Box.com instead.

> **NOTE** See Chapter 11, "Navigating Around iCloud," to discover strategies for making the most out of this feature-packed and free service. Thanks to iCloud, app-specific data can also be synced with compatible apps running on your iPhone, iPad, and iPod touch.

In addition to the apps available from Apple for the Mac, many third-party software developers offer a plethora of software that can be purchased, downloaded, installed, and run on your computer to handle an even greater range of tasks. Much of the software that's available for Macs, including free apps, is available through Apple's own App Store.

Beyond using the App Store to acquire software, there are other ways to install software onto your Mac, including the following:

- Software (apps) can be purchased and downloaded (or acquired for free in some cases) directly from a software developer's website.
- You can acquire software from online-based stores that cater to the Mac.
- Open source (free) software is available from a handful of online sources.
- Software can be purchased on CD or DVD from a retail store and then installed using your Mac's SuperDrive or optical drive.
- You can transfer most Mac apps between computers by linking the computers through a wireless network or by first copying the app files to a USB thumb drive or a CD/DVD.

☑ **TIP** If you don't want to network your Macs together to transfer apps/files and data, you can purchase the optional J5Create Wormhole JUC400 cable ($39.99, www.j5create.com/juc400.htm), which includes the software needed to automatically connect two Macs. You can then drag and drop or copy and paste content (including most apps) between them, with no special setup or configuration required. The J5Create Wormhole JUC400 is one of many products available that make syncing information between Macs easy using a USB cable.

📝 **NOTE** If you're using a MacBook Air (which has no SuperDrive built in), it's possible to connect an optional SuperDrive ($79, http://store.apple.com/us/product/MC684ZM/A). Alternatively, you can use the OS X drive sharing feature and use the SuperDrive that's connected to another Mac via a wireless network connection.

SHOPPING THE APP STORE

Mountain Lion comes bundled with an app called App Store. When your Mac is connected to the Internet, this app is used specifically to grant you access to the online-based App Store, shown in Figure 9.1. From here, you can find, purchase, and download apps from Apple and third-party developers, plus keep all the apps that are installed on your Mac current.

📝 **NOTE** The Updates feature of the App Store only works with the Mountain Lion operating system itself, the preinstalled apps, and third-party apps you've purchased from the App Store. If you acquire apps from another source, you'll need to learn about app updates and install them using the process outlined by that app developer. For example, the app may have a Check for Updates option built in.

📝 **NOTE** The App Store also offers a large and ever-growing selection of free apps. Some of these are demo versions or advertiser-supported versions of paid apps. Others are full-featured apps that the software developer does not charge for. When you look at an app's listing or description, the word *free* appears within the price button for an app that is free of charge.

FIGURE 9.1

Operated by Apple, the online-based App Store offers a one-stop shop for finding, purchasing, downloading, and installing apps for your Mac.

ADVANTAGES OF APP STORE APPS

In addition to the convenience of being able to shop online from a central location for your Mac software, there are some definite advantages to acquiring apps from the App Store, including the following:

- Most apps featured within the App Store all have star-based ratings, sales, or popularity rankings, and most have detailed reviews associated with them. Therefore, you can quickly obtain information about an app before installing it. Keep in mind, newly released or unpopular apps may not yet have ratings associated with them.

- When you purchase an app from the App Store, your purchase history is retained by Apple. As a result, you can click the Purchased tab at the top of the main App Store screen anytime and reinstall previously purchased apps for free on any Mac linked to your Apple ID account.

- Apps purchased from the App Store can be downloaded and installed on all of your Macs that are linked to the same Apple ID account, for no additional charge.

- Once an app is purchased from the App Store, if new updates for the app are released, the App Store will notify you, and you'll be able to download the latest version of the app, for free, using the App Store's Updates feature.

- After you select, purchase and download an app from the App Store, the installation process happens automatically.

■ All App Store purchases automatically get billed to the credit card or debit card linked to your Apple ID. You never have to manually enter your name, address, phone number, billing information, or other details about yourself when making a new purchase.

NOTE Aside from using a credit card or debit card, purchases from the App Store can be paid for using iTunes gift cards, which are available from Apple Stores, Apple.com, and wherever gift cards are sold. They're available in denominations between $10 and $50, and can easily be redeemed online. To learn more, visit www.apple.com/gift-cards.

TIP To redeem an iTunes gift card while visiting the App Store, access the main App Store page, and then click the Redeem option on the right side of the screen, below the Quick Links heading. When prompted, enter the card's unique gift card or download code. Figure 9.2 shows the gift card redemption screen of the App Store. Click the Redeem button to continue.

When you enter the card's code, the value of the gift card is credited to your Apple ID account and can be used to make app purchases.

You can also manage your Apple ID/iTunes account (to update your credit card or debit card information, for example) by clicking the Account option under the Quick Links heading.

FIGURE 9.2

The gift card redemption screen within the App Store.

USING THE APP STORE APP

If you're already an iDevice user, you're probably familiar with the App Store. Although the overall layout of the App Store for Mac software is very similar to Apple's iOS App Store, the two should not be confused. The App Store accessible using the App Store app from your Mac is designed to offer Mac software (apps) only, and is the focus of this section.

> **NOTE** Apple's App Store for iOS apps is accessible from the iTunes software on your Mac and from the App Store app on your iPhone, iPad, or iPod touch. This App Store, however, is exclusively for finding, downloading, purchasing, or acquiring iOS apps for your mobile device.

As long as your Mac is connected to the Internet, you can launch the App Store app on your Mac from the Applications folder or from the Dock (shown in Figure 9.3) or by using Launchpad. The App Store app connects automatically to Apple's online App Store and enables you to find, purchase, download, and install Mac apps (or acquire free apps, when applicable).

App Store

FIGURE 9.3

By default, the app icon for the App Store is on the Dock.

> **TIP** All purchases made from the App Store require a valid Apple ID account. You also need to have a credit card or debit card associated with that account or have a positive balance from redeeming iTunes gift cards. To create and manage your Apple ID account, or recover a forgotten Apple ID password, launch the Safari web browser and visit https://appleid.apple.com.

FINDING APPS IN THE APP STORE

Once you've accessed the App Store, use one of the following strategies to find and acquire the apps you're looking for:

■ If you know the exact name of the app, or can describe a specific app using keywords or a search phrase, enter this information into the Search field near the upper-right corner of the App Store app window (shown in Figure 9.4). The search results will reveal a selection of related app listings.

Search Box

Search results

FIGURE 9.4

You can use the Search field within the App Store to find any app that's available by entering its title or a related keyword or search phrase. The search results will be displayed as app listings in the main area of the App Store app window.

- Click the Featured tab near the top center of the main App Store screen to view a collection of apps from a variety of genres and categories that Apple is currently showcasing. Scroll down to view the New and Noteworthy (shown in Figure 9.5) and What's Hot sections.

FIGURE 9.5

The New and Noteworthy section of the App Store displays listings for apps that Apple chooses to promote. These listings change regularly.

- Click the Top Charts tab near the top center of the main App Store screen to view a listing of Top Paid, Top Free, and Top Grossing apps (shown in Figure

9.6). Next to the category headings, click the See All option to display the top 180 ranked apps, based on sales or download popularity.

FIGURE 9.6

View a general Top Charts list, or choose a specific category of apps and then view a more defined Top Charts list that will be sorted by Top Paid, Top Free, and Top Grossing apps.

> **TIP** After you click the Top Charts tab, a sidebar on the right side of the screen displays the Top Charts categories. Click any category to view the most popular category-specific apps. There are 21 app categories to choose from, including Business, Education, Finance, Games, Social Networking, and Utilities.

■ Click the Categories tab near the top center of the main App Store screen to view a listing of 21 app categories (shown in Figure 9.7). Click a category that's of interest, and then browse all the apps within that category that are available from the App Store. When you do this, on the right side of the screen look for the Quick Links menu, which offers a listing of specialized subcategories. For example, if you select the Games category, the Quick Link menu offers options for Gorgeous Games, Retro Games, Multiplayer Games, Adventure Games, Popular Puzzlers, and so on.

■ To view all the apps you've previously purchased from the App Store, on any of your Macs, click the Purchases tab near the top center of the main App Store screen. A listing of apps you've purchased will display, along with their date of purchase. If the app is currently installed on the computer you're using, a button labeled Installed will display. If the app has been purchased, but not yet downloaded and installed on the Mac you're using, an Install button will display.

FIGURE 9.7

Just like a traditional bookstore or library displays books on its shelves based on subject matter or category, the App Store does the same with apps. This makes it easy to narrow down your search and find what you're looking for faster.

■ Displayed along the right side of the main App Store window is a Quick Links menu, from which you can also browse through apps that fall into specific categories that Apple periodically creates, such as Apps Starter Kit, which describes apps that are ideal for new Mac users.

> **☑ TIP** Looking for great games? In addition to the App Store, you can find, purchase, and download popular Mac games from the Mac Games Store (www. macgamesstore.com) or directly from the websites of game developers such as Electronic Arts (www.ea.com/mac).

LEARNING ABOUT APPS FROM LISTINGS

Regardless of how you browse for apps in the App Store, initially what displays is a collection of individual app listings, as shown in Figure 9.8.

Each listing offers information about a specific app, including its name, category, average star-based rating, the number of ratings it has received, its price, and an icon that represents the app.

Rating   App name

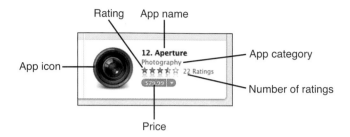

App icon

App category

Number of ratings

Price

FIGURE 9.8

A sample app listing from the App Store.

TIP   To immediately purchase an app (or acquire a free app) when viewing its listing, click the Price button. If it's a free app, click the Free button. You'll be prompted to enter your Apple ID and password. The app will then download and automatically install itself on your Mac. The app icon for it will appear within your Applications folder, at which time you can add it to your Dock. During the download and install process, you can watch a progress bar that appears below the Launchpad icon on the Dock.

LEARNING MORE ABOUT APPS

Instead of immediately clicking the Price button for an app to purchase or acquire it, click the app's icon or name to display its detailed Description screen (shown in Figure 9.9).

FIGURE 9.9

A sample Description screen for an app that's available from the App Store. You have to scroll down to view all the information included.

An app's Description screen includes the following:

- The app's name (at the top).
- The app's icon or logo (near the top left).
- The app's price icon (or Free icon), below the app's graphic icon.
- A text-based description of the app that's written by the app developer.
- An Information window that contains specific details about the app, including its Category, Release Date, Version Number, Price, File Size, Language, and Seller, as well as its age-related Rating and System Requirements.
- Sample screenshots from the app. This allows you to see an example of what the app looks like. In some cases, the app developer also makes short movie clips showing highlights from the app available.
- A link to the software developer's own website / support website.
- The Customer Ratings chart, shown in Figure 9.10, which shows the app's average star-based rating, the number of ratings the app has received, and how many one, two, three, four, and five star ratings it has earned.
- Under Customer Reviews section, you can read detailed, text-based reviews of the app written by your fellow Mac users.

FIGURE 9.10

The Customer Ratings chart shows you an average star-based rating for the app, how many ratings the app has received, as well as how many one, two, three, four, and five star ratings it has earned from your fellow Mac users.

TIP Apple's star-based rating system goes from one to five stars, with five stars being the highest possible rating. Look for apps with a high number of four or five star ratings. As a general rule, avoid apps with a significant number of one or two star ratings. Anyone who acquires the app can rate it. So, reviewing an app's star-based ratings and reviews provides you with unbiased information about the overall quality of the app.

To purchase the app from an app's Description screen, click the Price button near the top of the screen. When prompted, enter your Apple ID and password. The app will be downloaded and installed on your Mac. Keep in mind that if you're acquiring a free app from the App Store, you'll still need to supply your Apple ID before downloading and installing it; however, you will not be charged for the app.

OBTAINING APPS VIA OTHER MEANS

Apple designed the App Store to be a one-stop shop for all of your Mac app needs. However, not all Mac software developers offer their apps through the App Store. Therefore, to acquire certain apps, you might need to purchase and download them directly from the app developer's website or from an independent online software store, such as Amazon.com.

NOTE Some traditional consumer electronics stores (such as Best Buy), mass-market superstores (such as Target), and office supply stores (such as Staples) also sell Mac software on CD, which you can purchase and install on your computer. However, this option is quickly becoming obsolete.

TIP To purchase and download Microsoft Office for the Mac, visit Microsoft's own website (www.microsoft.com/mac). To purchase and download popular Adobe applications for the Mac, such as Photoshop CS6, visit www.adobe.com. The popular accounting and bookkeeping software from Intuit, including Quicken for Mac and QuickBooks, can be purchased and downloaded directly from Intuit's website (www.intuit.com). These apps are also available from other sources, as well, even though you won't find them on the App Store.

A handful of online services also offer Mac software for purchase and download. These online services offer free software as well as shareware, open source, and paid apps.

Amazon (www.amazon.com/software, click the Mac option), C/Net's Download.com (http://download.cnet.com/mac), MacMall (www.macmall.com), Softpedia (http://mac.softpedia.com), and MacWorld (www.macworld.com) are examples of these services.

> ☑️ **TIP**   If you're a high school or college student (or a teacher/professor), some software developers and resellers (such as the Academic Superstore, www.academicsuperstore.com) offer significant discounts on popular Mac apps.

OPEN SOURCE VERSUS PAID APPS

Companies like Apple, Microsoft, Adobe, and Intuit design software applications for the Mac with the purpose of hopefully selling many copies and earning a profit. However, many programmers throughout the world create software that's just as good as commercially available paid apps but choose to give away their software for free. This is called freeware or open source software.

When it comes to word processing, spreadsheets, and digital slide presentations, you can purchase the Microsoft Office software suite or Apple's iWork suite. However, several open source equivalents are offered for free and are fully compatible with the Microsoft Office / iWork apps.

Examples of such include Open Office (www.openoffice.org/porting/mac), NeoOffice (www.neooffice.org/neojava/en/index.php), and LibreOffice (www.libreoffice.org).

> ☑️ **TIP**   To find other open source software available for your Mac, visit www.freemug.org, www.opensourcemac.org, www.freeware.com/category/open-source-mac-software, or http://mac.appstorm.net/general/60-open-source-and-free-mac-apps.

INSTALLING SOFTWARE FROM OTHER SOURCES

When you seek out apps from other sources, finding, purchasing, downloading, and installing the app becomes a multistep process that is not as automated as when making app purchases from the App Store.

Typically, once you purchase an app from another source, you are directed to download the app first. The compressed download file is stored in your Downloads folder. You then might need to decompress the file before beginning the installation process, which involves choosing where you want the app installed. This requires you to manually choose the Applications folder on your computer (or another destination) and then enter your computer's password.

> **NOTE** The computer's password was created when you first set up your Mac. It must be entered before installing new apps or making significant changes to apps running on the computer. The computer's password may differ from your Apple ID.

> **TIP** If the app file you download had been compressed into a SIT file, you must decompress it before installing it. You can use free decompression software such as Stuffit Expander for Mac (www.stuffit.com/mac-stuffit.html). OS X will decompress ZIP files automatically for you.

Also, when you purchase and download software from sources other than the App Store, you may be supplied with a special Unlock or Registration key for that software. This will often include a large chain of numbers/letters that must be entered when you initially install the software. Keep in mind that the Unlock or Registration key is often case sensitive, so enter it into the app exactly as it's supplied to you.

> **NOTE** Some Mac software is still being distributed on CD/DVD and being sold through traditional retail stores, including Apple Stores, Best Buy, and office supply superstores. However, this option for acquiring software has become somewhat outdated and will probably be eliminated altogether within the next few years.

INSTALLING SOFTWARE FROM A CD/DVD (ON MACBOOK AIR)

If you've have software on a CD/DVD that you want to install using an optical drive, but your MacBook Air doesn't have a SuperDrive built-in, you have two options.

First, you can purchase an external SuperDrive and connect it to your computer via the USB port. Second, if you have an iMac, Mac Pro, or MacBook Pro that does contain a SuperDrive or optical drive, you can use OS X DVD/CD Sharing feature.

To use this feature, both computers need to be connected to the same wireless network, and both computers need to be running Lion or Mountain Lion. After linking the computers to the same wireless network, follow these steps:

1. On your iMac, Mac Pro, or MacBook Pro (which has a SuperDrive or optical drive installed), launch System Preferences, and select the Sharing option.

2. On the left side of the Sharing window, select and activate the DVD or CD Sharing feature.

3. Exit out of System Preferences on your iMac, Mac Pro, of MacBook Pro.

4. On the MacBook Air, launch System Preferences.

5. On the left side of the Sharing window, select File Sharing, and then exit out of System Preferences.

6. Insert a CD or DVD into the SuperDrive or optical drive installed in your iMac, Mac Pro, or MacBook Pro.

7. On your MacBook Air, launch Finder.

8. Within the sidebar of the Finder window on the MacBook Air, under the Devices heading, look for the Remote Disc option. Click it.

9. On the right side of the Finder window of the MacBook Air, a graphic icon or the name the CD that's been inserted into the iMac's or MacBook Pro's SuperDrive or optical drive will be displayed. Double-click it.

10. On your MacBook Air's desktop, a CD-shaped icon will appear. The contents of the CD will display within the right side of the Finder window that's open on your MacBook Air. Your MacBook Air is now sharing the SuperDrive or optical drive that's installed within your other computer. If the software on the CD doesn't begin auto-installing, click the Install icon for the software that's on the CD and follow the onscreen prompts. From this point forward, your MacBook Air will act as if a SuperDrive or optical drive is connected directly to it.

KEEPING APPS CURRENT

Whenever Apple makes a significant update to the OS X operating system, or as individual software developers choose to incorporate new features or functionality into their software (or fix known bugs), updated versions of apps are released.

In most cases, updates to software (apps) you've already purchased are free. For apps that were purchased from the App Store, you can manually check for new updates by launching the App Store app and clicking the Updates tab near the top center of the screen (shown in Figure 9.11).

FIGURE 9.11

If updates to any apps purchased from the App Store (including Mountain Lion itself) are available, they'll be listed when you click the Updates tab.

If updates to apps are available, you just need to click the appropriate Update button to download and install the latest version of the app. For apps that are purchased from other sources, you need to check for updates from within the app itself.

Most apps offer a Check for Updates option accessible from one of the pull-down menus on the menu bar. Other apps automatically check for new updates whenever they're launched and have access to the Internet.

> **NOTE** Especially after Apple releases a periodic update to OS X, you'll want to make sure you're running the most current version of your favorite or most frequently used apps to ensure ongoing stability and compatibility. If you recently upgraded your Mac to Mountain Lion, you may discover that some of your third-party apps will not operate at all until you download and install updated versions of them that are Mountain Lion compatible.

DISCOVERING NEW SOFTWARE

In addition to periodically visiting the App Store and perusing around the Featured, What's Hot, New and Noteworthy, and Top Charts sections, you can discover details about newly released Mac software by subscribing to a magazine such as *Macworld* or *MacLife*. These publications are available from newsstands, but they also have informative websites that you can access by visiting www.macworld.com and www.maclife.com, respectively.

Another option is to follow popular Mac-oriented news blogs and websites, such as Apple Insider (www.appleinsider.com) or Mac Daily News (www.macdailynews. com). The Unofficial Apple Weblog (TUAW) is another excellent source for discovering timely information about new app releases. Visit www.tuaw.com to read Apple-related news, how-to-articles, app reviews, and more.

> **TIP** To learn about Mac software developed and published by Apple, visit Apple's website (www.apple.com), click the Mac tab near the top of the screen, and then choose the Applications option. Or to learn about Apple's iLife apps, visit www.apple.com/ilife. You can find information about Apple's iWork apps at www. apple.com/iwork.

SETTING UP PARENTAL CONTROLS ON YOUR MAC

To help control your kids' spending online when it comes to apps, as well as their spending in the iTunes Store and for other content (including music, TV show episodes, movies, games, audiobooks, and eBooks), as a parent, you can easily set up an iTunes Allowance for your children.

By setting up an iTunes Allowance, you can automatically add between $10 and $50 to your child's iTunes account each month. This iTunes feature can be set up in minutes, be put on hold, or canceled at anytime.

To set up an iTunes Allowance, launch the iTunes software on your Mac and connect to the iTunes Store. (An Internet connection is required.) From the Quick Links menu on the right side of the screen, click the Buy iTunes Gifts option. When the iTunes Gifts screen appears, scroll down to the Allowances heading and click the Set Up an Allowance Now option.

Fill in the fields of the online form shown in Figure 9.12 to activate an ongoing iTunes Allowance for a specific recipient. You need to know the recipient's Apple ID.

> **NOTE** Instead of setting up the iTunes Allowance feature and giving someone a predetermined iTunes credit each month, you can send a one-time iTunes gift to anyone online, as long as you know that person's email address.

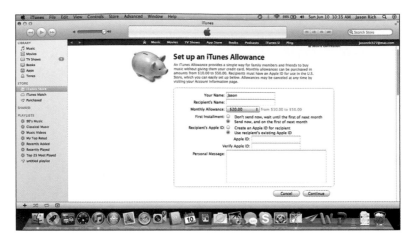

FIGURE 9.12

Control how much your child spends online buying apps and iTunes content by setting up an iTunes Allowance.

The monthly allowance you allocate for the recipient gets paid for each month using the credit card associated with your Apple ID. That amount automatically gets credited to the recipient's iTunes account.

> **NOTE** Keep in mind that even though it's called an iTunes Allowance, the funds can be used to purchase any content from the iTunes Store, Mac App Store, iOS App Store, iBookstore, or any of Apple's other online content stores.

SETTING UP PARENTAL CONTROLS

As a parent, you can also set up the Parental Control features on the Mac, which will control the types of apps and iTunes Store content someone other than yourself can purchase and install on the Mac you're using.

To set up Parental Controls, launch System Preferences on your Mac and click the Parental Controls option. When prompted, select the Create a New User Account with Parental Controls option, and click the Continue button.

You are then prompted to enter your computer's password. When the Create a New User Account with Parental Controls window appears, enter the full name of your child and create an account name for him or her. The account name is what they'll use to sign in to the Mac. Next, create a password for the account and verify that password by entering it a second time. You can also include a password hint to help remind you (or your child) of the password.

You are then prompted to add specific parental controls that ultimately determine how the Mac itself can be used, as well as what can be acquired online from the App Store. Near the top of the Parental Controls window (shown in Figure 9.13), you'll see five command tabs: Apps, Web, People, Time Limits, and Other. Click each tab to add or adjust a different selection of parental controls.

FIGURE 9.13

You can set many different types of parental controls for when your child uses your Mac or tries to acquire apps from the App Store.

When you have finished setting the various parental controls, which involves checking various check boxes and making selections from pull-down menus, just exit out of System Preferences to save and implement your changes.

In the future, your child can sign in to the Mac using his or her own account. That account will have the limits that you've set preinstalled. In addition to the parental controls you set through System Preferences, you can set additional parental controls within the iTunes software to further limit or control your child's access to content.

SETTING UP ITUNES PARENTAL CONTROLS

To set parental controls related to iTunes content, launch the iTunes software on your Mac. Select iTunes, Preferences from the menu bar.

When the General Preferences window appears, click the Parental tab near the top center of the window. You can then disable specific types of content and add content restrictions related to what TV shows, movies, and apps a child can access. Figure 9.14 shows the Parental Control window from which you can block specific types of content from your child.

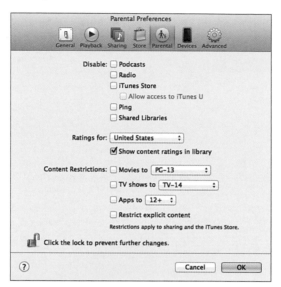

FIGURE 9.14

The iTunes software has its own Parental Controls feature that's separate from what's offered from within System Preferences when running Mountain Lion on your Mac.

To block explicit content, check the Restrict Explicit Content check box. Click the OK button to save your change.

USING GATEKEEPER TO PROTECT AGAINST MALWARE

Built in to Mountain Lion is a feature called Gatekeeper. It can help protect you from accidently downloading malware onto your Mac. Malware is software created by hackers and can potentially damage your system, erase files, or corrupt your data, for example.

Use this Gatekeeper tool to determine where new apps can be downloaded and installed from. For example, you can make it so that your Mac can download and install apps only from the App Store.

If you opt to broaden your Mac's ability to download software from other sources, you can set it up to be alerted if the app you're about to download and install was not created by a developer who has an Apple authorized Developer ID. Manual overrides for Gatekeeper are available, so if you know an app is legit and want to acquire it, you still can.

To configure the Gatekeeper options, launch System Preferences and select the Security & Privacy feature. Then, click the General tab on the Security & Privacy window shown in Figure 9.15.

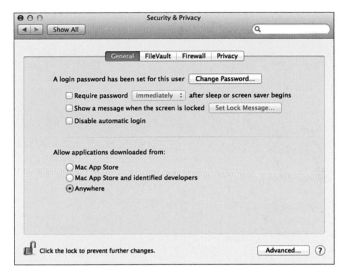

FIGURE 9.15

Using Mountain Lion's Gatekeeper feature, you can avoid accidently downloading and installing malware onto your Mac.

Within the Security & Privacy window, under Allow Applications Downloaded From, select Mac App Store, Mac App Store and Identified Developers, or Anywhere.

IN THIS CHAPTER

- Strategies for viewing, organizing, and editing digital photos
- Tips for creating prints from your digital images
- Sharing your digital photos and creating photo projects with them

10

GET BETTER RESULTS FASTER USING IPHOTO

Apple's iLife apps consist of iPhoto, iMovie, and GarageBand. Although these apps are not part of OS X Mountain Lion, they do initially come preinstalled on all Macs. Although minor updates to these three apps are provided for free, every two to three years, Apple gives the iLife apps a major overhaul, and an upgrade fee applies to install them. After a brief discussion about the apps available in iLife, this chapter focuses exclusively on iPhoto. For more information about iMovie or GarageBand, visit the App Store, or visit www.apple.com/imovie or www.apple.com/garageband, respectively.

> **NOTE** If you're using an older version of iPhoto, iMovie, or GarageBand and want to upgrade to the latest edition, you may need to visit the App Store and pay $14.99 each. For example, if you're still using iPhoto '09, you'll need to pay for the upgrade to iPhoto '11. However, if you already have iPhoto '11, but just need to upgrade to the latest version (iPhoto '11 version 9.3 or later), that is free.

ILIFE PRIMER

iPhoto is a feature-packed app designed to help you handle all aspects of digital photography after you've actually taken pictures using any type of digital camera (including the camera that's built in to your Mac, iPhone, or iPad). Once you import your digital images into iPhoto, you can use the app to view, organize, edit, print, and share the photos.

> **TIP** If you already have prints of your images and want to transform them into digital files, connect an optional scanner to your Mac, scan the prints, and save the images in JPEG (JPG) or TIFF format so that they can be imported into iPhoto.

iMovie enables you to take raw video footage you've shot using any digital video camera, edit it, and then share it. During the editing process, you can add titles, animated scene transitions, voiceovers, background music, and a wide range of other Hollywood-style effects to make your videos look amazing. Then, from within the app, you can preview your video or share it with other people by creating DVDs or uploading them to an online service, such as YouTube.

If you're an experienced musician who enjoys composing, recording, and producing your own music, the GarageBand app allows you to transform your Mac into a basic multitrack recording studio. For people who know less about music, but want to learn, the GarageBand app has built-in tutorials to teach you how to play an instrument, such as guitar or piano.

GarageBand can also be used to compose digital music from scratch, even if you don't know how to play an instrument, or you can edit and produce iPhone-compatible ringtones using this versatile app.

> **☑ TIP** The iLife apps are designed to meet the needs of average consumers. They each offer some really impressive functionality that's pretty easy to use. However, if your needs go beyond what iPhoto, iMovie, or GarageBand are capable of, Apple offers some more advanced apps for the Mac that provide truly professional-level features.
>
> iPhoto offers some basic photo-editing features, but if you want professional-level photo editing and enhancement tools at your disposal, you'll want to upgrade to Apple's Aperture app ($79.99) or another photo management and editing app, such as Adobe's Photoshop Elements or Photoshop CS6 (sold separately).
>
> For editing home videos, iMovie offers a suite of tools that are impressive, but to do professional-level video editing, you'll probably want to upgrade to Apple's Final Cut Pro software ($299.99).
>
> When it comes to recording and editing audio, to transform your Mac into a professional-quality digital recording studio, instead of GarageBand, consider upgrading to Apple's Logic Pro software ($199.99).

In addition to the iLife apps that are available for your Mac, fully compatible versions of the iPhoto, iMovie, and GarageBand apps are available (and sold separately) for the iPhone, iPad, and iPod touch. These iOS editions of the iLife apps are available from the Apple's iOS App Store for $4.99 each. Data between the Mac and iOS editions of these apps can be exchanged easily via iCloud.

> **☑ NOTE** To learn more about what iMovie is capable of, and to access free online tutorials for using this app, visit www.apple.com/ilife/imovie or www.apple.com/ilife/resources.
>
> To learn more about what GarageBand is capable of, and to access free online tutorials for using this app, visit www.apple.com/ilife/garageband or www.apple.com/ilife/resources.

GETTING STARTED WITH IPHOTO '11

Ever since iPhoto '11 was initially released, subsequent updates to this app have delivered a wide range of major enhancements, including the iCloud Photo Stream feature, more tools for sharing photos, and tools for creating prints or photo products (such as albums, photo books, greeting cards, calendars, and slideshows) using your digital images.

Especially if you want to take advantage of the iCloud Photo Stream feature, you'll want to make sure you're using the most recent version of iPhoto with Mountain Lion.

> **TIP** iCloud's Photo Stream feature works seamlessly with iPhoto. It enables you to automatically share up to 1,000 of your most recent digital photos with your Macs, iOS mobile devices (iDevices), and Apple TVs that are linked to the same iCloud account. All images you add to iPhoto automatically get uploaded to your Photo Stream and will remain there for up to 30 days (or until you reach 1,000 images, at which time older images are replaced by new ones), but you can manually add and delete images within your Photo Stream while using iPhoto. More information about Photo Stream is included later in this chapter.

ORGANIZING YOUR PHOTOS

Once you start taking pictures with your digital camera (or the camera that's built in to your smartphone or tablet), you'll quickly discover that it's fun and can be addicting. As a result, your personal digital photo collection will probably grow to be rather large, rather quickly. After all, you'll probably find yourself shooting pictures of your friends, family, pets, vacations, and the world around you as your life unfolds.

With so many digital images being shot, it's important to keep them well organized so that you can find them again quickly. Keep in mind that your digital camera probably uses a sequential numbering system to name your images, which isn't too descriptive. As a result, if you don't organize your digital photos properly into custom-named folders or digital albums, finding an image is equivalent to looking for a needle in a virtual haystack.

One of the main functions of iPhoto is to help you easily organize and manage your photos, enabling you to sort and search for them in a variety of ways so that you can find and share them quickly and effortlessly.

SORTING YOUR PHOTOS INTO EVENTS/ALBUMS

iPhoto serves multiple purposes. It can and should be used to organize your digital photos. When you import images into iPhoto, it automatically sorts them into separate events, based on the date images were shot. You can then add a custom title to those events or merge multiple events into one.

Click the Events option on the left side of the screen, within the sidebar, to view thumbnails for all the events currently stored within iPhoto, as shown in Figure 10.1.

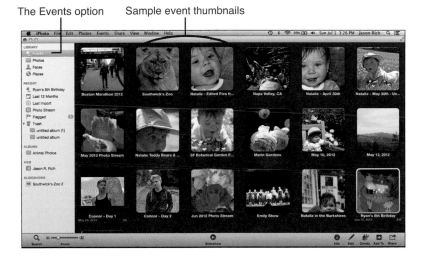

FIGURE 10.1

To view thumbnails that represent each event stored within iPhoto, click the Events option within the sidebar.

> **TIP** To merge events, click the Events option in the sidebar. As you're viewing the thumbnails that represent each event, select and highlight one or more of them. Drag the selected events on top of another event that you want to merge it with.

Beyond the events that iPhoto automatically creates, you can further organize your digital images by manually creating albums, into which you can group together images from separate events. You can create as many albums as you want by selecting File, New Album from the menu bar. Each album is then listed separately within the sidebar.

> **TIP** You can also create Smart Albums within iPhoto that automatically gather together and display images that meet specific criteria. To create a Smart Album, select File, New Smart Album. A new window will appear in which you can name the new album. Plus, using a series of pull-down menus, you can choose the criteria for which photos will be automatically added to that album. For example, you can choose photos by filename, event, place, face, rating, keyword, or date.

SORTING IMAGES WITH THE FACES FEATURE

iPhoto enables you to sort your digital images based on the people who appear within them. This is done using the Faces feature. As you begin using this app and viewing your images, click the Info button near the lower-right corner of the app window. A new column will appear on the right side of the app window and include the Faces option, as shown in Figure 10.2.

The Faces option

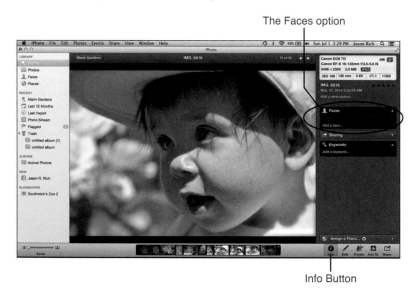

Info Button

FIGURE 10.2

Each image stored within iPhoto can be sorted based on who appears within the photo. To accomplish this, iPhoto uses advanced face-recognition technology.

Choose one image at a time with the Info button selected, and then click the Add a Face option. For each face that appears within each image, a caption bubble appears within the photo that says Unnamed, as shown in Figure 10.3. Click each caption bubble, and type the name of the person featured. Another option is to click Faces in the sidebar and then choose the Find Faces option near the bottom-right corner of the app window. Doing this will display the various faces that appear within your photos and allow you to either identify them by entering a name into the Unnamed field or confirm someone's identity whom iPhoto has automatically matched up with a photo.

Over time, iPhoto will utilize its face-recognition technology and learn to automatically identify the people repeatedly appearing within your photos. Then, when you click the Faces option within the sidebar (on the left side of the app window), you'll see separate folders representing the people featured in your pictures, and your applicable images will be sorted based on who appears within them.

FIGURE 10.3
Until iPhoto gets to know the people you frequently photograph, you'll need to manually associate names with the faces in your pictures.

NOTE Once iPhoto learns who the people in your photos are, instead of having to manually enter their names, you'll be asked to confirm their identity, as shown in Figure 10.4. This only needs to be done once per image. One way to access the listing of photos that iPhoto has matched up to the faces in your pictures is to click Faces in the sidebar and then choose the Find Faces option near the bottom-right corner of the app window.

FIGURE 10.4
Over time, iPhoto will begin to recognize the people you photograph the most often, and will automatically associate names to the faces. You will, however, need to confirm the matchups.

SORTING IMAGES WITH THE PLACES FEATURE

Yet another way iPhoto allows you to sort and search through your digital images is based on where they were shot. If your digital camera records geo-tagging information as you snap photos, this data is used by the iPhoto app to sort and display your photos based on location. Click the Places option within the sidebar to sort images within iPhoto based on where they were shot.

As you're looking at the map view within iPhoto which shows where your pictures have been shot, you can access the Country, State, City, and Places pull-down menus near the top-left corner of the map to zoom in on a particular region or area and see the photos shot there.

NOTE The iPhone and iPad, for example, automatically include geo-tagging within the photos you take, as long as you have the device's Location Services feature turned on to work with the Camera app.

TIP If your digital camera does not have a geo-tagging feature built in, when you click the Info button while looking at an image within iPhoto, click the Assign a Place option, and you'll be able to manually enter a geographic location where the photo was taken. Then, you can display detailed maps using iPhoto that showcase your shooting locations, as shown in Figure 10.5.

FIGURE 10.5

iPhoto can sort and display your images on maps, based on where they were shot.

> **NOTE** Use the New Smart Album command to create a Smart Album that contains only images that were shot at a specific location. You can choose a country, or narrow down the album to display photos shot in a particular state, city, or a specific location.

FLAGGING YOUR FAVORITE IMAGES

From the iPhoto '11 sidebar, you can always view images based on when they were shot. Or, it's possible to manually flag your favorite photos and then display only flagged images, regardless of which event or album they're stored in.

To flag an image while looking at its thumbnail, move the cursor over the image's thumbnail and click the gray flag icon that appears in the upper-left corner. The gray flag will turn orange, as shown in Figure 10.6, indicating that it's been flagged. Then, to view all your flagged images, click the Flagged option on the sidebar.

FIGURE 10.6

Manually Flag your favorite images so that you can quickly find and view them later.

> **TIP** Another way to flag an image is to click its thumbnail to view a larger version of the image, or select Photos, Flag Photo from the menu bar, or use the ⌘-. (period key) keyboard shortcut.

GIVING YOUR PHOTOS THE STAR TREATMENT

In addition to flagging your favorite photos, you can rate each image stored within iPhoto using a star-based system. It's then possible to sort the images using their star-based ratings.

To rate a photo, select and highlight its thumbnail, or view the photo and then select Photos, My Rating from the menu bar (shown in Figure 10.7). It's also possible to add ratings to your photos as you're looking through an event or album. As you're doing this, select View, Ratings from the menu bar. Then, when you hover your mouse over a photo thumbnail, you'll see empty stars appear under the image. Click the number of stars you want to rate the photo. For example, to rate it with one star, click the leftmost star. To rate it with three stars, click on the middle star, or to rate it as a five-star photo, click the rightmost star.

FIGURE 10.7

You can rate a photo with between zero and five stars, and then sort and view images based on their star rating.

When the cursor passes over the My Rating option on the Photo pull-down menu, a submenu that has between zero (none) and five stars will display. Click your rating choice. You can also use one of the following keyboard shortcuts to rate a photo:

- None: ⌘-0
- One star (★): ⌘-1
- Two stars (★★): ⌘-2
- Three stars (★★★): ⌘-3
- Four stars (★★★★): ⌘-4
- Five stars (★★★★★): ⌘-5

After photos have been rated, select View, Sort Photos from the menu bar, and then select the By Rating option as you're looking at events, albums or folders that contain image thumbnails. You can also create a separate Smart Album that includes only images with a five-star rating, for example. Thus, you can find and view those images quickly and easily.

> **TIP** As you're viewing image thumbnails, to view its rating as well as its filename and the keywords associated with the image, select View, Title (or Ratings or Keywords) from the menu bar.
>
> You can also wave your mouse cursor over an image thumbnail, and then click the down-pointing arrow icon that appears. A pop-up window containing additional commands, as well as the photo's rating, will appear, as shown in Figure 10.8.
>
> From this menu, you can assign a particular image to be the Key Photo when viewing an event or album thumbnail. Use the Make Key Photo command to do this.

FIGURE 10.8
Click the down-pointing arrow icon within an image thumbnail to view the rating you've assigned to it.

ASSOCIATING KEYWORDS WITH EACH IMAGE

To assign keywords to the images that you're viewing within iPhoto, click the Info button near the bottom-right corner of the app window. Then, select View, Keywords. Within the Info window for each image on the right side of the app window, a new Keywords area is created. Click this area, and one at a time, enter any number of keywords that you want to associate with the photo. You can enter one keyword at a time and then press the Return key, or enter multiple keywords by separating them with a comma as you enter them. For example, you can enter "Florida, Vacation, Disney World, Kids, Summer, Trip, Orlando, Mickey Mouse," and iPhoto will associate that photo with these individual keywords.

Later, you can sort and view your images based on a keyword. You can also create a Smart Album that gathers together and allows you to view images with the same keywords. Each photo can have any number of keywords associated with it.

> ☑ **TIP**   One way to quickly find images store within iPhoto that have specific keywords associated with them is to use the Search field in the lower-left corner of the app window.

RENAMING EVENTS, ALBUMS, AND IMAGES

When photos are first imported into iPhoto, the event they're placed in is created and named based on the date the images were shot. To change the name of your events to something more descriptive, such as Summer Vacation Photos 2012, Ryan's 8th Birthday Party, or Botanical Gardens, click the Events option in the side-bar under the Library heading.

Thumbnails representing each of your events will appear. Click the current title (below a thumbnail) for any event. Type the new event name you want to associate with that event, as shown in Figure 10.9.

FIGURE 10.9

You can change the name of an event, album, or individual image.

To create an album from scratch, select and highlight one or more pictures from an event and then select File, New Album from the menu bar, or use the ⌘-N keyboard shortcut. A new, but untitled album will be created and displayed on the screen. A listing for that album will also appear under the Albums heading on the sidebar.

As soon as you create a new album, you'll be given the opportunity to give that album a custom name to replace the Untitled Album title. Then, at anytime later, to rename the album, either click the album title near the top center of the window when you're viewing the album or click the album's title shown under its thumbnail image, and then just type in the new name.

When you're viewing thumbnails for individual images or looking at the images themselves within iPhoto, you can easily rename them, as well. As you're shooting digital photos, your digital camera will most likely automatically name each image using a sequential numbering system. In iPhoto, to rename an image, click the current filename shown below its thumbnail and type in the new name.

DELETING PHOTOS FROM IPHOTO

From within iPhoto, you can delete entire events or albums, or individual pictures within an event or album. When images are deleted from iPhoto, they are initially placed within iPhoto's Trash folder, which is separate from the Trash icon on the right side of the Dock.

The Trash folder for iPhoto is displayed within the app window's sidebar, as shown in Figure 10.10. Once images, Events or Albums, for example, are placed into the Trash folder, they remain there until you manually empty the Trash.

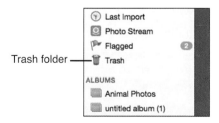

FIGURE 10.10

The iPhoto app has its own Trash folder that requires you to manually empty it before images sent to the trash actually get deleted (erased) from your Mac.

To empty the Trash folder within iPhoto, select iPhoto, Empty iPhoto Trash from the menu bar, or use the Control-⌘-Delete keyboard shortcut. Emptying the Trash periodically frees up storage space within your Mac's internal hard drive or flash drive.

! CAUTION Once you empty the Trash, images are deleted permanently from your Mac. The only way to recover them is from a backup or possibly from your Photo Stream (if the erased images were recently imported). When activated, Time Machine, for example, maintains a complete backup of your photos and all files and data on your Mac. See Chapter 12, "Backing Up Your Mac," for more information about backing up your important files and data.

DELETING EVENTS

To delete an event from iPhoto, click the Events option in the sidebar. Select and highlight the events you want to delete, and then drag the thumbnails associated with those events to the Trash option within the sidebar. You can also press the Delete key to delete the selected events, or select and drag the event thumbnail to the Trash.

DELETING ALBUMS

To delete an album from iPhoto, click the Albums option in the sidebar. Select and highlight the albums you want to delete, and then drag the thumbnails associated with those events to the Trash option within the sidebar. You can also press the Delete key to delete the selected albums. Another option is to click on the album title while holding down the Control key. When the context menu appears, select the Delete Album option.

DELETING INDIVIDUAL IMAGES

As you're looking at an image's thumbnail (after opening an event or album, for example, or by choosing the Faces or Places option), select and highlight the images you want to delete and drag them to the Trash option in the sidebar. Or, once the images are selected, press Delete.

NOTE When you drag an event, album, or image to the Trash, a pop-up window appears asking you to confirm your deletion decision. Click the Delete button to confirm.

If you delete an event, album, or image that's been published online (on Facebook, for example), iPhoto automatically deletes those published photos as well. Plus, any photo projects you've created within iPhoto using those images will also be impacted.

USING IPHOTO'S SIDEBAR OPTIONS

The sidebar along the left side of the iPhoto app window is where you can quickly access and view your digital images. At the top of the sidebar, a Library heading is displayed. Under the Library heading, you'll see Events, Photos, Faces, and Places options to sort and display images, as shown in Figure 10.11.

FIGURE 10.11

Access events, photos, faces, or places, as well as albums and folders from iPhoto's sidebar. It's displayed along the left margin of the app window.

When you click the Events option, separate thumbnails representing each event stored within the app display within the main area of the app window. Click the Photos option to display a complete listing of image thumbnails that represents all of the individual images stored within iPhoto. As you scroll downward to view your images, you'll see labeled divider bars that separate each event or album, as shown in Figure 10.12.

Event divider bar

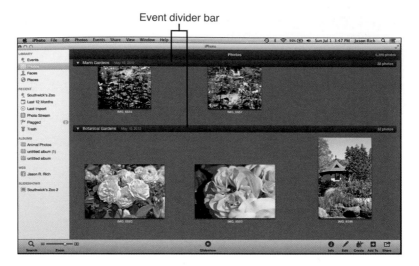

FIGURE 10.12

Using the Photos option, view thumbnails representing each image stored within iPhoto. Click the image to see a larger version of it and to then edit or work with that photo.

Click the Faces option to view thumbnails representing each person whom iPhoto "knows," and then view all the pictures featuring that person. When you choose this option to view individual thumbnails sorted by the Faces feature, if there are images that iPhoto has identified as being a specific person, but you haven't confirmed that person's identity, a message will appear along the bottom of the window. Click Confirm Additional Faces to confirm the identity of people whom iPhoto thinks belong in the Faces folder you're viewing.

When you click the Places option in the sidebar, a map appears showcasing the locations where your photos have been taken. Click one of the red pushpins on the map to view photos from a particular location, or use the pull-down menu options to narrow down your geographic search by selecting a country, state, city, or specific place.

Under the Recent heading within the sidebar, you'll discover a number of options that allow you to revisit events, albums, or photos you've recently viewed or worked with, or that you've recently imported into the app.

> **NOTE** Under the Recent heading, you'll also find the Photo Stream option, from which you can view and manage your Photo Stream, if you have this iCloud-related feature turned on.
>
> Also under the Recent heading is where you'll find the Flagged option (used for viewing all the images that you've flagged), as well as the Trash folder that's related specifically to iPhoto.

Working your way down along the sidebar within iPhoto, under the Album heading is where listings for the various albums that you've manually created will be displayed. Meanwhile, under the Projects heading, you can access iPhoto-related photo projects you've already created, such as slideshows, greeting cards, and photo books. This heading only appears after at least one project has been started and saved.

Thanks to iPhoto's integration with the Internet, if you've posted photos on Facebook or Flickr through the iPhoto app, any online albums you've created are listed here. From within the iPhoto app, any updates you make to these albums are reflected online, almost immediately, as long as your Mac is connected to the Internet.

> ☑ **TIP** If you publish and share your digital images using another online photo service, such as Google's Picasa or Smugmug.com, you can download free iPhoto Downloader plug-ins that enable you to upload images from iPhoto to a specific online service that is not currently supported using the app's Share options.

> ✎ **NOTE** To increase or decrease the size of the thumbnail images displayed within iPhoto, use the Zoom slider near the lower-left corner of the app window. Move the slider to the right to increase the size of the thumbnail images, or to the left to make them smaller. The smaller the thumbnail size you choose, the more thumbnails that will fit on the screen at any given time.
>
> When looking at individual images with iPhoto, the slider can be used to zoom in on specific areas of the image. Then, use the navigation window that appears to move around within the zoomed-in view of that image.

EDITING PHOTOS WITHIN IPHOTO

As you're looking at image thumbnails or individual images, click the Edit button near the lower-right corner of the app window to reveal the app's selection of photo-editing tools.

Displayed on the right side of the screen is a column of new command options related to photo editing, as shown in Figure 10.13. Along the top of this column, three command tabs appear: Quick Fixes, Effects, and Adjust. Each reveals a different selection of photo-editing tools.

FIGURE 10.13

iPhoto offers a nice selection of easy-to-use photo-editing tools.

The Quick Fixes options enable you to quickly rotate or enhance an image, fix red-eye that occurs because of a "bad" flash, straighten a photo that was shot with a camera that wasn't held level, crop an image, and retouch a specific part of an image. (For example, you can use Retouch to remove a blemish from someone's face in a portrait.)

The fastest and easiest way to edit a photo is to click the Enhance button. This automatically adjusts the various settings relating to contrast, color, and the other options that can otherwise be adjusted manually using the sliders displayed when you click the Adjust button at the top of the Edit window.

> **TIP** If you use an editing tool and don't like the results, click the Undo button near the lower-right corner of the app window when in editing mode. You also have the option to revert the photo to its original appearance at anytime by clicking the Revert to Original button.

> **NOTE** Like most commands available within iPhoto, many of the photo-editing commands that are displayed as buttons along the right side of the app window while in photo editing mode also have pull-down menu options and keyboard shortcuts associated with them.

From the Effects tab, you can quickly lighten or darken an image, enhance its contrast and color saturation, plus utilize eight different photo effects, which you can mix and match as you click them. In addition to turning on or off specific effects, like B&W, Sepia, or Antique, by clicking them, some of the effects are adjustable.

These options are shown in Figure 10.14. All of these effects alter the entire image. Your ability to alter only one part of a photo is limited when using iPhoto as a photo-editing tool.

FIGURE 10.14

iPhoto offers a variety of clickable effects options you can incorporate into your individual photos.

> 📋 **TIP**   To increase the intensity of an effect like Matte, Vignette, Edge Blur, Fade, or Boost, click repeatedly on the particular effect button. As you do this, a small number, along with a left- and right-arrow icon will appear at the bottom of the Effects button. To increase the intensity of an effect, click either the effect button itself or on the right-pointing arrow icon. To decrease the effect, click the left-pointing arrow or hold down the Option key while clicking the specific effect button.

Click the Adjust tab to access a collection of sliders that enable you to alter the appearance of a photo manually, as shown in Figure 10.15. Separate sliders allow you to adjust things like Exposure, Contrast, Saturation, Definition, Shadows, Sharpness, De-Noise, Temperature, and Tint. All these options impact an entire photo.

FIGURE 10.15

The Adjust tab reveals a collection of user-adjustable sliders that enable you to further edit or enhance each of your digital images.

> **TIP**   As you're using iPhoto, a lot of information gets displayed within the app window simultaneously. To maximize the onscreen real estate, iPhoto's Full Screen mode is extremely useful. To enter Full Screen mode, click the Full Screen mode icon in the upper-right corner of the app's window, or select View, Enter Full Screen on the menu bar. The Control-⌘-F keyboard shortcut is also available.
>
> When you enter into Full Screen mode, many of the folders, photo groupings, and options that were displayed within the sidebar become accessible using icons and buttons displayed along the bottom of the iPhoto app window.

CREATING PHOTO PROJECTS USING IPHOTO

Apple owns and operates its own photo-processing lab, which works seamlessly with the iPhoto app. If you want to design and publish a photo book, greeting card, or printed calendar using your images, click the Create button near the lower-right corner of the app window.

Depending on which option you choose, you'll be guided step by step through the process of designing and ordering the photo product you've selected. Products you order are then created by Apple, paid for using the credit card or debit card linked to your Apple ID, and shipped to your door within a few business days.

NOTE The Letterpress photo greeting cards you can order from Apple's photo lab allow you to custom design professional-quality greeting cards for any occasion that feature your images and personalized message. Apple will print the 5" x 7" custom cards and send them to their intended recipient for a flat fee of $2.99 each. These cards are as nice, if not nicer, than any greeting card you can purchase from a greeting card store. Plus, they're fully personalized.

The only drawback is that if you have Apple send the card to the recipient directly, you can't hand sign the card first. Of course, you can have the card shipped to you, and then you can sign it and mail it to the recipient.

TIP Two other options available after clicking the Create button are the ability to create an album from selected images and the ability to create and customize a digital slideshow that can be viewed on your computer screen, saved on DVD, transferred to your Apple TV, and viewed on your HD television set, or published online, for example.

After choosing to create a slideshow, you have the opportunity to select any number of your images to include within the presentation. You can then add a title slide, incorporate a pre-created theme, add background music, and utilize slide transition effects.

The slideshow can ultimately be viewed in Full Screen mode by clicking the Play icon, or be exported from within iPhoto so that it becomes a standalone file that can be transferred to an iDevice, another computer, DVD, or an Apple TV device.

Each slideshow you create is listed separately in the sidebar, under a Slideshows heading that appears when you create your first slideshow.

As you're creating photo projects, you can add additional images to the project by highlighting and selecting image thumbnails from their respective events or albums, for example and then clicking the Add To button near the lower-right corner of the app window. You can also drag them over the project name that's listed in the sidebar.

SHARING PHOTOS FROM IPHOTO

Like many Mountain Lion apps, iPhoto has a Share button. Within iPhoto, you can find the Share button near the lower-right corner of the screen. Options available from it include the following:

- **Order Prints**: Select images that are stored in iPhoto and order 4" x 6", 5" x 7", 8" x 10", 16" x 20", or wallet-size prints from Apple's own photo lab. The images you order will be printed and shipped to your door within several business days. The prices are pretty comparable to using any one-hour or professional photo lab, but shipping charges also apply. To learn about additional options for creating prints from your digital images, see the "Additional Options for Creating Prints" section, later in this chapter.

- **Flickr**: Upload photos to your Flickr account so that you can share them with other people in the form of digital albums. From the Flickr website, you can also create and order photo products that feature your photos, including traditional prints. To use Flickr with iPhoto, you have to set up a free Flickr account by first visiting www.flickr.com and clicking the Create Your Free Account option. Then, the first time you try to publish photos from iPhoto to Flickr, you must enter your username and password for Flickr into the iPhoto app when prompted.

- **Facebook**: Publish your digital images from iPhoto directly to your Facebook account so that you can share them with your online friends. When you do this, the online albums you create can then be managed, edited, or deleted either from the Facebook website or from within iPhoto. iPhoto gives you the option to add captions/tags to your images. Even online albums created directly from Facebook's website can be edited and managed from within iPhoto. The first time you use this feature within iPhoto, you must supply your Facebook login information to the iPhoto app.

> **NOTE** In late 2012, Apple will be reworking how Facebook integrates with Mountain Lion, as well as with iPhoto. As a result, the features and functionality for creating, managing, syncing, and sharing your digital photos between iPhoto and Facebook will be dramatically improved.

> **CAUTION** One problem people have when they begin syncing their digital images between iPhoto and Facebook is that when they edit or delete images within iPhoto, those changes almost immediately impact the images stored on Facebook (and vice versa). If you don't want this syncing process to take place, turn off the feature by selecting iPhoto, Preferences and then clicking the Accounts tab near the top center of the window. Starting in late 2012, you'll be able to better customize the behavior of the syncing feature between iPhoto and Facebook, however.

■ **Email**: Send photos directly to one or more people using email from within the iPhoto app. There's no need to launch the Mail app to do this. Simply select and highlight the images you want to email, click the Share button, and then choose the Email option. A compose email window will appear, as shown in Figure 10.16, and the photos you've selected will already be embedded within the message.

By adding a check mark to the Attach Photos to Message check box, you have the option of also including the photos as separate email attachments within the outgoing email. This makes it easier for the recipient to then work with the files or import them into their own photo-management or photo-editing software.

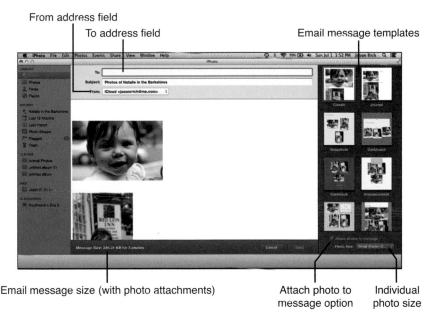

FIGURE 10.16

Email one or more photos to individual recipients from directly within the iPhoto app.

> **TIP**   On the right side of the compose email window, you'll discover a handful of email themes you can use. To send the email, fill in the To field with one or more email addresses (separated by commas). iPhoto links automatically with your Contacts database. So if you're sending an email to someone who already has a entry that includes their email address within the Contacts app, you can type their name into the To field, as opposed to their email address.

You can then modify the default Subject of the message and select which of your email accounts you want the email to be sent from (by clicking the From field).

!CAUTION Displayed in the lower-left corner of the email window is the message size. Most email accounts do not allow you to send or receive an email message that's larger than 5MB. If the photos you're trying to send are high resolution, you may need to adjust their file size (and lower their resolution) to email them. This is done from the File Size pull-down menu in the lower-right corner of the compose email window.

Your file size options include Optimized (meaning the file size and resolution will be adjusted by iPhoto to best accommodate email), Small, Medium, Large, or Actual Size. If you select the Optimize, Small, Medium, or Large options, the file size and resolution of the images you want to email will be reduced automatically.

- **Photo Stream**: Use this option to manually add selected and highlighted photos to your Photo Stream, if you have this iCloud feature turned on and active.

USING THE ICLOUD PHOTO STREAM FEATURE

If you opt to use iCloud's Photo Stream feature, up to 1,000 of your most recent images will become available on all your Macs and iDevices (as well as your Apple TV). As you shoot new photos using the cameras built in to your iPhone or iPad, or import photos into iPhoto, these images will automatically be added to your Photo Stream.

Photos added to your Photo Stream will remain there for up to 30 days, or until you reach 1,000 images, at which point they're automatically replaced by your newer images.

To get Photo Stream to work, the iCloud feature must be turned on, and then you need to activate the feature on each of your Macs and iDevices. When you do this, you must decide whether all your newly shot or imported images should be automatically added to your Photo Stream, or if you'll update your Photo Stream manually from each computer or device that's linked to your iCloud account.

An iCloud account is required to use the Photo Stream feature. To turn it on, launch System Preferences and select the iCloud option. Then, on the right side of the iCloud window within System Preferences, check the Photo Stream check box. You can now exit out of System Preferences.

From within the iPhoto app, select iPhoto, Preferences from the menu bar. Then, click the Photo Stream button along the top of the Preferences window (shown in Figure 10.17).

FIGURE 10.17
Enable the Photo Stream feature within the iPhoto app.

Check the Enable Photo Stream check box. Next, decide if you want to utilize the Automatic Import or Automatic Upload feature on the Mac you're using.

> **TIP** Activate the Automatic Import feature if you want to include your Photo Stream photos when using the Events, Photo, Faces, and Places options within iPhoto on the particular Mac you're using. If you activate the Automatic Upload option, iPhoto uploads and sends all newly imported photos to your Photo Stream.

After the Photo Stream has been enabled on your Mac, from within iPhoto click the Photo Stream option within the sidebar to view the images currently available within your Photo Stream. At the top of the display, the Photo Stream heading is displayed. Part of this heading information includes the date range in which the photos were added to the Photo Stream, and the total number of photos in your Photo Stream.

Keep in mind, as you view your Photo Stream, that these images are not permanently stored on your Mac within iPhoto. However, you can manually delete images from the Photo Stream by highlighting and selecting their thumbnails and pressing the Delete key (or by using any of the other photo-deletion techniques outlined earlier in this chapter).

To manually download and transfer images from the Photo Stream into iPhoto, so you can edit them, share them, or store them, select and highlight the images or their thumbnails, and then drag them into an event, the Photos folder, or an album that's listed within the sidebar.

If you want to manually transfer images currently stored within iPhoto to your Photo Stream, select and highlight those images or their thumbnails, and then drag them to the Photo Stream heading within the sidebar.

> **NOTE** To use the Photo Stream feature, your Mac needs continuous access to the Internet. However, if you disconnect the computer from the Internet, the next time it regains access, your Photo Stream will re-sync automatically.

> **! CAUTION** If you have the Automatic Upload feature turned on, any and all images that are imported into iPhoto will be synced with your Photo Stream. Within a very short period, these images will be accessible and viewable on all the other Macs, iDevices, and Apple TV devices linked to the same iCloud account. As a result, other people who might be using your Macs or devices will potentially be able to view the images.

After the 30-day period or before images are replaced within your Photo Stream once you reach the 1,000 image limit, those images will be automatically saved on the computer or iDevice from which they originated. They'll be saved in an event called Photo Stream, along with the month and year. However, unless you manually save those images on your other computers or devices, they will no longer be available via your Photo Stream.

> **NOTE** Since the iCloud Photo Stream feature was first introduced, Apple has continuously updated it with new functionality. Therefore, in conjunction with the anticipated overhaul of the iTunes app, for example, it's expected that Photo Stream functionality will be added to the iTunes app, as well, as will new functionality for viewing or working with images which are part of your Photo Stream. Starting in late 2012, you'll also most likely be able to access and view your Photo Stream directly from the iCloud.com website, and share your Photo Stream with other people.

CREATING PRINTS FROM YOUR DIGITAL IMAGES

In addition to allowing you to import, view, organize, edit, and share your digital images, the iPhoto app has a feature-packed Print option, which is compatible with the printers connected to your Mac. However, to create good-quality prints from your digital images from home, you'll definitely want to invest in a high-quality photo printer and premium-quality photo paper.

Instead of ordering prints from Apple's photo lab, if you have a photo printer connected to your Mac, use the Print command under File on the menu bar to create prints from your digital images stored within iPhoto. You can also use the ⌘-P keyboard shortcut. (Of course, you might want to edit the images first using iPhoto's photo-editing tools.)

From iPhoto's Print window, shown in Figure 10.18, you can create traditional prints in almost any popular size (or create your own custom print size). To do this, click the Standard option from within the Print menu. Before clicking the Print button, however, make sure you select your photo printer, and that you choose the correct paper size and print size from the pull-down menus within the Print window.

FIGURE 10.18
You can access the Print window of iPhoto by selecting File, Print from the menu bar.

> **TIP**   Photo paper comes in several different sizes, including 4" x 6", 5" x 7", and 8.5" x 11". Before purchasing anything but 8.5" x 11" photo paper, make sure the paper tray built in to your photo printer can accommodate smaller sizes, and then be sure to choose the appropriate paper size using the Paper Size pull-down menu within the Print window.

> ☑️ **TIP** Even if you're using 8.5" x 11" photo paper in your home photo printer, keep in mind, you can create 4" x 6", 5" x 7", or 8" x 10" prints (or prints of any custom size) using the Print Size command within the Print window. You can then trim the photo paper as needed to create the smaller size prints, which will be suitable for framing or inserting into a photo album.

From the Print window, also select the appropriate preset from the Presets pull-down menu. The option you select will be based on the type of paper you're using, as well as the desired results. Your options from the Presets pull-down menu may include the following (but will vary based on your printer make and model):

- Black and White - Draft
- Black and White
- Color
- Photo on Plain Paper
- Photo on Plain - Fine
- Photo on Glossy Paper
- Photo On Glossy Paper - Fine

Also from the Print window, you have the option of clicking the Customize button. This reveals a separate window in which you can adjust your print settings, plus choose from a handful of themes, backgrounds, borders and layouts. For example, you can add text (a caption) to your images before printing them, or create collages that contain multiple photos on a page by clicking the Layout button.

Beyond creating traditional prints from images stored within iPhoto using your home photo printer, you can click the Contact Sheet option in Print window to create a contact sheet containing thumbnails from a group of preselected images (such as the images in a particular event or album).

To add a digital border around an image before printing it, click Simple Border. You can also add a digital colored mat or double mat to the image by clicking Single Mat or Double Mat, and then clicking Customize.

When you're ready to send an image to your home photo printer to create one or more copies in traditional print form, click the Print button near the bottom-right corner of the Print window.

WHAT YOU SHOULD KNOW ABOUT PHOTO PAPER

To create the best quality prints from digital images stored within iPhoto using a home photo printer, you need to purchase photo paper for the printer. Photo paper is very different from the copy paper you typically use in a home inkjet or laser printer.

Photo paper comes in a variety of popular sizes, as well as in different qualities and in different finishes. So, when shopping for photo paper, consider the following:

- **The size of the photo paper**: Your options for a typical home photo printer include 8.5" x 11", 5" x 7", or 4" x 6". Photo paper is usually sold in packs of 25, 50, or 100 sheets.

- **The quality of the photo paper**: Among other things, this determines the paper's thickness, how well the photo printer's ink will adhere to the photo paper, the drying time of your prints, and how long the images will last without fading. The quality of photo paper is measured using a star-based rating system, between one and five stars.

> **☑ TIP**   For the best quality prints possible from your home photo printer, use five-star rated photo paper. Anything less than three-star quality isn't worth using. The higher the star rating, the more expensive the photo paper will be.

- **The finish of the photo paper**. The most common choices are glossy, semi-glossy, and matte. However, professional photo supply stores may also offer photo paper with a professional-level luster or satin finish. Luster- or satin-finished paper is usually more costly, but the results are often vastly superior in terms of the quality and appearance of the prints you create.

> **✎ NOTE**   Luster- or satin-finish photo paper is typically used by professional photographers who create portraits or wedding albums, for example, for their clients. These prints are suitable for framing or inclusion within a photo album or scrapbook.

> **☑ TIP**   If you'll be displaying your prints behind a glass frame, choose a semi-glossy or matte finish for your photo paper. However, a glossy finish looks nice if the prints will be displayed within a photo album or scrapbook, or kept loose.

Just about every photo printer manufacturer also sells its own branded photo paper, which you'll pay a premium for. However, most office supply superstores also sell generic brand photo paper that's significantly less expensive. As long as you go with a four-star or five-star photo paper, it does not matter who manufactured the photo paper or what type of photo printer you use it with.

Therefore, Epson photo paper can be used with an HP photo printer, for example, or generic branded photo paper can be used with any brand of photo printer.

ADDITIONAL OPTIONS FOR CREATING PRINTS

Instead of using Apple's photo lab and ordering prints from within the iPhoto app, or instead of creating your own prints at home using a photo printer, you have the option of exporting images out of iPhoto, and then either emailing, uploading, or hand delivering the files to a one-hour or professional photo lab.

To export images from iPhoto so that they can be burned onto a CD that's readable by computers not running iPhoto, or transferred to a USB flash drive, for example, select and highlight the images after clicking Events, Photos, Faces, or Places or any album in the sidebar.

When the images are highlighted and selected, select File, Export from the menu bar. From the first Export window, shown in Figure 10.19, choose the file format, and JPEG image quality if you selected this file format, and (if necessary) adjust the other options. If you plan on exporting images for the purpose of creating prints, choose either JPEG or TIFF for the file format (Kind), and select Maximum for the image quality (if you select JPEG format). Also, for the Size option, leave the Full Size selection (the default) as is. Click the Export button to continue.

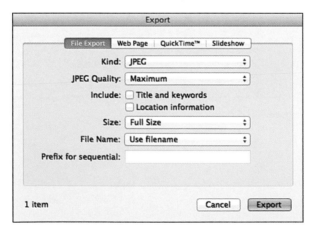

FIGURE 10.19

After editing images within iPhoto, you can export them out of the app in a popular file format, such as JPEG or TIFF, and then use those files with other apps or services.

From the second Export window that appears, shown in Figure 10.20, you have the option to rename the image by entering a new filename within the Save As field. Plus, you can select the destination drive and folder where the newly exported image will be stored. This can be a USB flash drive, for example, connected to your Mac.

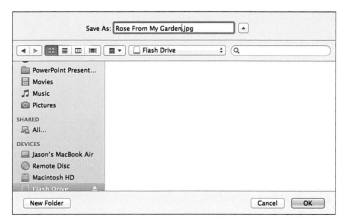

FIGURE 10.20

When exporting an image, choose where it will be exported and saved to.

Click the OK button to export the file. You can then email that exported image file to an online photo lab to order prints. There are hundreds of online photo labs you can use, but the quality of prints and their pricing vary greatly.

> **NOTE**   In addition to the iPhoto app window, if you open a Finder window or have another app running, you can copy and paste or drag and drop a full-size image from within iPhoto into another Finder or app window.

> **TIP**   Many one-hour photo labs that are available within mass-market superstores or pharmacies, such as Wal-Mart, Target, Walgreen's, Rite-Aid, and CVS, allow you to email your digital photos to their photo lab and then pick up your finished prints within an hour or so at your local retail location.
>
> You also have the option of uploading or emailing your prints to a higher-end professional photo lab and having the lab ship the prints to you.

If you transfer your exported photos from iPhoto to a CD or USB flash drive, for example, you can bring that media into a one-hour photo lab or professional photo lab in person and typically have prints created while you wait. Again, the pricing and print quality vary greatly between labs.

> **NOTE** In addition to creating traditional prints from your digital images, most photo labs (online or otherwise) can create a wide range of products from your photos, such as mugs, T-shirts, mouse pads, magnets, canvas prints, photo books, printed calendars, and many other types of products. These make great keepsakes and gifts.

CREATING A PHOTO BOOK

Using your 4" x 6", 5" x 7", or 8" x 10" prints, you can insert them into a traditional photo album or create a scrapbook. However, if you want to create a professionally printed photo book in much less time, consider creating a softcover or hardcover photo book from your prints.

From within iPhoto, you can design and upload a photo book, which will be printed by Apple's lab and shipped to you. When you do this, the photo book gets designed within the iPhoto app using the app's built-in page and cover design templates. iPhoto walks you through the process of designing your photo book's front and back cover, and then using templates, you choose what each page of the photo book will look like.

However, if you export your images out of iPhoto, you can then work with third-party services to create photo books using more powerful photo book layout and design tools, or that offer a greater selection of cover and page template options. For example, if you go to the Blurb.com website, you can download the free Blurb software, shown in Figure 10.21, and then design softcover or hardcover photo books in a wide range of trim sizes, using a vast selection of professionally designed templates.

> **NOTE** Within your photo book, you can easily add text, captions, and other graphic or design elements to create a truly one-of-a-kind publication that you'll cherish for years. Everything is done using a drag-and-drop method, so you see exactly what the photo book will look like on your screen before ordering it.

FIGURE 10.21

The free and feature-packed Blurb app for the Mac allows you to design photo books and have them printed by the Blurb.com service. Visit Blurb.com to download the software.

With a few clicks within the Blurb app, your photo book file gets uploaded to the Blurb service, and within a few business days, an extremely impressive photo book will be shipped to you. You can have just one copy of a photo book created, or order them in any quantity, based on your needs. Photo books make excellent gifts.

> **TIP**   One nice feature of the Blurb.com photo book service is that for an additional $1.99, you can purchase an eBook edition of your photo book, and immediately download it onto your iPad to view using the iBooks app (shown in Figure 10.22).

Regardless of which company you use to print your photo books, the end result will be a professionally printed book that looks like something you purchased at a bookstore, only it features your own photos. You can choose the book's trim size, paper quality, binding type, and whether it will be a soft cover, hard cover, or an image-wrapped book. Depending on the options you select, this will impact the photo book's price.

Photo books offer a contemporary alternative to traditional photo albums or scrapbooks and take a fraction of the time to create. Plus, the end result is a published book that will last for years.

FIGURE 10.22

A photo book created and printed using the Blurb.com service can also be turned into an eBook for the iPad. View the eBook using the iBooks app.

BACKING UP YOUR PHOTOS

It is absolutely essential that you maintain a current backup of your entire digital photo library. This can be done using Time Machine or another backup method, or you can utilize an online-based photo archival service. You also have the option to back up your digital images onto CDs or DVDs. Whichever option(s) you choose, make sure that it's used to backup all of your digital images and that it's reliable, in case something happens to your Mac.

! CAUTION Keep in mind that some online photo-sharing services, such as Facebook, Instagram, Twitter, or Tumblr, are not meant to archive your photos. These services are great for sharing photos with others, however.

When you upload photos from your Mac to some online services, the resolution and file sizes of the images are automatically reduced dramatically. Therefore, if your Mac gets lost, stolen, or damaged, and the only backup of your photos is stored on an online service that reduced the resolution and file sizes of your images, what you can do with those files later will be limited.

Other online-based photo services, such as Smugmug.com, Flickr.com, and Picasa.com, do not automatically reduce your image size or resolution when you upload them.

IN THIS CHAPTER

- ■ Discover what the iCloud service is and how to use it
- ■ Set up your free iCloud account
- ■ Configure iCloud-related features on your Mac
- ■ Keep tabs on the location of your Macs and iDevices

11

NAVIGATING AROUND ICLOUD

The concept of and technology behind a cloud-based data backup and file sharing service has been around for years. However, when Apple introduced iCloud, it not only made this web-based technology more accessible and affordable for consumers, it also made it practical to use in conjunction with the average person's everyday computing needs.

Apple's iCloud is a free service. When you sign up for your own iCloud account, it comes with 5GB of online storage space and a free email account. Unlike other cloud-based services, iCloud functionality has been integrated into the OS X Mountain Lion operating system itself, as well as into many of the preinstalled apps that come with every Mac. Some third-party apps also offer iCloud integration.

> **NOTE**   All of your iTunes Store, App Store, iBookstore, and Newsstand purchases automatically get stored within your iCloud account. However, the additional online storage space that's needed for this content is provided free of charge, above and beyond the 5GB that's allocated for your personal files, documents, and data.
>
> Also, the online storage required to maintain your iCloud Photo Stream, if you opt to use this feature, is also provided by Apple for free, and it does not impact your 5GB of personal online storage space.

As a result, backing up data in the cloud, as well as syncing app-specific data with other Macs, is now a truly automated process. Unlike when you use Time Machine to back up data to an external hard drive connected to your computer (or on the same wireless network as your computer), the data stored within your iCloud account is kept secure on a remote server in cyberspace. So, if your computer gets lost, damaged, or stolen, your data is retrievable.

In addition, iCloud functionality is fully integrated into the iOS5 and iOS6 operating systems, which run on the Apple iPhone, iPad, and iPod touch mobile devices. Therefore, it's become an automated and easy process to wirelessly sync documents, files, and app-specific data between a Mac and iOS mobile device (iDevice). For example, if you add an appointment to the Calendar app on your iPhone or iPad, that new event gets added to the Calendar app on your Mac, as well as to the Calendar app (or a compatible scheduling app) running on your other computers or mobile devices. It also becomes accessible directly from iCloud.com.

> **TIP**   Content from iCloud, including your digital music and Photo Stream, and any TV show episodes or movies you've purchased from the iTunes Store, can also be accessed from your Apple TV and viewed on your HD television set.

DISCOVERING ICLOUD'S MANY USES

Apple has built a lot of functionality in to its iCloud service, and with each new update to the OS X and iOS operating system, iCloud features are constantly being added or enhanced.

Once you set up your free iCloud account, you can pick and choose which iCloud features you want to utilize. However, you're not obligated to use all of them, or any of them for that matter.

The core functionality of iCloud includes the following:

- **Email**: You can access and manage your iCloud-related email account (*username*@me.com): This can be done from iCloud.com or from within the Mail app.

- **Online storage for your music library**: You can store all your online digital music library so that it's accessible from all of your Macs, iDevices, and Apple TV. This includes all music purchases made from the iTunes Store. However, to manage your entire personal digital music library using iTunes (regardless of where the music was acquired from), you'll need to upgrade to the iTunes Match service for $24.99 per year.

> **NOTE** To learn more about using iCloud and the iTunes Match service with the iTunes app, see Chapter 8, "Getting the Most from iTunes and Games Center."

- **Online storage for all your apps**: You can store all of your Mac and iDevice apps from the App Store so that you can reinstall any of them, on any compatible device linked to your iCloud account, without having to repurchase the app. So, if you purchase an app from the App Store on your iMac, you can also download and install it on your MacBook Air or MacBook Pro (or vice versa), without having to purchase that app from the App Store again.

- **Online storage for all your digital publications**: You can store all your eBooks and digital publications purchased (or acquired for free) from iBookstore and Newstand so that you can access them from any iDevice using the iBooks or Newsstand app. This content can be stored and organized on your Mac.

> **NOTE** For more information about how iCloud can be used to manage your online purchases from the iTunes Store and Apple's other online business ventures, see Chapter 9, "Installing New Software."

- **Manage Photo Stream**: You can create and manage your Photo Stream, so up to 1,000 of your most recently shot or imported digital photos are accessible and viewable on all of your Macs, iDevices, and Apple TV. Starting in late 2012, you'll also be able to share your Photo Stream with other people, even if their computer isn't linked with your iCloud account.

NOTE To learn more about using the iCloud Photo Stream feature in conjunction with the iPhoto app, see Chapter 10, "Getting Better Results Faster Using iPhoto."

- **Back up and sync app-specific data**: You can back up and sync app-specific data related to several of the preinstalled apps that come with Mountain Lion, including Contacts, Calendar, Reminders, and Notes. This backup and syncing process happens automatically and in the background, once the feature is turned on for each compatible app. It can also be used with Apple's iWork apps, including Pages, Numbers, and Keynote.

NOTE Refer to specific chapters of this book that focus on using various apps to discover how iCloud works with them. For example, when it comes to using iCloud with the Contacts and Calendar app, see Chapter 3, "Optimizing Preinstalled Apps." From Chapter 6, "Making the Most of Reminders and Notes," you'll learn how to use iCloud in conjunction with these two popular apps.

- **Access your open Safari web browser tabs on all of your computers and iDevices**: You can begin web surfing on one computer or device and then switch to another Mac or iDevice linked to the same iCloud account and pick up exactly where you left off, with the same web browser window tabs accessible. iCloud can also sync your Safari Bookmarks menu, bookmarks bar, and Reading List with other computers and devices.

  You can also remotely access open web browser tabs on other computers or devices linked to the same iCloud account. Figure 11.1 shows Safari running on a MacBook Air. By clicking the iCloud Tabs icon, you can view and access Safari tabs currently open on an iPad.

TIP How to use tabbed web browsing with the Safari app is covered within Chapter 7, "Improved Web Surfing and Email Management." As long as you have the iCloud option for Safari turned on (from within System Preferences), your Safari-related Bookmarks menu, bookmarks bar, Reading List, and open tabs will automatically sync with your other computers and iDevices linked to the same iCloud account.

iCloud icon   iCloud menu

FIGURE 11.1

Use iCloud to sync Safari related information in real-time with your other computers and iDe-vices. Shown here, Safari running on a MacBook Air but it is accessing web browser tabs open on an iPad that's also running Safari.

- **Back up wirelessly**: You can create and maintain a full backup of your iDe-vice so that it can be restored wirelessly from anywhere a Wi-Fi Internet connection is available. The backup files are stored in the cloud, as opposed to on your computer which is the case if you use the iTunes Sync process to backup your iDevice.

- **Keep track of your Mac and iDevice**: You can almost instantly pinpoint the exact location of your Mac or iDevice using the free Find My iPhone, Find My iPad, or Find My Mac feature (which collectively are referred to as the Find My iPhone feature).

- **Store and manage documents on your iCloud account**: This can be done automatically from within the iWork apps, or manually using the Preview or TextEdit apps when working with Microsoft Office files, PDF files, or other document files. Preview can also be used to manually store photos on iCloud, separately from your Photo Stream. Figure 11.2 shows documents and files that have been manually transferred to iCloud from a Mac using the Preview app.

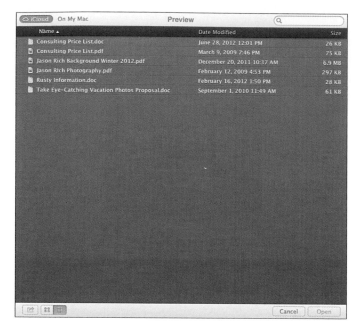

FIGURE 11.2

The Preview app that comes preinstalled with Mountain Lion now offers full iCloud integration. It allows you to utilize iCloud's Documents in the Cloud feature.

- **Access to data, documents, and files**: You can access data, documents, and files stored within your iCloud account from any computer or mobile device that has Internet access. This includes PCs and non-iDevices. When you visit iCloud.com and sign in using your iCloud username and password, you can then use online-based apps that replicate Contacts, Calendar, Reminders, and Notes, plus access your manually stored "Documents in the Cloud."

> **TIP**   If you also use a PC running Microsoft Windows, you can download the free iCloud Control Panel for Windows software from Apple's website (http://support.apple.com/kb/DL1455). This control panel enables you to incorporate iCloud functionality and sync app-specific data with your PC, as opposed to, or in addition to, using it with a Mac or iDevice.

SETTING UP YOUR FREE ICLOUD ACCOUNT

Setting up an iCloud account takes just a minute or two, and it only needs to be done once. Your single iCloud account can then be used in conjunction with all of your Macs, iDevices, and Apple TV, which you'll want to link to the same iCloud account.

To set up a new iCloud account from your Mac, launch System Preferences and click the iCloud option. Then, on the left side of the iCloud window, enter your existing Apple ID and password. This makes your Apple ID and iCloud account username and password the same.

> **TIP** It is possible to enter a different email address than your Apple ID when setting up an iCloud account. However, if you do this, your iTunes Store, iBookstore, Newsstand, App Store, and other purchases will not sync up with your iCloud account, and you will miss out on some of the core functionality that iCloud offers.
>
> One reason to separate your Apple ID and iCloud username and password is so that as a family you can share your iTunes purchases between computers and iDevices (for example, using the same Apple ID, but still allowing each person to have his or her own iCloud separate account for syncing personal app-specific data or using FaceTime or Messages).

At the same time your iCloud account is set up, you'll be provided with a free email address that ends with a me.com extension (*username*@me.com). All emails associated with this free email account will automatically sync with your iCloud account and your other Macs and iDevices if you select the Mail option on the right side of the iCloud window (within System Preferences).

> **TIP** You can also access and manage your iCloud email account from any computer or mobile device with Internet access by signing into the iCloud website (www.icloud.com/#mail). Even if you have other email accounts set up to work with the Mail app, only your iCloud-related email account will sync up with iCloud and be accessible from the iCloud website.

> **NOTE** Your iCloud-related email account will automatically configure itself to work with the Mail app. To adjust these settings, launch the Mail app, select Mail, Preferences from the menu bar, and then click the Accounts tab. Select and highlight the iCloud email account listing. Or from System Preferences, click the Mail, Contacts & Calendars option.

Once your iCloud account is created and verified, on the right side of the iCloud window pick and choose which features you want to turn on and use. Keep in mind that each iCloud feature needs to be turned on separately on your Mac, and then on each of your other computers and iDevices that will be linked to the same iCloud account.

As you use some specific apps, from within those apps, you'll also need to manually turn on iCloud functionality. However, you only need to do this once per app. This is necessary within iPhoto, as well as for all three of the iWork apps (Keynote, Pages, Numbers).

It's also necessary to configure the iTunes app to work with iCloud. This is done from within the iTunes app. Just select iTunes, Preferences from the menu bar, and then click the Store button near the top center of the screen (shown in Figure 11.3). You can then turn on or off automatic downloads related to music, apps, and books.

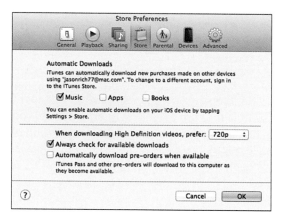

FIGURE 11.3

Decide whether you want your Mac to automatically download new music, apps, or books by adding a check mark to the box associated with each type of content. (This includes free content acquired from the iTunes Store, iBookstore, or App Store.)

> ☑ **TIP**   When you turn on Automatic Downloads from within the iTunes app on the Mac you're using, anytime you purchase new music, apps, or eBooks on any computer or device linked to your Apple ID/iCloud account (assuming they are the same), those purchases will be automatically downloaded to the Mac you're using.
>
> For example, if you use your iPhone to buy a new song from the iTunes Store, that song will download to your iPhone immediately. At the same time, if your Mac is also connected to the Internet, the song will download to iTunes on your

Mac, as well, automatically. If the Mac isn't currently turned on or connected to the Internet, when the Mac is next turned on or regains Internet access, the new iTunes purchases will be automatically downloaded.

PURCHASING ADDITIONAL STORAGE SPACE

The 5GB of online storage space provided to you for free from Apple is used to store your personal data, files, and documents as well as your iDevice backup files.

NOTE If you were a former Apple MobileMe user (a service which has been discontinued by Apple as of June 2012), you may have been given extra online storage space when you created your new iCloud account and migrated over from MobileMe.

If you need additional online storage space within iCloud, you can purchase it using your Apple ID. Just launch System Preferences and click the iCloud option. When viewing the iCloud window, click the Manage button near the bottom-right corner of the window (shown in Figure 11.4).

FIGURE 11.4

To manage your iCloud account, launch System Preferences and select the iCloud option.

A new window will appear that displays specifics about how your 5GB of online storage space is currently being utilized. To purchase additional online storage, click the Buy More Storage button in the upper-right corner (shown in Figure 11.5).

FIGURE 11.5

In addition to seeing how your iCloud online storage is being utilized, you can purchase more online storage space.

As you can see from Figure 11.6, the price of an additional 10GB of online storage (which gives you 15GB total) is $20 per year. For an additional 20GB of online storage (which gives you 25GB total), the price is $40 per year. To acquire 50GB of online storage, the price is $100 per year. Choose your upgrade option and click the Next button to initiate the purchase. Once the purchase is finalized, the additional online storage space becomes instantly accessible.

Keep in mind that once you acquire additional online storage space, this becomes a autorenewal purchase. At the end of the 12-month period, the credit or debit card that's linked to your Apple ID will automatically be billed for the next year's service. You can cancel this autorenewal using Apple's online-based tools for managing your Apple ID account.

> **NOTE** If you use iCloud to wirelessly back up two or more iDevices, or heavily use the Documents in the Cloud feature, in addition to iCloud's other functions, the 5GB of free online storage space might not be enough. For most users, however, the 5GB of free iCloud online storage space provided by Apple is more than adequate.

FIGURE 11.6

Click the amount of additional online storage space you want, and then click Next to finalize the purchase.

CONFIGURING ICLOUD TO WORK ON YOUR MAC

From the iCloud window within System Preferences, when you select an iCloud feature, that feature will become active on the Mac you're using. So, if you activate iCloud to work with Contacts, for example, your Contacts app on your Mac will automatically sync with iCloud. Your Contacts database will also almost immediately become accessible on the iCloud website.

However, if you also want to sync your Contacts database with your other Macs, PCs, or iDevices, you have to turn on the iCloud feature to work with Contacts on those other computers and devices separately. Again, this only needs to be done once.

If you purchase and install any of the iWork apps onto your Mac, be sure to access the Share pull-down menu within Pages, Numbers, or Keynote and select the Sign In option. Then, when the Sign In window appears, enter your Apple ID and password. This allows the iWork apps to automatically sync with iCloud, and thus makes your iWork-related documents and files accessible from your other Macs and iDevices that are also running the iWork apps.

KEEPING TRACK OF YOUR MACS AND IDEVICES

One of the features that iCloud offers that is not tied specifically to another app is called Find My iPhone. This name is somewhat misleading, because the feature also works with the iPad, iPod touch, and any Mac. As the name suggestions, Find My iPhone enables you to pinpoint the exact location of your computer or iDevice if it gets lost or stolen.

For this feature to work, however, it must be initially activated in advance. Then, to pinpoint the location of the lost or stolen device, that device must be turned on and have access to the Internet.

When the Find My iPhone feature makes contact with the lost or stolen device (which takes just seconds), you have several options. In addition to pinpointing its exact whereabouts on a detailed map, you can remotely have your computer or device emit a sound or display a message on the screen.

At the same time, you can remotely lock down your device by setting up the passcode lock feature, or you can erase the contents of your computer or device remotely to ensure someone can't access your data. (You can later restore your device using a Time Machine backup, for example.)

Be sure to set up the Find My iPhone feature on each of your Macs and iDevices. On a Mac, this is done by launching System Preferences, selecting the iCloud option, and then checking the Find My Mac check box (shown in Figure 11.7).

FIGURE 11.7

Activating the Find My Mac feature on your Mac only needs to be done once. However, it must be done before the computer gets lost or stolen.

> **TIP** For the Find My Mac feature to function properly, your Mac must be connected to the Internet using a Wi-Fi connection, as opposed to an Ethernet or cable-based connection.

> **NOTE** On your iDevices, turn on the Find My iPhone feature by launching Settings. Then, select the iCloud option, and tap on the virtual on/off switch that's associated with the Find My iPhone option to turn it on. Again, make sure your device is connected to the Internet using a 3G, 4G, or Wi-Fi connection.

Once the Find My iPhone feature is turned on, from any computer or Internet-enabled device use the web browser and visit www.icloud.com/#find. Log in using your iCloud username and password (which is most likely your Apple ID and password).

> **NOTE** You can also visit iCloud.com and click the Find My iPhone icon, or from your iDevice download and install the free Find My iPhone app and then run it from that device (to pinpoint the location of your other computers and iDevices).

On the left side of the browser window, shown in Figure 11.8, under the My Devices heading, a listing appears of your Macs and iDevices linked to your iCloud account. A green dot to the left of any listing means that the Find My iPhone feature has pinpointed that device's location.

> **TIP** When viewing the map that displays your computer or device's location, click the plus or minus sign buttons near the upper-right corner of the map to zoom in or zoom out. By zooming in, you can see the pinpointed location down to the specific address on a street. Click the target button to the left of the plus sign to center the map around the pinpointed location.

From the right side of the browser window, you can then choose to remotely play a sound on that device, send a message to be displayed on the screen, lock down the device, or erase the contents of the device. Click one of the listings to view the location of your computer or device on a map.

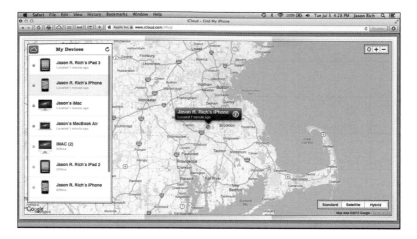

FIGURE 11.8

From any web browser, visit www.icloud.com/#find to pinpoint the location of a Mac, iPhone, iPad, or iPod touch that has the Find My iPhone, Find My iPad, or Find My Mac feature activated.

TIP While looking at the device's location on the map, click the Information button (the circled *i* icon) to access the options for taking control of the computer or device to lock it down or erase its contents, for example.

! CAUTION Cheating spouses beware! If you have the Find My iPhone feature turned on and active on your MacBook or iDevice, anyone with access to your iCloud account, such as your spouse, children, parents, or boss, can pinpoint your exact location, anytime and anywhere, as long as your computer or iOS device is turned on and has Internet access.

NOTE If you encounter a problem using iCloud, but you're not sure if it's an issue with your computer, your Internet service provider, or the iCloud service, you can access the System Status of iCloud by visiting www.apple.com/support/icloud/systemstatus, and quickly pinpoint or rule out one cause of the problem.

12

BACKING UP YOUR MAC

Just about everyone stores important information on his or her computer. Whether it's your contacts database, your schedule that you'd be utterly lost without, personal or business financial data, your digital photo albums, or your music library, this is data that you want to protect against loss.

When it comes to backing up your data, you have a variety of options. Some of those options happen automatically and in the background after they're set up. Others require you to manually copy files and data from your computer's primary hard drive or flash storage drive to an auxiliary storage medium.

> **NOTE** iMacs and Mac Pros (as well as older MacBooks) use a built in hard drive as their internal storage; Newer MacBook Pro and MacBook Air notebook computers use flash storage technology. One benefit to flash storage is that you do not need to manually save your work before shutting down your computer or placing it in Sleep or Power Nap mode.

> **! CAUTION** Every available backup solution for the Mac has pros and cons. To fully protect your data and important files against almost any foreseeable situation, consider using multiple backup solutions for your most important or irreplaceable data. For example, if you use Time Machine with an external hard drive that connects to your computer via a USB or Thunderbolt cable, and your computer gets stolen or damaged by flood, fire, or a power surge, chances are this will also directly impact your backup media. In these situations, having your data also backed up on a remote and secure cloud-based server will ensure its protection.

It's a good strategy to create a backup for your Mac starting immediately (if you're not already doing so), and then regularly update your backup files. As you'll discover, some backup solutions update your backup files hourly, while others backup files as soon as modifications are made to them. Some backup solutions work on a daily basis, or only when manually activated by the user.

> **TIP** Regardless of how you back up data, if you want to encrypt your files and information, first launch System Preferences and select the Security & Privacy option. Click the FileVault tab near the top center of the window. Make sure the security lock in the lower-left corner of the window is unlocked. To do this, click the lock icon, and when prompted, enter your computer's password. Next, click the Turn On FileVault button to activate the data encryption feature. After you do so, you will need your computer password or the generated data recovery key to access your data; otherwise it will become inaccessible. Write down the data recovery key before clicking the Continue button.
>
> Keep in mind, to make changes to these features within System Preferences, your user account must be labeled as an admin account.

YOUR MAIN BACKUP OPTIONS

Some of the easiest and most cost-effective backup solutions for your Mac include the following:

■ Using Time Machine with an external hard drive (that's directly connected to your Mac) to back up your entire computer. You also have the option to use third-party data backup software, such as SuperDuper ($27.95, www. shirt-pocket.com/SuperDuper/SuperDuperDescription.html), with an external hard drive.

■ Using Time Machine or the third-party software in conjunction with an external hard drive that's wirelessly connected to your Mac (such as Apple's optional Time Capsule), via a wireless network.

> **NOTE** Time Machine comes bundled with OS X Mountain Lion. Once set up, it automatically creates and maintains a backup of your entire Mac, which is updated hourly. Your backup files get stored on an external hard drive that's connected to your Mac using a USB cable, Thunderbolt cable, or via a wireless network.

■ Using iCloud to backup app-specific data online.

■ Using another remote, cloud-based file sharing or data backup service. (An Internet connection is required.)

■ Archiving important data, documents, and files by saving them onto a CD or DVD or a USB thumb (flash) drive.

PLANNING A BACKUP STRATEGY

Because not all backup solutions are right for everyone, you must determine your needs and objectives before you implement your backup strategy. As you do this, ask yourself the following questions:

■ Do you want to backup your entire Mac or just your most important data, documents, and files?

■ How often do you want an updated backup to be created? The more often a backup is created, the better off you are if something goes wrong. However, creating frequent backups may temporarily slow down your computer while the backup files are being created and saved.

■ Do you want to store your backup files on an external hard drive or other storage media that's directly connected to your Mac via a USB or

Thunderbolt cable, use an external storage device that's connected to your Mac via a wireless connection, or maintain an off-site remote backup using an online service? If your computer gets stolen or caught in a flood or fire, whatever backup storage you have directly connected to your computer will most likely also be impacted negatively.

- How much data (in terms of gigabytes of storage space) do you require?
- What are you protecting your data against (computer theft, hackers, fire, flood, power surges, computer hardware malfunctions, user mistakes)?
- For whatever backup solution you choose, what are its potential drawbacks?

BACKING UP VIA TIME MACHINE

The Time Machine software that comes bundled with your Mac is designed to automatically create and maintain a complete backup of your entire computer. At anytime, you can retrieve specific files from your backup, or restore your entire computer, with a few clicks of the mouse.

Once turned on and set up (a process which takes less than two minutes), as long as your Mac is connected to an external hard drive, the Time Machine software functions automatically and in the background.

Time Machine begins by creating a complete backup of your Mac. It then updates that backup as needed every hour, and also stores daily backups on your external hard drive that remain accessible for one month. As space on the hard drive permits, it also makes weekly backups for all previous months. These backups automatically get overwritten as needed to make space for newly created backups.

> **!CAUTION** Although you can use the name networked external hard drive to back up multiple Macs using Time Machine, unless you have plenty of storage space on that drive, you could run into storage space issues that result in Time Machine not being able to maintain achieved back ups for each computer.

Time Machine enables you to retrieve files that you used on your computer up to at least a month earlier, even if they have since been deleted or somehow removed from your Mac's primary storage drive.

> **✔ TIP**   As you're seeking files to restore using Time Machine, within the Finder window click the Listing View icon near the top center of the window to see the filename, the date it was last modified (or created), its file type, and its file size. Shown in Figure 12.1, this information may change as you go back in time using Time Machine. So, you can choose which specific version of a file to restore, based on when it was created or last modified.

FIGURE 12.1

The Listing view within the Finder window shows when a file was created and last modified. You can then go back in time within Time Machine to retrieve that file from a specific date, as opposed to when it was last backed up.

CHOOSING AN ADEQUATE EXTERNAL HARD DRIVE

For Time Machine to work properly, you must connect an external hard drive with an available storage capacity greater than the size of your Mac's internal hard drive or flash storage drive.

To figure out the size of your Mac's internal hard drive (or flash storage drive), click the Apple icon on the menu bar, select the About This Mac option, and then click the More Info button. When the About This Mac window appears, shown in Figure 12.2, click the Storage tab.

FIGURE 12.2

To discover the storage capacity of your Mac's internal hard drive or flash storage drive, click Storage tab in the About This Mac window.

A colorful chart displays how your Mac's internal storage is currently being used, for audio, movies, photos, apps, backups, and other data, as shown in Figure 12.3. On the left side of this window, a computer hard drive icon displays. Below it, as well as near the upper-right corner of the window, the storage capacity of the Mac's internal hard drive (or flash storage device) is displayed.

NOTE Details about the other external drives that are also connected to your Mac (including the one being used by Time Machine) show within the About This Mac window, as well. When setting up your storage drives, be sure to give them easily identifiable names so that you can readily tell them apart and identify them.

FIGURE 12.3

After clicking the Storage tab, see the left side of the About This Mac window to determine the size of its internal storage drive.

> **☑ TIP** Ideally, you'll want to connect an external hard drive to your computer with at least double the storage capacity of your Mac's internal hard drive or flash storage drive. For most computer users, a 1TB or 2TB drive is more than sufficient. However, if you'll be storing a large audio, video, or photo library, invest in a 2TB or larger external storage drive.

> **✎ NOTE** Your Time Machine drive can also be used to manually store data or files, and multiple Macs with Time Machine can use the same drive. The Time Machine app keeps the backup files created by different machines separate.

In addition to considering the storage capacity of the external drive, focus on how the drive will connect to your computer. A USB drive connects to the computer using a USB cable. For an even faster data transfer speed between your Mac and the external drive, spend a bit more to purchase an external hard drive with a Thunderbolt connection (assuming your Mac has a Thunderbolt port built in).

> **✎ NOTE** Macs sold after June 2012 support USB 3.0, which is significantly faster than USB 2.0 when used with a USB 3.0 compatible external hard drive.

If you plan to share the external drive with multiple computers, or you want to keep the drive physically away (separate) from your Mac, consider investing in a backup external drive that offers wireless connectivity. For this type of connection to work, both the Mac and the external drive need to be connected to the same wireless network.

One last thing to consider when choosing an external hard drive is the drive's read/write speed. Invest in a drive with the fastest read/write speed you can afford. Otherwise, during the hourly backups, you may notice your Mac will slow down temporarily while the new backup files are being created and transferred to the external storage device.

> **✎ NOTE** Time Machine works only with an external hard drive that connects to your computer via a USB, Thunderbolt, or a wireless connection. It will not work with remote, online, or cloud-based data backup services.

!CAUTION If you're a MacBook Air or MacBook Pro user, even if you have Time Machine turned on, an external hard drive still needs to be connected to your computer for backup files to be created. So, if you're using your notebook computer with a portable hard drive that connects using a USB or Thunderbolt cable, get into the habit of connecting the external drive to the computer regularly to create backups, because you probably won't keep the external drive connected to your notebook computer when using it on the go.

TIME MACHINE AND TIME CAPSULE

Dozens of manufacturers, including Seagate, Western Digital, Iomega, Samsung, ioSafe, Data Robotics, Toshiba, and Verbatim, offer various external hard drives that are fully compatible with the Mac. They are available with different storage capacities, offer various read/write speeds, plus provide different connection options. Prices vary greatly based on brand name and the hardware configuration of the drive.

TIP An external hard drive's capacity, read/write speed, and connection options all impact its price. Once you know your needs, consider shopping for an external hard drive online to save money. Use a price comparison website, such as Nextag.com, to help you find the lowest price possible for the drive make and model you're interested in purchasing. Within the main Nextag.com search field, enter the exact make and model of the hard drive you want, such as "Seagate Agent GoFlex 1TB Portable Hard Drive," or use a search phrase like "External hard drive Mac" or "Seagate external hard drive."

In addition to what's available from third parties, Apple offers its Time Capsule external storage solution (www.apple.com/timecapsule), which is designed to work seamlessly with the Time Machine app.

Apple's Time Capsule comes in a 2TB or 3TB version, priced at $299 and $499, respectively. Either version can be connected to a Mac via a USB, WAN, or Ethernet cable or wirelessly linked to your Mac via Wi-Fi, as long as the Mac and Time Capsule are connected to the same wireless network.

One nice feature of Time Capsule is that it can serve as a wireless backup solution for multiple Macs simultaneously. So, if you have an iMac and MacBook Air, for example, you can set up the Time Machine app on each machine to wirelessly backup to your single Time Capsule drive.

The Time Capsule drive itself measures 7.7 inches by 7.7 inches by 1.4 inches, and it weighs 3.5 pounds. It plugs into a standard electrical outlet. The device can also serve as a wireless Internet router for your home or office network. Plus, Time Capsule makes it easy for you to share printers between computers (including Macs, PCs, and iOS mobile devices [iDevices]).

> **TIP** You can manage your wireless network and Time Capsule from your iPhone or iPad using a free app called AirPort Utility App. It's available from the App Store.

Once the Time Capsule device is plugged in, set up, and connected to your Mac (wirelessly or via a cable), it works seamlessly with Time Machine to create and maintain a backup of one or more computers.

SETTING UP TIME MACHINE

After you've connected an external hard drive to your Mac, you have to turn on and set up Time Machine just once. After that, it's designed to work automatically and in the background.

To set up Time Machine, launch the Time Machine app. You can do so from the Applications folder, Dock, Launchpad (from the Other folder) or by clicking the Time Machine icon that by default is on the right side of the menu bar, as shown in Figure 12.4. After clicking the Time Machine command icon on the menu bar, for example, choose Open Time Machine Preferences.

Time machine icon

FIGURE 12.4

The Time Machine icon can be found among the command icons on the right side of the menu bar.

Once the Time Machine app is launched, on the left side of the Time Machine app window (shown in Figure 12.5), you'll see a virtual on/off switch under the large Time Machine heading. Click this switch to turn it on. Next, on the right side of the app window, click the Select Disk button and choose the external hard drive that you've connected to your Mac and that you want to use to store backup files.

FIGURE 12.5

From the Time Machine app window, you can configure the app to back up your Mac to a specific external hard drive if two or more drives are connected to the computer.

> **TIP** If you want to remove the Time Machine icon from the menu bar, deselect Show Time Machine In menu bar.

At this point, you can exit out of the Time Machine app. It is now activated and ready to begin creating and maintaining a complete backup of your Mac. If there are files or data that you don't want to maintain a backup of, or if you're using a MacBook and don't want Time Machine to run while the notebook computer is being operated on battery, click the Options button in the lower-right corner of the Time Machine window and customize the app's options.

The Time Machine window shows details about when the oldest backup and latest backup were created, along with the schedule for the next backup.

> **TIP** To exit Time Machine, either click the red dot near the upper-left corner of the app window or select System Preferences, Quit System Preferences from the menu bar.

The first time you activate Time Machine, the app creates a complete backup of your Mac. This could take up to several hours, depending on the capacity of the Mac's internal storage drive and how much data is stored on it. After that, when hourly backups are created, only new or revised files are backed up, so the backup process happens much faster (usually in between 30 seconds and 3 minutes).

> **TIP** To manually initiate a Time Machine backup at anytime, click the Time Machine icon on the menu bar and choose Back Up Now.

RESTORING FROM A TIME MACHINE BACKUP

If you need to restore a single file from your Time Machine back, click the Time Machine icon on the menu bar and select Enter Time Machine (shown in Figure 12.6).

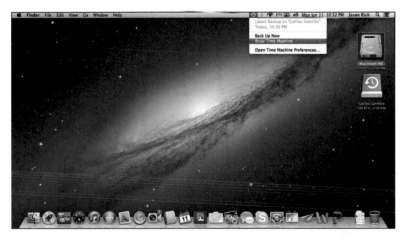

FIGURE 12.6

To retrieve and restore a file, folder, or data from Time Machine, choose the Enter Time Machine option after clicking the Time Machine icon on the menu bar.

In the main area of your desktop, you'll see a handful of Finder windows, one behind the other, as shown in Figure 12.7. Each represents a backup made at a different time. When a specific backup was created (time and date) is displayed near the bottom center of the screen. A detailed timeline also shows along the right margin of the desktop.

> **NOTE** The further back you go in terms of Finder window layers, the older the backup files are.

FIGURE 12.7

Each Finder window displayed on the desktop represents a separate backup made at a different time.

Within the appropriate Finder window, locate the file, folder, or data you want to restore. Click that item to select and highlight it. Then, click the Restore shown in Figure 12.8. The items or files you've selected will be restored and saved.

> 📝 **NOTE**   From within the Finder window, you can also highlight and select multiple items and restore them all simultaneously.

Time Machine can restore system files, applications, account data, preferences, music, photos, movies, documents, and other files.

FIGURE 12.8

From a Finder window, select and highlight the file, folder, or items you want to restore and then click the Restore button that appears.

TIP   Once you locate the appropriate Finder window, based on a specific time/date of a backup, you can use the Search field in the upper-right corner of the window while in Time Machine to quickly locate a specific file or folder.

If the restored file will be replacing a file or folder with the same name as one that's already stored on your Mac, a pop-up window appears with three command buttons, as shown in Figure 12.9: Keep Original, Keep Both, and Replace. To keep the original file and ignore the restored file from the backup, click Keep Original. To keep both the original file and the restored file, click Keep Both. To replace the original file with the restored file, click the Replace button. If you select the Keep Both option, each will be given a slightly different filename so that you can tell them apart.

FIGURE 12.9
You can restore an older version of a file currently stored on your Mac and either keep or replace the existing file.

NOTE   You can also restore an item (or items) that have been erased from your Mac altogether but that are stored within an archived backup on the external hard drive being utilized by Time Machine.

Once a file is restored, your Mac exits Time Machine and returns you to the current Finder window.

TIP   Use this file/item Restore feature if you've accidentally deleted a file, you've made unwanted changes to a file that can't otherwise be undone, or if the current version of a file has become corrupted or somehow lost.

If you purchase a new Mac and want to transfer your existing files from your original Mac to the new one, you can restore the entire system from a Time Machine backup using the Migration Assistant app that comes preinstalled on the computer.

However, if you need to restore your current Mac because of a catastrophic computer failure that results in data loss, as you boot the computer press and hold down the ⌘-R. When prompted, select Restore from Time Machine Backup. Doing this erases everything currently stored on your Mac and replaces it with the contents of a specific Time Machine backup.

> ☑ **TIP**   If you have AppleCare for your Mac, consider visiting an Apple Store or calling AppleCare's toll-free technical support number (800-APL-CARE) for help with the data-restoration process to avoid further complications. You can find additional information about using Time Machine online at http://support.apple.com/kb/HT1427.

BACKING UP VIA ICLOUD

In conjunction with the release of Mountain Lion, Apple added additional app-specific functionality to its free iCloud service. It's now possible, using iCloud, to automatically sync app-specific data related to Contacts, Calendar, Reminders, and Notes, as well as the iWork apps and your iPhoto photo stream.

You have to turn on data syncing for each app separately, in addition to turning on iCloud functionality from the iCloud option within System Preferences. Then, as long as your computer is connected to the Internet, any changes you make to the app-specific files are automatically synced and backed up to your iCloud account.

Once your app-specific data is stored on iCloud, it can automatically be synced with your other Macs and iDevices linked to the same iCloud account. You can also access your app-specific data using any computer (Mac or PC), or any Internet-enabled device, by visiting www.iCloud.com and signing in using your Apple ID and password (or iCloud account details).

> ✐ **NOTE**   The computer or device you use to access iCloud.com and your data does not need to be linked to your iCloud account. When you visit iCloud.com, you are prompted to sign in using your iCloud username and password (which for most people is their Apple ID and password). You're then given access to online-based apps similar to Contacts, Calendar, Notes, Reminders, and Mail (for managing your iCloud-specific email account only).

From iCloud.com, you can run online-based apps that are nearly identical to the Contacts, Calendar, Reminders, and Notes apps on your Mac, and you can access your personal app-related data using these apps.

The benefit of storing your app-related data securely online is that if your computer gets lost, stolen, or damaged, or if your Mac or iDevice crashes, you can always access your most current data, and can then later restore your app-specific data as needed.

> **NOTE** See Chapter 11, "Navigating Around iCloud," for more information about how to use Apple's free, online-based file-sharing and backup service. You can also visit www.apple.com/icloud.

To set up iCloud to work with your specific apps, launch System Preferences and click iCloud. From the left side of the iCloud window, confirm that you're signed into your iCloud account. Then, from the right side of the app window, select each app that you want to back up and sync with iCloud. When you're done, exit System Preferences to activate this feature.

From this point forward, as long as your computer has access to the Internet, the apps you selected automatically back up and sync data with iCloud each time the app is launched.

> **NOTE** This option works with specific apps that come bundled with your Mac (as well as the iWork apps, by clicking System Preferences, iCloud, Documents & Data). Some third-party apps also offer iCloud backup and syncing capabilities.
>
> This is not a solution for backing up your entire Mac. However, by default, iCloud automatically keeps a backup of all iTunes Store, iBookstore, and App Store purchases you make. This includes music, TV shows, movies, and eBooks purchased from Apple.

BACKING UP ONLINE

You have many options for remotely backing up other app-specific data or specific file types (such as photos) online. For example, many third-party apps work with independent services, like Dropbox (www.dropbox.com). Microsoft, Google, and Amazon also offer cloud-based file-sharing services that are compatible with the Mac and that offer somewhat similar functionality to iCloud.

When it comes to storing your photo library online, cloud-based services allow you to store or archive hundreds or thousands of high-resolution digital images within online albums: Flickr (www.flickr.com), SmugMug (www.smugmug.com), Google Picasa (http://picasa.google.com), and Photobucket (www.photobucket.com), to name just a few. From many of these services, you can also order prints or photo gifts from the images you store on the service.

!CAUTION Some online photo-sharing services (Facebook, Tumbler, and Instagram, for example) automatically reduce the resolution of images you upload. So although these services are ideal for sharing photos, you should not use them to store or achieve high-resolution images, because you will not be able to recover the high-resolution version of the image from the service later.

Google, Yahoo!, and other online services offer cloud-based backup options for some app-specific data. These services are fully compatible with Contacts and Calendar, for example, and work very much like iCloud for backing up, syncing. and remotely accessing this data.

Yet another option is to pay for a remote backup service that automatically backs up and stores the contents of your entire Mac online. These services charge by the month or year, as well as by how much online storage space is required. They also come with their own automatic backup software.

Before paying for one of these services, make sure that the upload speed for the backups does not get throttled after a predetermined amount of data has been transferred. Otherwise, you could wind up in a situation where your Mac never gets fully backed up onto the remote backup service, which basically renders the service useless if you experience catastrophic data loss on your Mac.

TIP Some third-party apps, from companies like Microsoft, Adobe, and Intuit, offer their own online data backup solutions specifically for their Mac apps. In these cases, this remote backup option is free. Other companies, however, charge for this added feature.

BACKING UP VIA THIRD-PARTY SOFTWARE

Just as the Time Machine software is used to create and maintain a backup of your entire Mac on an external hard drive, if you launch the App Store and within the Search field enter the keyword "Backup," you'll discover a handful of third-party apps that offer Mac backup functionality, as shown in Figure 12.10. Each app offers slightly different features, such as data encryption options, a disc cloning feature, or the ability to pick and choose exactly what files, folders, and data you want to back up.

FIGURE 12.10

Browse the App Store to discover alternatives to using Time Machine to back up your Mac.

Some external hard drives also come with free automatic backup software for the Mac that you can use rather than Time Machine. From any Internet search engine, enter the search phrase "Mac Backup Software" to find additional options not necessarily available through the App Store.

BACKING UP MANUALLY

Using Finder, you always have the option to select and then copy and paste or drag and drop files, folders, or items from your Mac's main internal storage to external storage media, such as a CD or DVD, an external hard drive, or a USB thumb drive (also called a USB flash drive).

> **TIP** When using most apps, you can also use the Save As or Duplicate command to store a copy of a file (or app-specific database) to a location other than the app's default folder on your Mac's internal storage drive. For example, use Save As to store a copy of a Microsoft Word document on a USB flash drive connected to your Mac.

Manually backing up extremely important documents, files, folders, photos, or data to a USB thumb drive allows you to then store that drive in a safe location, or carry it with you wherever you go. Thumb drives have become extremely inexpensive, and they're now available with large storage capacities (4GB, 8GB, 16GB, 32GB, 64GB, 128GB, and larger).

What's nice about USB thumb drives is that they're extremely portable, require no external power source, and they're reliable. They're also readily available from computer stores, consumer electronics stores, and office supply superstores, or can be ordered online. Some USB flash drives are as small as a quarter, and some are designed in whimsical casings.

> **NOTE** Are you a fan of *Star Wars*? If so, a company called Mimoco (www. mimoco.com/mimobot-flash-drives) offers a line of portable USB thumb drives that take on the shape of popular *Star Wars* characters. The company also has USB thumb drives modeled after Hello Kitty and superheroes from DC comics. They're priced as low as $15 for a 2GB model or $94 for a 64GB model.

A USB thumb drive simply gets inserted into the USB port of your computer and then provides a place to store any type of data. Once connected to your Mac, the drive shows up on your desktop, and also displays under the Devices heading within the sidebar of the Finder window.

After you manually copy data, documents, files, folders, apps, or other items to the drive, it can then be ejected from your Mac, and stored, carried with you, or placed into another Mac or PC to access what you stored on it.

> **! CAUTION** To avoid corrupting the data, be sure to eject the USB thumb drive from your Mac before removing it. To do this, select and highlight the drive in the Finder window or on your desktop, then press the Eject key on your Mac's keyboard. You can also drag the drive's icon from your desktop to the Trash icon on the Dock. Or, highlight the icon for the drive on your desktop (or within Finder) and select File, Eject from the menu bar (when running Finder). With the drive listing highlighted, you can also press Control and click at the same time to access the context menu and then select the Eject option from it.

13

SYNCING INFORMATION WITH OTHER MACS AND IDEVICES

Built into Mountain Lion are a handful of different ways you can link your computer with other Macs, PCs, and iDevices to share or sync files, documents, and data. Some of these options require the Internet, others utilize a wireless network, and some involve connecting your Mac to another computer or device using a USB cable.

What you're trying to send, receive, or sync, and whether the computers and devices are in close proximity to each other, will best determine which method to use.

Beyond using the data syncing and transfer methods described in this chapter, you can also use iCloud to sync and share app-specific data with another Mac or iDevice. When you use iCloud, app-specific data, documents, and files can be shared with other computers or devices linked to your iCloud account.

The benefit of using iCloud is that as long as your Mac and the other computers or devices have Internet access, the app-specific data syncing process (or backup process) happens automatically and in the background once you turn on iCloud functionality.

As a result, whenever you modify your Contacts, Calendar, Reminders, or Notes databases, for example, regardless of whether you're using your Mac, iPhone, iPad, or iPod touch, those changes will be reflected within a few seconds on all your linked computers and devices, so the data is always up-to-date and accessible when and where it's needed.

NOTE One of the things you'll discover from this chapter is that there are cloud-based file sharing service alternatives to iCloud that enable you to share your documents, data, and files with your other computers and mobile devices, as well as with other people whom you grant access to. These services, such as Dropbox.com, don't always sync your data, documents, and files automatically, like iCloud, but they do offer other functionality that you may find beneficial based on your needs and work habits.

TIP Using your Mac's AirPlay feature (which is the focus of Chapter 14, "Optimizing AirPlay"), you can stream multimedia content from your Mac to other devices, including a high-definition television set with an Apple TV device connected.

EXPLOITING MOUNTAIN LION'S SHARING FEATURES

If your Mac is connected to a wireless network at home or work, consider setting up Mountain Lion's Sharing features so that you can easily share files, storage devices, optical drives, printers, scanners, and other peripherals with the other computers and users on the same network.

NOTE The Sharing features can be used wirelessly with your Macs, but for them to work, you must remain within the proximity of your wireless network. Some of the Sharing features work only with a Wi-Fi connection to a network. If your computer is connected to a local network via an Ethernet cable, for example, some Sharing features will not function.

> **TIP**   If you're a MacBook Air user, or you're using a Mac that does not have an optical drive or Apple SuperDrive built in, the Sharing feature built into Mountain Lion enables you to utilize the optical drive that's built in to another Mac so that you can access data or install apps from a CD-ROM, for example.

To set up the Sharing features, first make sure your Mac is connected to a wireless network via Wi-Fi. Then, launch System Preferences and select the Sharing option. At the top of the Sharing window, shown in Figure 13.1, within the Computer Name field, you'll see the name you assigned to your computer during the initial setup process. This is the name that will be used when Mountain Lion creates a unique identifier for your Mac on the local network it's connected to. You can enter a new name into this field to make your computer easier to identify on a network.

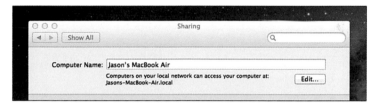

FIGURE 13.1

When setting up the Sharing features, make sure the computer you're using has an easily identifiable name.

For example, within the Computer Name field, you can use Jason's iMac, Work MacBook, Desktop Computer, or MacBook Air, so you can differentiate it from other computers connected to your local network with which you'll soon be sharing devices, drives, and data. You can name your computer just about anything, which will make it easier to set it apart from other computers it's connected to.

On the left side of the Sharing window is a list of available Sharing services you can activate on the Mac you're using (shown in Figure 13.2). Keep in mind that in most cases you'll need to also activate these same services on the other Macs on your local network for the specific Sharing features to function properly.

> **NOTE**   An optical drive is an internal or external storage device with CD/DVD-ROM read/write capabilities. Apple's own optical drives for the Macs are called SuperDrives.

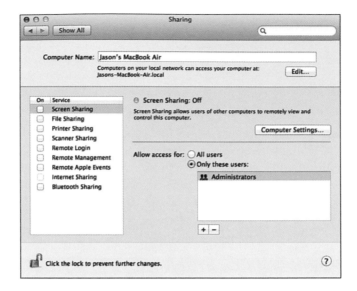

FIGURE 13.2

Each Sharing feature built in to Mountain Lion needs to be activated and customized individually from the Sharing window within System Preferences.

> ✅ **TIP** To activate specific Sharing features, select each Sharing service you want to turn on. You can then customize the settings for that feature from the right side of the Sharing window within System Preferences. For example, you can determine who will be given access to specific content or devices related to the Mac you're using.

The Sharing services available include the following:

■ **DVD or CD Sharing**: If your Mac has a built in optical drive or SuperDrive (or a drive connected to it via a USB or Thunderbolt port, for example), it can be shared with other Macs on the same network. This feature is particularly useful if you have an iMac (with a SuperDrive or optical drive) and a MacBook Air (without a SuperDrive) and want to install CD-ROM-based software onto your MacBook Air.

When a connection is made, the MacBook Air, for example, takes control over the optical drive or SuperDrive associated with the other computer and uses it while the connection is maintained, as if it were an internal drive.

NOTE The DVD or CD Sharing feature displays only if your Mac has an optical drive (or SuperDrive) connected to it. If you want to manually grant someone on your network permission before that person can access the optical drive on your computer, add a check mark to the Ask Me Before Allowing Others to Use My DVD Drive check box.

TIP If you're using a Mac that doesn't have an optical drive installed (or you want to use the optical drive on another Mac connected to the network), this is possible as long as the other Mac has the DVD or CD Sharing feature turned on. When your Mac is connected to that other computer via the network, under the Devices heading within Finder on your Mac, the drive will be listed (as Remote Disc, for example) and be fully accessible.

■ **Screen Sharing**: This feature allows other users, working on other computers, to remotely gain access to your Mac and control it. This includes remotely being able to see what's on your Mac's screen from their computer. When you activate this feature, when other people on your network access Finder on their Mac, under the Devices heading, your computer name will be displayed, giving them access to it (and vice versa when it comes to accessing other computers on the network).

After activating the Screen Sharing feature on your Mac, you can choose to allow access for all users on the network, or pick and choose specific users who can have access to your computer. This is done by customizing the Allow Access For option displayed within the Sharing window (shown in Figure 13.3).

FIGURE 13.3

In conjunction with the Screen Sharing feature, if you select Only These Users for the Allow Access For option, you can pick and choose who can access your Mac via the network.

☑ **TIP**   Once you turn on the Screen Sharing feature, within the Sharing window of System Preferences, click the Computer Settings button. This allows you to grant anyone on your network permission to control your Mac's screen, or to create a password that others will need to use in order to gain access to your Mac.

■ **File Sharing**: Without giving up control over your entire computer, this feature allows other people on your network (whom you preapprove) to access the contents of specific folders. After selecting the File Sharing feature to turn it on, click the Options button on the right side of the Sharing window to password-protect your files.

☑ **TIP**   When using the File Sharing feature, choose which folders on your Mac can be shared, and then select which other people on the network will be able to access them (shown in Figure 13.4). Under the Shared Folders heading, click the plus sign button to add folders you want to make accessible. (Select the individual folders from the Finder window that appears.) To remove access to folders listed under Shared Folders, click the minus sign button.

Then, to choose who will have access to your shared files, and to grant the other people the ability to either read, or read and write, click the plus sign button under the Users heading. When you grant someone Read Only access to files within a folder, that person can view the information but not alter it on your Mac. However, if someone has Read & Write privileges for files within one or more specific folders, that person can view/modify that content on your Mac.

One aspect of the File Sharing possible with Mountain Lion involves the Public folder that's pre-created on your Mac. It's located in your home folder. This has been set aside as a place where you can place files or items that you want to share with other people on your network. This folder is set up so that other people can both see and copy files from your Public folder (if they're granted permission to do this), but they cannot modify the files that are stored within the Public folder on your computer.

Your Public folder also offers a Drop Box folder, into which other people can place their files or items so that you can access them. When someone "drops" an item into your Drop Box, they will not be able to see the other contents within the folder.

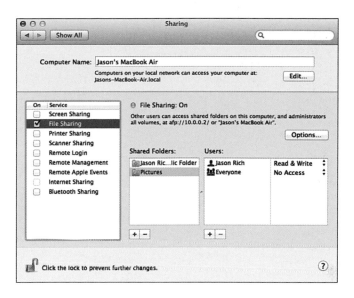

FIGURE 13.4

In conjunction with the File Sharing feature, preselect which folders other users can access on your Mac, and then select which users can access those folders.

- **Printer Sharing**: When it comes to sharing printers on a network, you have two options. You can connect the printer (wirelessly or via a cable) to the network itself, and then make that printer available to all computers and devices on the network. Or, you can connect a printer to a specific computer connected to the network, and then allow others on the network to access and share that printer. Using the latter option, you can control who has access to which printer that's directly connected to the Mac you're using.

  After selecting Printer Sharing, under the Printers heading within the Sharing window of System Preferences (shown in Figure 13.5), you'll see a list of printers currently connected to the Mac you're using. Select each printer you want to share on the network. Then, if you choose, click the plus sign button under the Users heading to select specific people on your network who can have access to those printers.

- **Scanner Sharing**: This feature works very much like the Printer Sharing feature, but it applies to scanners connected directly to your Mac.

- **Remote Login**: As you know, individual people who use your Mac can set up their own account on the computer. When those people log in to your Mac and begin using it, all of their files and user customizations become available. Using the Remote Login feature, someone on your network (using another computer) can log into the Mac you're using to access his or her account.

FIGURE 13.5

Choose which printers that are connected to your Mac that you want to share with other people on your network, and then pick and choose who will have access.

After turning on the Remote Login feature, from the Allow Access For option choose either All Users or manually select other people who will be granted permission to remotely log in to the Mac you're using.

> **✓ TIP** To set up or manage user accounts on your Mac, launch System Preferences and select the Users & Groups option. To add new users, click the plus sign button near the lower-left corner of the window. To modify permissions given to specific users who already have accounts, highlight their name within the Users & Groups window and click Login Options.

■ **Remote Management**: Using Apple Remote Desktop, other people can access the Mac you're currently using if this feature is turned on and under the Allow Access For option you've selected either All Users or have included a specific person on the list. Click the Options button in the lower-right corner of the Sharing window to further customize this option and choose what things someone who is remotely accessing your computer will be able to do, as shown in Figure 13.6.

FIGURE 13.6
After activating the Remote Management option, click Options to select what functionality
people "managing" your Mac can utilize.

> **NOTE** The Apple Remote Desktop app is available from the App Store.
> It enables you to easily access and manage the other Macs on a network or via
> the Internet. For example, you can use it to remotely install apps on computers
> connected to the network. To learn more about this app, visit www.apple.com/
> remotedesktop.

■ **Remote Apple Events**: When turned on, this feature allows apps running on
other Macs within the network to send and share events with the computer
you're using. After activating this feature, you can pick and choose which
other users on the network will be allowed to share events with your Mac.

> **NOTE** Not to be confused with events from the Calendar app, an Apple
> event is an AppleScript program that activates a specific process that can happen
> on your computer, such as the ability to remotely open and print a file stored on
> your Mac.

■ **Internet Sharing:** If your Mac has Internet access, but other computers on your network don't, you can share your Internet access via Wi-Fi, USB Ethernet or Bluetooth PAN by turning on this feature.

■ **Bluetooth Sharing**: Instead of two Macs being able to share files over a network, Bluetooth Sharing allows two computers to create a private connection via Bluetooth that can be used to share data, documents, and files. For this feature to work, it must be activated on both computers that are attempting to make a Bluetooth connection. After turning on the Bluetooth Sharing feature, you can further customize it from the Sharing window (shown in Figure 13.7).

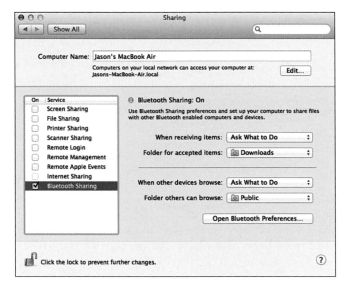

FIGURE 13.7

Choose how you'll handle incoming content sent via Bluetooth from another computer, as well as how your Mac will respond to requests to establish a Bluetooth connection.

📝 **NOTE** While a Bluetooth connection between two computers is wireless, the distance the computers can be from each other is limited by the strength of the Bluetooth signal. This is typically around 33 feet (or just under 11 yards).

EXCHANGING DOCUMENTS AND FILES WIRELESSLY VIA AIRDROP

When two or more Macs are linked to the same wireless network or Wi-Fi hotspot, an instant connection between those computers can be created automatically, using AirDrop, to facilitate the exchange of files.

 NOTE The AirDrop feature works with all recently released Macs, but not older models.

To activate AirDrop, connect your Mac to any Wi-Fi hotspot or network. This can be done in a hotel, cafe, airport, or anyplace a Wi-Fi network is available. It only works with other Macs connected to the same wireless network or hotspot (not with PCs or iDevices).

Once the computer is connected to a Wi-Fi hotspot or network, launch Finder, and within the sidebar of the Finder window, click the AirDrop option under the Favorites heading.

TIP As you're looking at the Favorites listing within the sidebar of a Finder window, if AirDrop is not listed as a visible option, select Finder, Preferences from the menu bar. Then click the Sidebar tab near the top center of the window. Make sure the AirDrop option is selected and that it has a check mark in its check box. Keep in mind, however, that this feature is not compatible with older Macs, in which case, the feature will not be displayed or accessible.

The Finder window will transform into an AirDrop window, as shown in Figure 13.8. An icon representing your computer will appear near the bottom of the window. Displayed near the top of the window will be icons representing other Macs that are nearby and that have the AirDrop feature activated.

To transfer files or folders between computers linked via AirDrop, open a second Finder window and select what you want to send to the other computer. Then drag those files or folders to the AirDrop window, and place them over the icon that represents the other computer you want the files or folders sent to.

A pop-up dialog box then asks, "Do you want to send *file/folder name* to *destination computer name?* Click the Send button to send the content wirelessly to that other Mac (shown in Figure 13.9). The receiving party must then approve the file transfer.

FIGURE 13.8

When AirDrop is activated, an icon representing your Mac appears near the bottom of the window. All other Macs that have AirDrop active will be displayed as icons along the top portion of the app window.

FIGURE 13.9

You must click the Send button before files from your Mac will be sent to another Mac via AirDrop.

If someone is sending you files or folders via AirDrop, within the AirDrop window, over the icon that represents the other computer, a pop-up dialog box will appear with this alert: "*Computer name* wants to send you *file/folder name*." Three command buttons also display. You can choose to Save and Open the file, Decline the file transfer, or Save the file, as shown in Figure 13.10.

FIGURE 13.10
You must approve the receipt of a file from someone else when using AirDrop. The files or folders are then stored within your Mac's Downloads folder by default.

By default, any files transferred to your computer via AirDrop are placed within the Downloads folder (accessible from Finder). You can then copy and paste, drag and drop, or otherwise move the incoming files to whatever destination you choose and use those files with your own apps.

> **NOTE** Any type of file can be sent via AirDrop. What's nice about this feature is that it requires no setup, passwords, or configuration. If two Macs are connected to the same Wi-Fi hotspot or wireless network, and AirDrop is turned on, the feature simply works.

> **CAUTION** As long as the AirDrop window within Finder is kept open, your computer will show up in other people's AirDrop windows who also have this feature activated. This includes total strangers who may also be using their Mac at an airport, cafe, or hotel. To close the connection, simply close the AirDrop window. Keep in mind, however, that files or folders cannot be transferred to or from your computer using AirDrop without the approval of both parties.

USING THIRD-PARTY CLOUD-BASED FILE SHARING

As you know, iCloud functionality and integration is built in to Mountain Lion, as well as into many of the core apps that come preinstalled with your Mac, including Contacts, Calendar, Reminders, Notes, Safari, and iPhoto. A growing number of third-party apps are also starting to include iCloud integration, allowing those apps to automatically sync app-specific data, files, or content with your iCloud account and then make that content available on your other Macs and iDevices linked to the same iCloud account.

When using third-party apps that offer automatic cloud-based file sharing capabilities, you might discover that these apps are not compatible with iCloud, but they do work with other cloud-based services. Dropbox.com, Box.com, Microsoft SkyDrive and Amazon Cloud Drive are among the other cloud-based file sharing services that the apps you're using may support.

> **TIP** Depending on what apps you're using, and how you're using them, it may be necessary to have access to iCloud, as well as one or more other cloud-based file sharing services to back up, sync, or share all your app-specific data, documents, and files. In most cases, a basic subscription or membership to a cloud-based file sharing service is free, and it includes a predetermined amount of online storage space, such as 2GB or 5GB. Beyond that, you have to pay for additional online storage.

Beyond syncing app-specific data through other cloud-based file sharing services, these service can be used to back up information (either automatically or manually), as well as to share content with other people. This file sharing capability is password protected and secure, and allows you to collaborate with others. This is something iCloud isn't currently capable of, unless the other computer is linked to your iCloud account, in which case, the other user gains access to all your iCloud data, files, and documents.

Before you can use a third-party cloud-based file sharing service, such as Dropbox, you have to set up an account by visiting the service's website. If you want to use Dropbox, for example, visit www.Dropbox.com, and click the Download Dropbox button on home page.

After you have a Dropbox account set up, you can access it via your web browser, or you can use the free Dropbox app that you'll download from the company's website. If the apps you're using have Dropbox integration built in, after entering your Dropbox-related email address and password into the app once, that app will have access to your online-based Dropbox account whenever your computer is connected to the Internet.

While Dropbox and services like it can be used to back up, sync, or share any type of documents, data, files, or content, some cloud-based file sharing services have specific purposes. For example, Amazon's Cloud Drive works seamlessly with Amazon's MP3 Music Store for storing and managing your digital music library online. Microsoft SkyDrive functionality is integrated into Microsoft Office, so your Word, PowerPoint, and Excel documents and files can be synced, backed up, or shared. A service like Flickr is used to back up and share digital photos.

> **NOTE** Many companies also have their own private cloud-based file sharing services, allowing employees and customers to share data, documents, and files. Your Mac can be set up to work with those services, as well.

Just like iCloud, most cloud-based file sharing services can be used to back up data remotely, sync content within the cloud, and share content with other computers and mobile devices in a password-protected and secure manner. Keep in mind that you're not limited to using just one cloud-based file sharing service. For example, you can use iCloud for your Calendar, Contacts, Reminders, and Notes data, for example, but use Dropbox to store and share document files and other items.

When it comes to backing up and syncing your Contacts, Calendar, and to-do list data with iCloud, Google, or Yahoo!, however, you will need to choose just one service for this task. You cannot sync your Contacts database with both iCloud and Google, for example.

> **TIP** Cloud-based file sharing services require access to the Internet to upload or download files. So, if you're using a MacBook Pro or MacBook Air, for example, and will be using your computer where an Internet connection is not available, be sure to plan ahead and download the files you'll need from the cloud before losing the Internet connection; otherwise, you won't have access to that data.

CONNECTING YOUR MAC TO AN FTP SITE

An online-based server that can store your data, documents, and files may be referred to as an FTP site as opposed to a cloud-based file sharing service. If you're connecting and sharing data with an FTP site, you can do so with Safari or by using an FTP file transfer client app.

An FTP file transfer client app can be download from the App Store, for example, and will allow your Mac to easily transfer files to and from any FTP site that you have access to. Transmit ($33.99), Yummy FTP ($9.99), Captain FTP ($28.99), DropMeFTP ($1.99), ForkLift (19.99), and Fetch ($28.99) are just some of the many third-party FTP client apps available from the App Store. Free FTP file transfer client apps are also available for download, like Filezilla (http://filezilla-project.org) and Cyberduck (http://cyberduck.ch); these offer the same functionality as the paid apps.

SHARING INFORMATION USING YOUSENDIT.COM

YouSendIt.com is one of many online-based services that enable you to send large-size files or entire folders (containing multiple files) to other people. Most email accounts have a 5MB limit on all incoming or outgoing emails. YouSendIt.com allows you to upload your large files to a remote server, and then email the intended recipients a personalized and secure link for downloading the file, folder, or content via their web browser.

Using YouSendIt.com (or a similar service), you can send an unlimited number of files to anyone, anywhere. There's no need for the recipient to be linked to the same network or cloud-based service as you.

To make sending files easy using YouSendIt.com, you can download a free Mac app. The company also offers plug-ins, thus enabling you to send and receive files via YouSendIt from within other apps. However, files can be sent directly from the YouSendIt.com website, as well, after you set up a free account.

> **NOTE** The basic services offered by YouSendIt.com are free. However, for truly unlimited use of the service, without file-size limitations, it's necessary to pay a low monthly subscription fee. Various premium services, such as the ability to password-protect files and get a return receipt when the recipient accesses the files you sent, can be purchased on an à la carte basis.

> **TIP** If you set up a premium YouSendIt account, the service can also be used very much like a cloud-based file sharing service to automatically backup and sync data from your Mac.

A free YouSendIt account offers 2GB of online storage and the ability to send or receive files up to 50MB each. The Pro plan ($9.99 per month or $99 per year) offers 5GB of online storage space and the ability to send and receive files up to 2GB each. (Keep in mind YouSendIt will automatically compress and then decompress files). The Pro Plus plan ($14.99 per month or $149.99 per year) offers a handful of additional features, including unlimited online storage space.

SYNCING DATA BETWEEN MACS AND PCS USING A USB CABLE

If you have two computers within close proximity and want to be able to share data, documents, files, and content between them freely, without connecting the computers to any type of a network, consider establishing a USB cable connection between those computers.

> **TIP** Using a USB cable connection, you can connect two Macs together, or allow a PC and a Mac to exchange data freely, with no special configuration required.

The easiest way to set up a direct USB cable connection between two computers is to use a product like the J5 Create Wormhole cable ($39.99, www.j5create.com/juc400). This cable connects to the USB ports of both computers and has software built in that automatically configures both computers to send and receive data, whether it's a Mac or PC.

Once the cable connection is established, you can copy and paste or drag and drop files, folders, or content between computers. The connection process takes just seconds and happens automatically.

SHARING DOCUMENT FILES BETWEEN COMPUTERS

You already know that iCloud can be configured to seamlessly sync app-specific data related to Mountain Lion's preinstalled core apps and Apple's iWork apps (including Pages, Numbers and Keynote). Therefore, as soon as you create or modify a document in the Pages word processor, for example, that document gets uploaded to iCloud and made available to all your other Macs and iDevices that also run Pages and have the iCloud feature turned on.

However, if you're also Microsoft Office user (or sending files to an Office user), it's possible to export Pages, Numbers, and Keynote documents and files into the Microsoft Word, Excel, or PowerPoint format (respectively). You also have the option to export iWork documents and files in PDF format. However, if you're a

Microsoft Office user, automatic document and file syncing isn't available with iCloud. (You'll need to use Microsoft SkyDrive instead).

> **TIP** In late 2012, Microsoft is expected to release Microsoft Office apps for iDevices that will be fully compatible with Office for Macs and PCs and allow for seamless data and document syncing, most likely through the Microsoft SkyDrive cloud-based service.

Even though automatic document syncing via iCloud is not yet possible using anything but the iWork apps, iCloud does offer the Documents in the Cloud feature, which has been improved upon with the release of Mountain Lion. This feature enables you to manually back up and sync non-iWork documents and data files with iCloud.

To use this feature, first turn on iCloud's Documents & Data functionality by launching System Preferences, and then check the Documents & Data check box within the iCloud window of System Preferences.

You can then use the Preview or TextEdit apps (both of which come preinstalled on the Mac with Mountain Lion) to manually copy and paste or drag and drop files from within a Finder window on your Mac to your iCloud account's Documents folder, as long as you have an active Internet connection.

To use Preview to manually share files with your iCloud account, launch the Preview app. Near the upper-left corner of the Preview window, click the iCloud button (shown in Figure 13.11). Now, open a new Finder window on your Mac and select and highlight the files/folders you want to manually transfer to iCloud. Two separate windows should be visible on your desktop.

From the Finder window, select and highlight the files and folders you want to transfer to iCloud, and then drag them into the Preview window. The files will upload to iCloud and be stored there. Once stored on iCloud, those files become accessible from other Macs and iDevices linked to the same iCloud account, or can be accessed by logging in to the iCloud.com website.

> **TIP** Once files or documents are stored within your iCloud account, to open them on your Mac, launch the Preview app, click the iCloud button, and then highlight the file you want to open. Click the Open button near the lower-right corner of the Preview window. That document or file (if compatible with the Preview app) will then open and appear on your Mac's screen. You can then save it to your Mac's internal hard drive or flash drive, or modify it and save it back within iCloud.

FIGURE 13.11

With the Preview app running, click the iCloud button to access the files and documents you have stored there, or to drag and drop new files from your Mac to be uploaded to your iCloud account.

> **NOTE**   Although you can use the Preview app to view or access a wide range of compatible file types, if you want to modify text-based documents without using a full-featured word processor, it's possible to access documents stored on iCloud using the TextEdit app. TextEdit enables you to view Word, Pages, or other text-based documents, as well as modify, print, and save them. Like the Preview app, you can transfer document files from TextEdit on your Mac to iCloud from within the app, or load documents from iCloud into TextEdit on your Mac.

While using Preview with the iCloud button activated (and while viewing the compatible files and documents stored within your iCloud account), it's possible to highlight and select one or more items and then click the Share button near the lower-left corner of the Preview app in order to send that documents and files to other people via email, message, or AirDrop, as shown in Figure 13.12. Photos can also be shared with Facebook, Twitter, and Flickr.

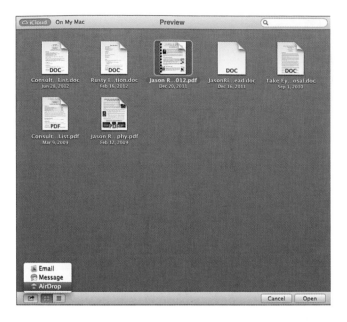

FIGURE 13.12

As you look at what's stored within your iCloud account from the Preview app, you can select and highlight an item and then use the Share button to send that item to someone else.

By clicking one of the two View icons, also near the bottom-left corner of the Preview window, you can display your documents and files stored within your iCloud account as icons (with the filenames displayed below the icons), or as a detailed file listing that includes the filename, file type, date modified, and file size.

> **TIP**   When you access the iCloud website (www.iCloud.com) using any computer or mobile device with Internet access, you can log in to your account using your iCloud username and password and then click the Documents & Data icon to access the files and documents you've manually transferred to your iCloud account. This includes your iWork-related documents and files.

IN THIS CHAPTER

- Display what's on your Mac's screen on your HD TV
- Discover what AirPlay can do
- Set up AirPlay to work with your Mac

14

OPTIMIZING AIRPLAY

In March 2007, Apple released a device that connected to a television set called Apple TV. It allowed people to experience their iTunes content, including purchased music, TV show episodes, movies and music videos, as well as their photos and home videos through their home theater system or high-definition television.

Five years later, in March 2012, the third-generation Apple TV device was released. It offered a true high-definition viewing experience in 1080p, plus better integration with iCloud and the AirPlay functionality offered by the iDevices with iOS 5.

A few months later, with the introduction of Mountain Lion, Apple brought the AirPlay feature to the Mac. What this means is that using a second- or third-generation Apple TV Device ($99, www.apple.com/appletv), anything that can be displayed on your Mac's screen can also be wirelessly simulcast on your television set or monitor—in high-definition (1080p) resolution and in Dolby Digital surround sound.

This includes purchased content from the iTunes Store, your photos, home videos, and your PowerPoint or Keynote presentations, for example.

> **NOTE** To use the AirPlay feature with your Mac, an Apple TV and high-definition television (or monitor) with an HDMI-In port is required. Both the Apple TV and Mac need to be connected to the same wireless network via Wi-Fi.
>
> Rumors suggest that in late 2012 or early 2013 Apple will be releasing its own line of high-definition televisions that will have Apple TV functionality, among other features, built in. Currently, a standalone and optional Apple TV device needs to be connected to your existing HD TV for the AirPlay functions of your Mac to work and for you to access your iTunes content on your TV.

> **! CAUTION** Airplay is a new feature added to Mountain Lion. However, it does not work with all Macs or older Apple TV devices. You must have an Apple TV Generation 2 or later (which means it had to have been purchased after September 2010). As for the computers AirPlay works with, you'll need an iMac (mid-2011 or newer), Mac mini (mid-2011 or newer), MacBook Air (mid-2011 or newer), or MacBook Pro (early-2011 or newer). The television you plan to connect your Apple TV device to must be high-definition and have an HDMI-In port.

DISCOVERING APPLE TV

Imagine a small black box that weighs 0.6 pounds and that measures just 0.9 inches high by 3.9 inches wide and 3.9 inches deep. When this small box is connected to your high-definition television set using an HDMI cable, it opens up a new way to experience on-demand TV programming and movies through Apple's iTunes service. Plus, this small box offers access to a vast selection of other programming through Netflix, YouTube, Vimeo, and Apple's other programming partners, including MLB.TV, the NBA, the NHL, and *Wall Street Journal* Live.

> **NOTE** A separate paid subscription is required to access certain content from third parties like Netflix, the MLB, NBA, and NHL.

This same black box also enables you to enjoy your entire digital music library on your home theater system in Dolby Surround sound, and to watch your home videos and view your digital photos on your big-screen television. In addition, anything that can be displayed on the screen of your Mac, iPhone, or iPad can also be displayed on your high-definition television using the AirPlay feature built in to the Mountain Lion and iOS operating systems.

> **NOTE** When AirPlay is activated, any multimedia content that is stored on your Mac (or iDevice) can wirelessly be streamed to your Apple TV and viewed on your HD television set or monitor through iTunes. This allows you to begin watching a movie, for example, on your MacBook Air while you're on the go, and with a single mouse click, continue watching it on your big-screen television when you get home.
>
> Likewise, if you want to present a PowerPoint presentation to a small group, instead of using cables to connect your computer to an LCD projector, the presentation can be displayed on your HD television screen or monitor. This can be done using AirPlay to wirelessly send what's on your Mac's screen to an Apple TV device (which, in turn, is connected to your TV and the same wireless network as your Mac).

Okay, you can stop imaging this device and purchase an Apple TV for $99 (shown in Figure 14.1). Apple TV is the perfect addition to any home theater system, especially if you often purchase or rent content from the iTunes Store and have already acquired a vast digital music, TV show, or movie library through iTunes.

FIGURE 14.1
The Apple TV device connects to your high-definition television set and your Internet connection.

☑ **TIP**   The Apple TV device comes with a handheld remote control. However, you can download the free Remote app for your iDevice from the App Store to wirelessly control some features of your Apple TV.

In addition to using AirPlay to stream content from another Apple computer or mobile device to your Apple TV, the Apple TV itself can connect to the Internet in order to access the iTunes Store and your iCloud account directly.

As a result, you can directly purchase music, TV show episodes, and movies or music videos from the Apple TV device using your Apple ID, or access any past iTunes Store purchases and experience those through the Apple TV for no additional charge. Movies can also be rented from the iTunes Store and viewed using your Apple TV device.

☑ **TIP**   When your Apple TV is connected to the Internet, it can access your iCloud Photo Stream and display those images one at a time or as an animated slide show (accompanied by background music) on your television set. Apple TV can also access your Flickr account and showcase your digital images that are stored on that service.

What's great about Apple TV is that it is easy to set up and use. The supplied power cable connects to the back of the Apple TV device and plugs into an electrical outlet. Then, using a standard HDMI cable (sold separately), your Apple TV box gets connected to your HD television set or home theater system.

When turned on, the Apple TV device will automatically connect itself to your wireless network and then display a graphic-based, menu-driven user interface that enables you to control the device using a supplied remote control (or the Remote app running on your iDevice).

☑ **TIP**   If you're connecting the Apple TV to a home theater system, in addition to the HDMI cable, you can connect an optional optical audio cable (sold separately) between your Apple TV device and the home theater system to enhance the audio quality when experiencing video content with Dolby Digital 5.1 surround sound.

When used with iTunes, AirPlay can stream content from your iTunes library to your Apple TV device, so that it can be viewed/heard on your television. The AirPlay Mirroring feature allows anything and everything that's displayed on your Mac's screen to also be displayed simultaneously on your television set. This includes any apps that are running, such as PowerPoint or your favorite games.

ENHANCING APPLE TV AUDIO WITH AIRPLAY-COMPATIBLE SPEAKERS

If you don't have a home theater system with surround sound, or you want to use wireless stereo speakers with your Mac, several speaker manufacturers, including Denon, Marantz, Bowers & Wilkins (B&W), JBL, and iHome, offer high-quality, external speakers that are AirPlay compatible. Using these speakers, you can transmit audio from your Mac to any room in your home via AirPlay (when using the iTunes app), or you can enjoy better-quality audio when watching video content on your Mac or using your Apple TV.

More than 15 different AirPlay-enabled speaker options are available from Apple.com, ranging in price from $199.95 to $799.95. To learn more about this wireless speaker option and how it works with your Mac's AirPlay feature, visit www.apple.com/airplay.

SETTING UP AIRPLAY TO WORK WITH YOUR MAC

After purchasing an Apple TV device and HDMI cable (sold separately), connect the Apple TV box to your television set using the HDMI cable, and also plug in the Apple TV to an electrical outlet (using the supplied power cable).

Make sure you set up the Apple TV in a room where the signal from a wireless network or Wi-Fi hotspot is available. Follow the onscreen prompts to initially set up the device using the Apple TV's remote control. This may involve downloading and installing the latest Apple TV operating system update (which will take approximately 10 minutes, depending on the speed of your Internet connection).

> **NOTE** Your Apple TV can also be plugged directly into an Internet router using an Ethernet cable so that it can access the Internet, iTunes Store, and iCloud. However, some of its functionality, including AirPlay, won't function unless you use a Wi-Fi Internet connection with the Apple TV.

You'll also need to enter your Apple ID and password when prompted. If your iCloud password is separate from your Apple ID, this information will need to be entered, as well, to access your Photo Stream, for example.

From the Apple TV main menu, to set up the AirPlay feature so that you can stream content from your Mac (or iDevices), use the directional arrow buttons on the Apple TV remote control to move the onscreen cursor to the right to highlight the Settings icon.

When Settings is highlighted, click the remote's center button to select it. Then, from the main Settings menu, scroll down and select the AirPlay option. Make sure that the AirPlay feature is turned on. If you choose, you can password-protect this feature by selecting the Set Password feature, and then create and enter a password that will then be needed to use the AirPlay feature with your Mac or iDevice. Press the Menu button twice on your Apple TV remote to return to the main menu.

Now, from your Mac, connect to the same wireless network as you Apple TV device. Launch System Preferences, and select the Displays option (shown in Figure 14.2). Near the bottom of the Displays window, select Apple TV from the pull-down menu associated with the AirPlay Mirroring option, and check the Show Mirroring Options in the Menu Bar When Available check box, as well as the Overscan Correction option.

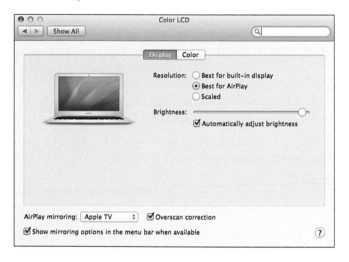

FIGURE 14.2

Configure your Mac to work with the AirPlay feature from within System Preferences.

In conjunction with the Resolution option, select the Best for AirPlay option. For the Brightness option, select Automatically Adjust Brightness. This only needs to be done once.

> **TIP**   Upon turning on the AirPlay option, an AirPlay icon will be displayed in blue on the menu bar if the feature is turn on, active, and communicating wirelessly with your Apple TV. If the AirPlay icon on the menu bar is black, click it and select the Apple TV option to turn on the AirPlay feature.

As long as the AirPlay feature is turned on within the Apple TV device and also on your Mac, an AirPlay connection will automatically be established.

If you haven't already done so, click the AirPlay option on the menu bar to turn on AirPlay Mirroring (shown in Figure 14.3). When you do this, anything and everything that appears on your Mac's screen will also be streamed to your Apple TV and be displayed on your television set. The Apple TV menu that was displayed on your TV will automatically be replaced by the streaming content from your Mac.

FIGURE 14.3

Once turned on, the AirPlay Mirroring option can be turned on or off by clicking the AirPlay icon on the menu bar.

Now, from your Mac, you're free to launch an app, such as iPhoto, PowerPoint, Keynote, or any other app that offers content you want to view on your television set and share with others.

> **TIP**   From iPhoto, you can create and display a slide show of your favorite digital images, for example, by selecting an event or album, highlighting the photos you want to include, and then clicking the Create button. Choose the Slide Show option, and then use iPhoto's slide show editing tools to add a title slide, theme, background music, and slide transition animations.

When you're ready to present your slide show on your television set, click the AirPlay icon on the menu bar, choose the Apple TV option, and then click the Play icon within iPhoto. Your slide show will be displayed on both your Mac's screen (shown in Figure 14.4) and streamed to your television set.

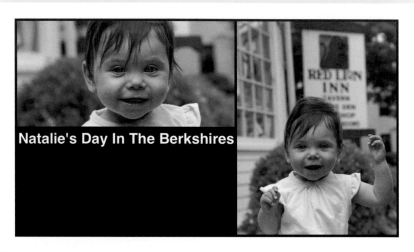

FIGURE 14.4

With the AirPlay feature turned on, your iPhoto slide shows can be viewed simultaneously on your Mac's screen and on your HD television set.

PLAYING ITUNES CONTENT VIA AIRPLAY

To use the AirPlay feature to stream music, TV show episodes, movies, or music videos from your Mac to your television set wirelessly, launch the iTunes app on your Mac and choose the content you want to experience.

In the lower-right corner of the iTunes app (in version 10), you'll see the AirPlay icon (shown in Figure 14.5). Click it to choose where you want to experience the content. Your options will include your computer or Apple TV. Select the Apple TV option. While the playback controls for that content will appear on your Mac, the content itself will be streamed to your television set via the Apple TV.

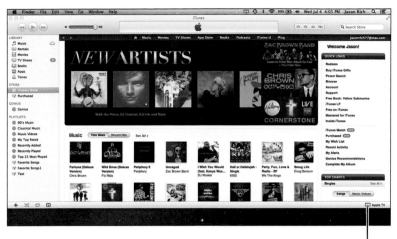

AirPlay icon

FIGURE 14.5

From the iTunes app, click the AirPlay icon to stream iTunes content from your Mac to your Apple TV and experience it on your HD television set or home theater system.

> **TIP** If you want to experience music/audio (from video content) on multiple speakers, including your computer speakers and TV speakers, and/or AirPlay-enabled external speakers, from the AirPlay icon select the Multiple Speakers option and then choose which speakers you want active while the AirPlay feature is being used to stream content from your Mac to your Apple TV device (or to stream audio from your Mac just to AirPlay enabled speakers).

When audio is streaming from your computer to your Apple TV via AirPlay, control the iTunes app from your Mac using the regular iTunes controls. For example, you can pick individual songs from your personal digital music library to play or choose to hear a playlist.

However, if you're streaming video content from your Mac to Apple TV via AirPlay, it's possible to control the video playback from your Mac using the onscreen controls, the Apple TV remote, or the Remote app on your iDevice (shown in Figure 14.6).

Using the Apple TV remote, you can pause a video, play a video, fast forward, and rewind. Meanwhile, from your Mac, you also have full control over the iTunes content, just as you normally would when experiencing it on your computer screen.

FIGURE 14.6

The free Remote app for the iPhone, iPad, or iPod touch can be used to control your Apple TV.

PRESENTING PRESENTATIONS VIA AIRPLAY

To present a PowerPoint presentation from your Mac and display it on your HD television set or monitor via Apple TV and the AirPlay feature, launch PowerPoint or Keynote and load in your presentation, just as you would if you were to watch it on your computer screen.

Once the presentation is loaded, click the AirPlay icon on the menu bar and choose the Apple TV option. Then, from PowerPoint, for example, access the Slide Show pull-down menu and select the Play From Start option.

> **NOTE** Using the AirPlay Mirroring function, you can also experience your favorite Mac games on your home theater system, for example. The feature works with nearly all Mac apps and content.

AIRPLAY VERSUS HOME SHARING

The AirPlay feature enables you to stream content from your Mac to your Apple TV and then experience that content on your television set. Your Apple TV is not storing the content. It's simply acting as a conduit or receiver between your Mac and your television set.

The Home Sharing option that's also available is different. This feature allows your Apple TV to wirelessly access content that is stored on your computer, so you can experience it on your television.

In other words, you access and select the content from your Apple TV device (not your Mac), and it then acquires it from your computer wirelessly, as opposed to you using your Mac to send (stream) content to the Apple TV. Home Sharing works only with iTunes content and photos, and both the computer and Apple TV need to be connected to the same wireless network via Wi-Fi.

> **TIP** To view photos stored on your computer on your TV via the Home Sharing feature, from the iTunes app, select Advanced, Choose Photos to Share. Then, select the iPhoto albums, events, or folders you want to make accessible from your Apple TV, or select the regular folders on your Mac that have digital images stored within them, such as your Pictures folder. Using this feature, you can also access home videos stored on your Mac.

To set up the Home Sharing feature of Apple TV, from the Apple TV main menu, click the Computers icon. When the Home Sharing Setup screen appears, you'll be asked either to enter your Apple ID and password or, if you've already done this, to confirm that it's the Apple ID account you want to use.

Once turned on, your Apple TV device will access your computer, locate its iTunes libraries, and give you access to that content. Before this feature will function, you must also turn on the Home Sharing feature from the iTunes app on your Mac. To do this, launch the iTunes app and from the Advanced pull-down menu, select the Turn On Home Sharing feature. You'll be prompted to enter your Apple ID and password.

A message will appear on your Mac's screen: Home Sharing Is Now On. The display on your television set will also change. Instead of displaying the Apple TV main menu, you'll see your personal iTunes Library menu.

From this menu, you can select Music (including your iTunes playlists), Rentals, Movies, TV Shows, Podcasts, iTunes U content, or photos that are stored on your Mac, and view/experience it on your television set via Apple TV. From this point, to control the content, use the Apple TV's remote control (or the Remote app on your iDevice).

Meanwhile, the Home Sharing message is what will be displayed within the iTunes app window on your computer, regardless of what's being displayed on your television set (via Apple TV). Home Sharing does not allow you to run most other Mac apps and view what's on the computer screen simultaneously on your TV. To accomplish this, use the AirPlay Mirroring feature.

> **☑ TIP**   To access music videos stored on your Mac, from the iTunes Library menu on your Apple TV, select the Music option, and then choose the Music Videos options from the Music menu. Select the music video you want to watch and press the center button on the remote.

> **✎ NOTE**   If you're using Home Sharing from your Apple TV, but then activate the AirPlay feature from your Mac, the content you choose to experience via AirPlay will override the content selected from your Apple TV via Home Sharing. However, if AirPlay is turned off, you can use Home Sharing to experience music, for example, on your TV, but also listen to other music or watch different video content as you normally would using the iTunes app on your Mac. (Two different things can be happening simultaneously.)

Keep in mind that you can also use Mountain Lion's Sharing features (described in Chapter 13, "Syncing Information with Other Macs and iDevices") to share multimedia content between two Macs connected to the same wireless network. Do this by launching System Preferences and selecting the Sharing option. From the Sharing menu, choose File Sharing. Under the Shared Folders heading, be sure to add your iTunes Library folders and select which computers you want to share those folders with.

Using iCloud, however, your iTunes-related content can automatically be shared and synced with multiple computers linked to the same iCloud account, without having to use the Sharing feature.

15

USING PERIPHERALS AND ACCESSORIES

Depending on which model Mac you're using, either on its back (if you're using an iMac, Mac Pro, or Mac mini) or its sides (if you're using a MacBook Air or MacBook Pro), you'll discover a variety of different ports. For example, depending on which model Mac you have, you'll find two or more USB ports, as well as an Ethernet port, Thunderbolt port, a FireWire port, a display port, an IR receiver, a microphone (audio in) jack, and a headphone jack (audio out).

In addition, thanks to OS X Mountain Lion and the hardware built in to your Mac, the computer can also make wireless connections with other devices using Wi-Fi, Bluetooth, and AirPlay.

These ports and wireless communication methods allow you to connect a wide range of optional peripherals to your Mac and greatly expand its capabilities. As you'll discover from this chapter, each type of port or wireless connection method is best suited for use with specific types of peripherals or to accomplish specific tasks.

Peripherals commonly used with a Mac include the following:

- Additional or external displays
- Apple Magic Mouse (wireless) or another mouse
- Apple Multi-Touch trackpad (as an external and wireless add-on)
- External hard drives
- External Keyboard (wireless or via USB cable)
- External speakers
- Memory card reader or digital camera
- Microphone
- Printers (such as an inkjet printer, laser printer, photo/label printer)
- Scanner (flatbed or sheet fed)
- USB flash drives
- USB hub (giving your Mac additional USB ports)

> ☑️ **TIP**   If your MacBook Air, for example, doesn't have a standalone Ethernet port to establish a cable-based connection to a modem or router, you can use your computer's USB or Thunderbolt port with a special adapter, such as Apple's USB Ethernet Adapter ($29, http://store.apple.com/us/product/MC704ZM/A) or Apple's Thunderbolt to Gigabit Ethernet Adapter ($29.99, http://store.apple.com/us/product/MD463ZM/A).
>
> Other types of optional adapters are available from Apple that enable you to transform one type of port into another, based on what type of peripherals you want to connect to the computer. For example, the Mini DisplayPort to VGA Adapter ($29.99, http://store.apple.com/us/product/MB572Z/A) enables you to connect your MacBook Air to an external monitor or LCD projector.

REVIEWING YOUR MAC'S PORTS AND PERIPHERAL CONNECTION METHODS

Here's a quick summary of the different types of ports and wireless peripheral connection methods that your Mac may offer, including a synopsis of what each can be used for and how to use them. Keep in mind, however, that no single Mac model offers all of these options.

AIRPLAY

As you discovered in Chapter 14, "Optimizing AirPlay," the AirPlay feature that's built in to Mountain Lion enables you to use your computer's wireless Wi-Fi capabilities to stream content to other devices, such as to an Apple TV or external AirPlay-enabled speakers.

Using the AirPlay Mirroring function, anything that's displayed on your compatible Mac's screen can also be streamed to and displayed on your HD television or monitor via Apple TV. This includes PowerPoint presentations or your favorite games.

If you have external AirPlay-enabled speakers (such as Bang & Olufsen's BeoPlay A8 speakers, which are shown in Figure 15.1), audio from your computer (such as music from your personal digital music library) can be streamed to those speakers that are located within the wireless signal radius of your network.

FIGURE 15.1

Bang & Olufsen's BeoPlay A8 speakers are AirPlay-enabled.

BLUETOOTH

Bluetooth is another wireless technology that allows you to connect certain types of peripherals to your computer (wirelessly), as long as they're located within about 30 feet from your computer. Some of the more popular uses of Bluetooth are to connect an external (wireless) keyboard, mouse, trackpad, drawing tablet, numeric keypad, external speakers, or a wireless headset to your Mac.

> ☑ **TIP** If you use your Mac to communicate using video conferencing or as a voice over IP (VoIP) telephone (using Skype, for example), connecting a Bluetooth headset that has speakers and a microphone built in gives you added privacy (compared to using your Mac's built-in speakers), plus enhances the audio quality, allowing you to better be heard when you speak, and to better hear the other people speaking to you. A Bluetooth headset is what you may already use with your cell phone to achieve hands-free functionality.
>
> Depending on the app you use to video conference or use with your VoIP service, a headset (with built-in microphone) may need to be connected to your Mac via the USB port, as opposed to using a Bluetooth connection.

Your Mac is cable of connecting to multiple Bluetooth devices simultaneously. For the Bluetooth function to work on your Mac, you must turn on this functionality from within System Preferences. Then, it's necessary to initially "pair" each separate Bluetooth device to your Mac just once.

> ☑ **TIP** You can also turn Bluetooth functionality on or off by clicking the Bluetooth icon on the right side of the menu bar, shown in Figure 15.2. If this icon is not displayed, it's possible to add it to your menu bar from the Bluetooth window within System Preferences.

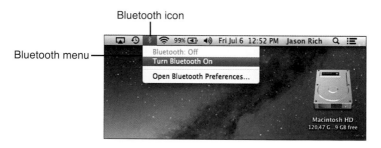

Bluetooth icon

Bluetooth menu

FIGURE 15.2

Access your Mac's Bluetooth functionality from the Bluetooth icon on the right side of the menu bar. You can set up Mountain Lion to display this icon by choosing the Bluetooth option from within System Preferences.

To turn on Bluetooth functionality and "pair" new Bluetooth devices, launch System Preferences and click the Bluetooth option. Check the On and Discoverable check boxes near the top of the Bluetooth window (shown in Figure 15.3). If you don't yet have any Bluetooth devices connected to your Mac, click the Set Up New Device button in the center of the Bluetooth window.

FIGURE 15.3

Configure Bluetooth functionality on your Mac and pair devices from within the Bluetooth window of System Preferences.

As you do this, make sure your new Bluetooth device is turned on and placed in pairing mode. How to do this will be described within the directions that came with the device.

Once the Bluetooth device has been paired with your Mac, as long as the Bluetooth feature and the device are turned on and within 30 feet or so from each other, a connection between the two will automatically be made, and the device will function with your computer.

> **TIP** If you're using a MacBook Air or MacBook Pro on battery power, and not currently using any Bluetooth devices, turn off the unused Bluetooth function to conserve battery power. Otherwise, your Mac will continuously look for Bluetooth devices to connect with. This also goes for Wi-Fi.

> **NOTE** Most Bluetooth devices, such as Apple's Magic Mouse or Apple's external Multi-Touch trackpad run on battery power. If a connection between your Bluetooth device and computer cannot be established, or the connection drops inexplicably, the battery within the device could be dead.

When using a Magic Mouse or Multi-Touch trackpad, for example, if you launch System Preferences and click the Mouse or Trackpad option, the current battery level (if applicable) will display in the lower-left corner of the window, as shown in Figure 15.4.

Also, if you click the Bluetooth menu bar icon and then hover your mouse over the Bluetooth device's name, its current battery level will display. A blinking icon means the battery level is running low.

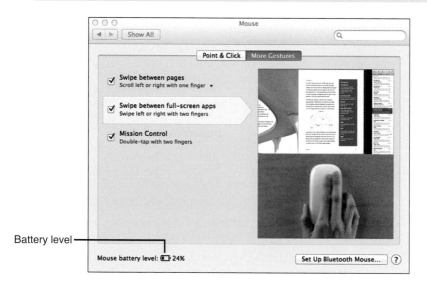

Battery level

FIGURE 15.4

You can check the battery level of some Bluetooth devices from within System Preferences. Shown here is an Apple Magic Mouse's battery level, which is accessible by clicking the Mouse option within System Preferences.

ETHERNET PORT

This port is used to connect a cable from your broadband, FiOS, or DSL modem or router to your Mac. It's an alternative to using a wireless router with your network to connect your computer to the Internet or a network.

Most public places, including airports, hotels, cafes, bookstores, schools, and libraries now offer Wi-Fi hotspots that allow your Mac to connect wirelessly to the Internet. However, if you don't have a wireless network at home or work, or the hotel you're staying at offers an Ethernet cable to connect to the Internet, you'll need to plug this cable into your Mac.

> **TIP**   If your MacBook Air, for example, doesn't have a standalone Ethernet port to establish a cable-based connection to a modem or router, use your computer's USB or Thunderbolt port with a special adapter, such as Apple's USB Ethernet Adapter ($29, http://store.apple.com/us/product/MC704ZM/A) or Apple's Thunderbolt to Gigabit Ethernet Adapter ($29.99, http://store.apple.com/us/product/MD463ZM/A).

FIREWIRE PORT

The FireWire port that is built in to some Mac models allows you to connect certain types of FireWire-compatible peripherals to your computer, such as external hard drives or an external display. A special FireWire cable is used to connect your computer with a compatible device.

The benefit to FireWire is that it can transfer data at speeds up to 800 megabits (Mbps) per second, which is significantly faster than USB 2.0 (which can send and receive data at speeds up to 480Mbps).

The drawback to FireWire is that the peripherals it's compatible with tend to cost significantly more than similar peripherals that use a standard USB 2.0 or USB 3.0 connection.

Like USB peripherals, FireWire peripherals are "plug and play." In other words, they don't need to be set up. When you plug the peripheral into your Mac, Mountain Lion installs the appropriate drivers automatically and makes the peripheral available to you.

> **NOTE**   If your Mac doesn't have a FireWire port, Apple offers a Thunderbolt to FireWire adapter. It connects to the Thunderbolt port that's built in to your Mac and allows you to connect a FireWire-compatible peripheral to it.

HEADPHONE JACK (AUDIO OUT)

If you want to connect external stereo headphones to your computer (to listen to the audio generated from it in private) or you want to attach external speakers to your computer to enhance the stereo sound, this can be done using the standard headphone jack that's built in to all Macs.

> **NOTE** The MacBook Air and Mac mini, for example, have a single audio in/out port that serves the same function as both the headphone jack (audio out) and microphone jack (audio in) found in other Mac models.

However, both wireless stereo headphones and external speakers that use Bluetooth technology are available, allowing you to connect these optional audio output devices to your computer via Bluetooth. In addition, wireless AirPlay-enabled external speakers for your Mac are available.

> **TIP** The same headphones that came with your Apple iPhone or iPod can be plugged into the headphone jack or audio in/out jack of your Mac.

IR RECEIVER

This feature allows you to use Apple's wireless handheld remote control with your Mac to control iTunes as you're playing music or watching video content. If your Mac didn't come with an Apple Remote, you can purchase one for $19 from Apple. com (http://store.apple.com/us/product/MC377LL/A).

MICROPHONE JACK (AUDIO IN)

Instead of using the microphone that's built in to your Mac, if you need higher-quality audio input, you can attach an external microphone to your computer using the microphone (audio in) jack.

Another option, however, is to acquire a USB microphone. For example, if you're recording music, vocals, or voiceovers (for a podcast or blog), a USB microphone offers a much better recording quality than the computer's built-in microphone.

Music stores, such as Guitar Center (www.guitarcenter.com), as well as Apple Stores and other consumer electronics superstores, offer a selection of optional, external microphones that can connect to your computer. For example, a company called BlueMic (www.bluemic.com) offers a selection of professional-quality microphones that can connect to your Mac using its USB port.

If you're using your computer for VoIP phone conversations or video conferencing, a wireless headset with built-in microphone will offer better audio quality than using your Mac's built-in speaker and microphone. The Plantronics Savi 440 ($279.95, www.plantronics.com/us/product/savi-440) is one example of a high-end wireless headset option. It's shown in Figure 15.5. Plenty of less-expensive options are also available.

> **NOTE** Hello Direct (www.hellodirect.com) is an online-based business that sells wired and wireless headsets from a handful of companies.

FIGURE 15.5

The Plantronics Savi 440 is an example of a high-end wireless headset with a built-in microphone that can be used with your computer.

THUNDERBOLT PORT

The Thunderbolt port built in to many Mac models uses technology that Apple helped to develop. When you connect a Thunderbolt peripheral to your Mac, using a special Thunderbolt cable, data can be exchanged extremely quickly between the two devices.

> **NOTE** Connecting certain peripherals to your Mac using the computer's Thunderbolt port offers an alternative to using a high-speed FireWire connection. Using Thunderbolt, data transfer speeds up to 8 to 10 gigabits (Gbps) per second are possible. This is significantly faster than FireWire or USB 3.0.

Like USB and FireWire, Thunderbolt technology is plug and play. Because it is capable of high-speed data transfers, it is ideal for connecting an external monitor/display or external hard drive to your computer.

The drawback to using a Thunderbolt-compatible display/monitor or external hard drive with your Mac is the cost of these peripherals. Expect to pay more for a Thunderbolt-compatible peripheral than an otherwise similar product that can connect to your computer using a standard USB 2.0 or USB 3.0 connection.

> ## NOTE
> Apple's own 27-inch Thunderbolt display ($999, http://store.apple.com/us/product/MC914LL/A) can be connected to any iMac, Mac Pro, MacBook Pro, or MacBook Air using a Thunderbolt cable.

The Thunderbolt port that's built in to your Mac can also be used with an optional adapter to easily connect your computer to any VGA monitor or display, as well as to an LCD projector. The appropriate adapters are available from Apple Stores or Apple.com. Which adapter you need will be based on the Mac model you own and the type of display or LCD projector you're connecting to the computer.

USB PORTS

The USB (Universal Serial Bus) ports that are built in to all Macs allow you to plug in and use a wide range of compatible peripherals and accessories, including printers, scanners, memory card readers, digital cameras, external hard drives, and USB flash drives. It's also possible to recharge the internal batteries of many mobile devices, such as your cell phone, tablet, eBook reader, or digital camera, by plugging these devices into the USB port of your computer.

USB offers plug-and-play connectivity. In most cases, this means you plug one end of the USB cable into your Mac and the other end into the USB-compatible accessory and it automatically configures itself and work.

However, in some cases, the first time you plug in some USB peripherals, Mountain Lion may need to access the Internet to download and install specific drivers for the peripheral you've connected. In other cases, the peripheral you've purchased may come with drivers on a CD-ROM that need to be installed before the device can be used with your computer.

What's great about USB technology is that you can connect multiple USB devices to your Mac simultaneously and they all run independently of each other. Plus, if you don't have enough USB ports built in to your Mac, you can easily connect an optional USB hub and connect four, six, eight, or more additional USB ports to your computer.

Since it was developed in the mid-1990s, USB technology has evolved somewhat dramatically. The first major innovation that increased the data transfer speeds this technology was capable of came about in April 2000, when the USB 2.0 standard was established. USB 2.0 offers data transfer speeds up to 480Mbps.

In 2008, USB 3.0 was introduced, which once again dramatically enhanced the data transfer speeds possible using this technology. However, it took Apple a while (until 2012) before it started introducing USB 3.0 compatible ports into its computers.

NOTE If your Mac has USB 2.0 ports built in, it can connect to USB 1.0- or USB 2.0-compatible devices. However, if your newer Mac has USB 3.0 ports built in, they are downward compatible and can be used with any currently available USB-compatible devices. When used with USB 3.0 devices, data transfer rates up to 5Gbps (which is about 10 times faster than USB 2.0) are possible.

TIP If your Mac has USB 3.0 ports built in, be sure to purchase USB 3.0-compatible peripherals, especially when it comes to external hard drives. When you use Time Machine (or another data backup application) with a USB 3.0-compatible external hard drive, every time your Mac needs to back up data, the process will happen much faster, compared to when using a USB 2.0 external hard drive. Thus, the overall performance of your computer won't slow down throughout the day when automatic data backups are being created.

The USB ports that are built in to your Mac use an industry standard USB Type A connection. However, some USB peripherals utilize one of more than six other USB connection plug types. If this is the case, the required USB cable needed to connect the peripheral to your computer will typically be included with the peripheral.

This is the case with all Apple iOS mobile devices (iDevices) that come with a white USB cable with a standard Type A plug on one end and Apple's proprietary 30-pin dock connector plug on the other. It's also the case with most digital cameras, eBook readers, and other types of peripherals, including some printers.

However, if the USB peripheral you want to connect to your Mac also has a standard Type A USB port, you can purchase a USB to USB cable from any computer, office supply, or consumer electronics store in a wide range of lengths, based on your needs.

WI-FI

The ability to connect to the Internet or a network wirelessly using Wi-Fi has become standard on most computers and mobile devices. Mountain Lion makes finding and connecting to a wireless network or hotspot a straightforward process.

To turn on the Wi-Fi capabilities of your Mac, click the Wi-Fi icon on the right side of the menu bar and select the Turn Wi-Fi On option (shown in Figure 15.6).

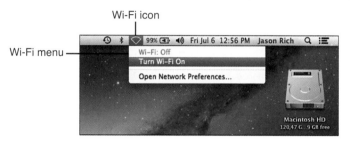

FIGURE 15.6

Turn on Wi-Fi from the Wi-Fi icon on the right side of the menu bar.

When turned on, this icon transforms into a Wi-Fi signal strength indicator. A listing of available networks displayed just below the menu bar. Click the network you want to connect to (shown in Figure 15.7).

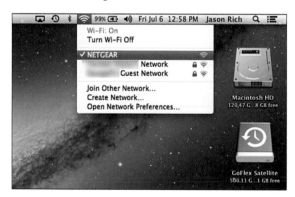

FIGURE 15.7

Once turned on, the Wi-Fi icon becomes a signal strength indicator and below the icon, a list of available networks is displayed when you click the icon.

Displayed to the right of each network listing is a signal strength indicator. The closer you are to the wireless router, the stronger the signal will be. If a lock icon appears to the right of a network's listing, this indicates the network is password protected. When you click its listing to connect to it, you'll be prompted to enter a password.

> ☑ **TIP** Configure Wi-Fi functionality by launching System Preferences and clicking the Network option. From here, you can also turn Wi-Fi on or off, plus choose whether the Wi-Fi signal indicator will display on the menu bar.

CONNECTING PERIPHERALS

Knowing you have several options for connecting most types of peripherals to your Mac, the trick is to choose the method that best meets your needs, based on whether you prefer connecting optional devices wirelessly or using a cable. Part of this decision should also take into account data transfer speed issues, when applicable.

For example, you can connect an external hard drive to your Mac using a standard USB connection, a Thunderbolt or FireWire connection, or use Wi-Fi, based on the external hard drive's make and model (and the ports built in to your Mac). The benefit to using a Thunderbolt or FireWire connection is significantly faster data transfer speeds between your computer and the external drive. The drawback of this option is the higher price tag for the drive.

However, if you want to share the external hard drive with multiple computers and/or want to use a wireless connection, choose a drive that offers Wi-Fi capabilities, such as one of Apple's own Time Capsule drives (http://store.apple.com/us/product/MD032LL/A/Time-Capsule-2TB). The most affordable external hard drives available for your Mac are those that connect via USB 2.0 or USB 3.0. These drives come in a wide range of storage capacities.

> ✑ **NOTE** See Chapter 12, "Backing Up Your Mac," for more information about external hard drives.

As soon as you plug an external hard drive into your Mac, Mountain Lion identifies it and makes it available. You'll find an icon for the drive displayed on your desktop, plus it'll be listed within the sidebar of the Finder window. Also, when using the Save As command within any app, any external drives you have connected to the computer are listed as possible destinations for the file.

With the exception of some printers and any Bluetooth devices, most peripherals you ultimately connect to your Mac automatically configure themselves as soon as they're connected to the computer. However, from System Preferences, you can custom configure the behavior of optional drives, displays, printers, scanners, speakers, as well as the keyboard, mouse, trackpad, and the Bluetooth devices you want to use with your computer.

CONNECTING PRINTERS/SCANNERS

Mountain Lion has the drivers to operate some popular printer and scanner makes and models built in. However, when initially installing many printers or scanners, it'll be necessary for your Mac to either connect to the Internet to find, download, and install the necessary drivers, or you'll need to load the drivers from the CD-ROM that came with the printer or scanner.

Your Mac can be connected to multiple printers simultaneously. For example, you may utilize an inkjet or laser printer to handle printing your traditional documents and files, but use a home photo printer to create prints from your digital images. It's also possible to connect a specialized label printer to your Mac that can print directly onto labels. Some label printers can print U.S. postage stamps directly from your Mac.

As soon as you plug in a new device, Mountain Lion identifies and either auto-configures it or walks you through the process of installing the necessary drivers. It's also possible to manually add a printer or scanner to your computer after connecting it by launching System Preferences.

From System Preferences, choose the Print & Scan option, and then click the plus sign icon under the Printers list on the left side of the window (shown in Figure 15.8). If the printer make and model is listed within the menu that appears, click it. Otherwise, select the Add Printer or Scanner option and follow the onscreen prompts.

> **TIP** If your printer can utilize Bluetooth or Wi-Fi instead of a cable to connect to your Mac, refer to the directions that came with the printer to configure the Bluetooth or Wi-Fi functionality it offers, and then make sure you turn on your Mac's Bluetooth or Wi-Fi function.

> **NOTE** Your Mac can also connect to and utilize a printer that's on your network, but not directly connected to the computer itself. Again, if your printer has this capability, refer to the manual that came with it to determine how to set it up on your network. When your Mac is connected to the same network, it will then automatically detect the printer and make it accessible.

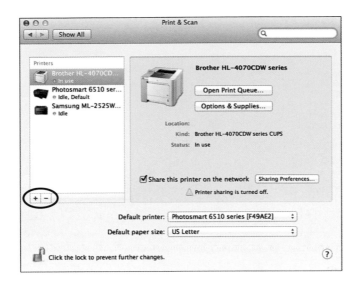

FIGURE 15.8

Configure your printers from the Print & Scan window within System Preferences.

CHOOSING A PRINTER FOR YOUR MAC

When it comes to shopping for a quality printer for your Mac, you don't have to spend a fortune, but you should consider your needs before making a purchase. The following are a few things to consider:

- What you'll be printing. Do you need to print in color? Your basic printer options include the following:
    - Personal laser printer
    - Workgroup laser printer (Designed for a home office or work environment. The page-per-minute speed of these printers is faster and the resolution is often better than a personal laser printer.)
    - Inkjet printer (capable of printing in black and white or color)
    - Multifunctional/all-in-one device (a printer/scanner/copier/fax machine)
    - Photo printer (Used for creating prints on photo paper from your digital photos. The Epson Artisan 835 Angle, shown in Figure 15.9, is one of hundreds of different photo printers that are Mac compatible.)

FIGURE 15.9

The Epson Artisan 835 Angle is an example of a home photo printer.

- Color laser printer (These printers are ideal for printing in full-color and high-resolution, but not for creating prints from your digital images. They're also more costly to maintain, in terms of toner cost, than an ink-jet printer, making the color laser printers better suited for business use.)
- Label printer (Print directly on labels. Some of these printers, such as those from Dymo, allow you to print U.S. postage stamps.)

- Will you need to print on paper that's larger than 8.5" x 11"?

> **⌇ NOTE** Depending on your needs, wide-carriage printers are available that allow you to print posters or banners.

- For your basic documents and files, do you want or need the print quality offered by a B&W or color laser printer, or will a quality inkjet printer meet your needs? Pay attention to the printer's resolution.

> **☑ TIP** A printer's resolution is measured in dots per inch (dpi). The more dots, the better the resolution. When the printer's dip is listed with two numbers (for example, 600 x 600), this refers to the number of dots per inch horizontally and vertically.

- Will you be printing long documents? If so, the number of pages per minute the printer is capable of printing is an important feature to consider.

- If you'll be using the printer extensively, especially for longer documents, the capacity of the paper tray is important. After all, you don't want to constantly have to refill the paper tray during large print jobs.

- Will you often be switching between paper sizes? If so, choose a printer with two or more adjustable paper trays. For example, one paper tray can hold basic, white 8.5" x 11" paper, while the other can hold legal size paper or your company letterhead.

- What connection options does the printer offer? Most printers have USB built in, but some also support Bluetooth or Wi-Fi. Higher-end printers may also support other connection options.

- In addition to the price of the printer itself, take into account the cost of the replacement ink or toner cartridges. Some printer manufacturers set the printer prices extremely low, but then charge a fortune for ink.

- The number of ink cartridges the printer requires to function. Some color printers have a black ink and a single multicolor ink cartridge. Others require you to install up to six cartridges (one for each color), and the printer won't function unless all of the cartridges are installed. In general, the more printer cartridges that are required, the higher the ink costs will be to keep that printer operational.

- How long does the ink or toner cartridge last, in terms of the average number of pages you can print?

> **☑ TIP** Although the printer manufacturers all recommend always using the company's own branded replacement ink or toner cartridges for your printer, to save money consider using generic ink or toner cartridges available from a wide range of Internet vendors.
>
> To find low-cost generic ink or toner cartridges, use any Internet search engine or price comparison website (such as Nextag.com), and enter the exact make and model of your printer, followed by the phrase "replacement ink" or "replacement toner cartridge." You can often save even more if you buy three or more replacement cartridges at the same time.
>
> Most companies that sell generic replacement cartridges use high-quality inks, but some don't. Pay attention to customer reviews and when using a new ink supplier, buy one cartridge to test it with your printer before stocking up.

> **TIP** For a laser printer, most manufacturers offer standard capacity and high-capacity replacement toner cartridges. The high-capacity toner cartridges are more expensive, but they last up to three times longer than a standard capacity toner cartridge.

CONSIDERING A MULTIFUNCTIONAL/ALL-IN-ONE OPTION

Although you can invest in a standalone printer, for consumers and small businesses, many printer manufacturers offer all-in-one solutions that include a laser or inkjet printer, scanner, fax machine, and copier all in one device that's usually about the same size as a standalone printer. These all-in-one solutions are also economically priced and can help you save physical space on your desk.

> **NOTE** Some of these all-in-one devices offer photo printing and traditional printing capabilities, with multiple paper trays that can accommodate letter or legal size paper, as well as 4" x 6" or 5" x 7" photo paper.

When choosing an all-in-one printer option, pay attention to the printer's specifications to make sure it can handle your needs from a quality and speed standpoint.

IN THIS CHAPTER

■ Transferring your PC files and
   data to your Mac
■ Learning the differences
   between Windows and
   Mountain Lion
■ Running Windows on your Mac

16

TRANSITIONING EASILY FROM A WINDOWS PC TO A MAC

Many Windows PC users who switch to a Mac find the differences between the two operating systems to be a bit confusing at first. With just a little bit of practice, however, they become acclimated to the Mac. But, you should expect a short learning curve and adjustment period when making the switch from a PC to a Mac.

TRANSFERRING YOUR PC FILES TO A MAC WITH MIGRATION ASSISTANT

Mountain Lion includes an app, called Migration Assistant, that offers the tools needed to quickly transfer your Windows PC-based data, documents, files, photos, and multimedia content to your Mac and organize the information in appropriate folders.

Before using Migration Assistant on your Mac, be sure to download the Windows edition of Migration Assistant on your PC and install it. You can download this free software from www.apple.com/migrate-to-mac. It's also a good strategy to backup all of your files before starting this process.

> **TIP** On the Mac, you'll find Migration Assistant within the Utilities folder. One way to access and launch it is to open Finder and then click the Applications folder option along the sidebar. Scroll down to the Utilities folder and double-click it. Locate the Migration Assistant app icon and double-click it to launch it.

From the Introduction window of Migration Assistant, choose how you want to transfer your information. Choose the From a Mac, PC, Time Machine Backup or Other Disk option, and then click the Continue button (shown in Figure 16.1). When prompted, enter the computer password for your Mac, and then click the OK button.

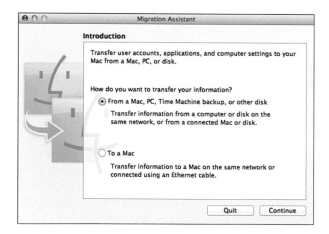

FIGURE 16.1

The Introduction window of Migration Assistant.

> **NOTE** When using Migration Assistant, be sure to save all your work associated with other apps running on your Mac, and then close those apps. When the Quit Other Applications window appears, other apps that are running will be closed for you when you click the Continue button.

When the Select a Migration Method window appears, choose the From a Mac or PC option, and then click Continue. At this point, your Mac attempts to establish a connection with the PC that's also running Migration Assistant.

Once the connection is made, you are prompted to select the items you want to transfer. For each Windows account, select each type of file or content. Your options include: Desktop, Documents, Downloads, Movies, Music, Pictures, Public, and All Other Folders and Files.

As soon as you click the Continue button, your files are copied from your PC to your Mac and placed in the appropriate folders or imported into relevant apps. This process could take a while, depending on how much information needs to be transferred.

> **NOTE** Part of the transfer process includes transferring app-specific data and customized settings. For example, if you have a custom wallpaper displayed on your PC's desktop, that same image will be used for your Mac's wallpaper and be displayed on your Mac's desktop.

Your email account information, Contacts database, schedule data, web browser bookmarks, and other personalized settings will also be transferred and automatically imported into the appropriate apps on your Mac.

So, you'll find your Outlook contacts data from your PC loaded into the Contacts app on the Mac, and your scheduling data will be loaded into the Calendar app. Your email account information will be imported into the Mail app, and your web browser bookmarks and data will be imported into Safari.

> **TIP** Another method for connecting a PC to a Mac is to use the J5 Create Wormhole cable ($39.99, www.j5create.com/juc400.htm). This special USB cable connects a PC to a Mac via their respective USB ports, and automatically loads the necessary software on both computers to instantly establish a connection. You can then copy and paste or drag and drop files, folders or content between computers freely.

> 📝 **NOTE** The Move2Mac software ($39.95 www.detto.com/move-2-mac-overview.php) is a software-based solution for moving information from a PC to a Mac. The functionality of this software is similar to Migration Assistant. This software automatically moves your documents, folders, photos, music, files, wallpapers, web browser favorites, and Outlook-related emails, contacts, and scheduling data.
>
> On a PC, Move2Mac works with Windows XP, Vista, Windows 7 and Windows 8. It allows your Mac and PC that are connected to the same network to transfer information, or you can use an external USB hard drive to go from the PC to the drive, and then from the drive to the Mac.

If you plan to go back and forth between your PC and Mac, after the initial transfer of your data and files is made using Migration Assistant, you can then link your PC to your iCloud account and transfer or sync certain types of app-specific data that way as well. To use iCloud with your PC, you first need to download and install the free iCloud Control Panel (http://support.apple.com/kb/DL1455).

From the Windows Start menu on your PC, choose Control Panel, followed by Network and Internet. Then select the iCloud option. When prompted, enter your Apple ID and password. Next, select the iCloud services you want to enable on your PC.

> 📝 **NOTE** The iCloud Control Panel for Windows looks very similar to the iCloud menu on your Mac that's accessible by launching System Preferences and then clicking on the iCloud option.

> ☑️ **TIP** Using iCloud, your Outlook contacts and scheduling data from your PC can continue to remain synchronized with the Contacts and Calendar apps on your Mac, while your Microsoft Internet Explorer bookmarks will remain synced with Safari. Your iCloud Photo Stream can also be viewed on a PC or Mac, and all your past and present content purchases from the iTunes store are also accessible on your PC or Mac (including music, TV shows, movies, music videos, eBooks, audiobooks, and iOS mobile apps).

MICROSOFT WINDOWS VERSUS MOUNTAIN LION

For a variety of logistic and legal reasons, Microsoft Windows and OS X have some major and some more subtle differences. Initially, as someone makes the switch from being a PC to Mac user, it's what sets these two operating systems apart that often causes the most confusion or frustration.

YOUR MAC'S MOUSE OR TRACKPAD HAS NO BUTTONS

The mouse used with Windows typically has a left and right mouse button. However, a mouse or trackpad used with a Mac has only one button equivalent on which to click.

To access the shortcut menu or utilize the equivalent of a right mouse click on your Mac, press the Control key and the mouse button at the same time. For example, when using Mountain Lion, Figure 16.2 shows the shortcut menu within Finder that is accessed using this method.

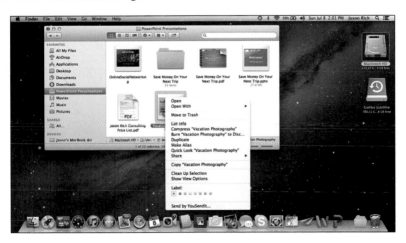

FIGURE 16.2

The shortcut menu can be accessed for files or folders, for example, within Finder.

> 📝 **TIP**   If you're using an Apple Magic Mouse with your Mac, you can configure it so that if you click the top-right side of the mouse, this will simulate a right-click of the mouse. To make this customization, launch System Preferences and select the Mouse option. At the top of the window, click the Point & Click tab. Then select the Secondary Click option (shown in Figure 16.3).

If you're using a built-in Multi-Touch trackpad on a MacBook Pro or MacBook Air, or using an optional Apple Magic Trackpad with any Mac, to activate a figure gesture that simulates a right-click of the mouse, launch System Preferences and click Trackpad.

Next, click the Point & Click tab at the top of the window, shown in Figure 16.4, and select the Secondary Click option.

By doing this, you'll discover that if you now tap on the trackpad with your index finger and middle finger simultaneously, this simulates a right-click of the mouse.

You can also purchase a USB or wireless mouse from a third party, such as Targus (www.targus.com), Belkin (www.belkin.com), or even Microsoft (www.microsoft.com/hardware/en-us/mice), that offers a traditional right and left mouse button, but that's also fully compatible with your Mac.

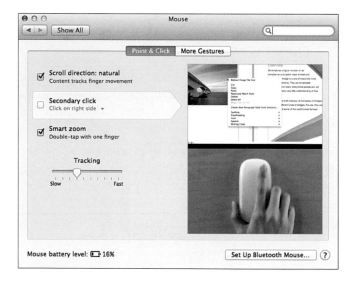

FIGURE 16.3

You can configure the Apple Magic Mouse to simulate a right-click of the mouse.

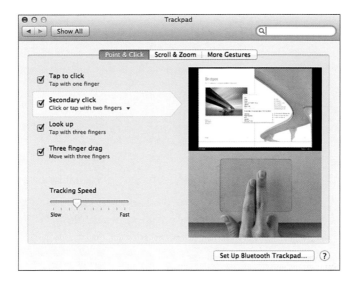

FIGURE 16.4

You can configure the trackpad to work with a two-finger tap to simulate a right-click of the mouse.

DIFFERENT ICONS USED TO CLOSE, MINIMIZE, OR MAXIMIZE WINDOWS

On your PC that's running Windows, when a window is open, there's typically an X icon in the upper-right corner of it that's used to close that window. On a Mac, to close a window, click the red dot icon near the upper-left corner of the window (shown in Figure 16.5).

FIGURE 16.5

Click the red dot icon to close an active window that's displayed on your Mac's desktop.

> **TIP**   On the Mac, another way to close an active window is to select File, Close Window from the menu bar, or use the ⌘-W keyboard shortcut. Keep in mind that closing a window does not cause the app to quit or stop running. It simply closes the window, allowing the app to continue running in the background.

> **TIP** When using Windows, closing an app window also quits the app. This is not usually the case on a Mac running Mountain Lion.
>
> To actually quit most apps so that they stop running altogether on a Mac, access the pull-down menu to the right of the Apple ( ) icon on the menu bar. This menu bears the name of the app you're using (for example, Word or Safari). From it, select the Quit command. Or use the ⌘-Q keyboard shortcut.

Likewise, instead of the Minimize icon being displayed to the left of the X icon (near the upper-right corner of the screen) on your PC, you'll discover a yellow dot icon displayed near the upper-left corner of windows displayed within Mountain Lion. Click the yellow dot to minimize a window.

> **TIP** On the Mac, you can also access the Minimize command from the Window menu on the menu bar, or use the ⌘-M keyboard shortcut to minimize the active window on your desktop.

To maximize the active window, instead of clicking the Maximize icon near the upper-right corner of the window of your PC that's running Windows, you click the green dot icon near the upper-left corner of the window. When you do this, the Dock at the bottom of the screen will stay visible. However, from within System Preferences, you can automatically hide the Dock so that it appears only when you hover the mouse over where it should be. This will save additional onscreen real estate. To automatically hide the Dock, from System Preferences click the Dock option and then add a check mark to the Automatically Hide and Show Dock option.

> **TIP** In addition to maximizing a window, when running many apps on your Mac, you can also enter into Full Screen mode. This allows the app to utilize the entire screen. Upon entering into Full Screen mode, where app-specific command icons appear may be different, plus the Dock and menu bar become hidden.
>
> To enter into Full Screen mode when it's available, click the Full Screen icon near the upper-right corner of an app window. Or select View, Enter Full Screen from the menu bar. You can also use the Control-⌘-F keyboard shortcut.
>
> While in Full Screen mode, to access the now hidden menu bar, hover your mouse near the very top of the screen where the menu bar would typically be displayed

and the menu bar will appear. Likewise, to access the Dock while in Full Screen mode, hover your mouse over where the Dock would normally be located (typically at the bottom of the screen), and it will appear.

To exit out of Full Screen mode, press the Esc key. Especially if you're using a MacBook, you'll discover that Full Screen mode works exceptionally well on some apps where having extra onscreen real estate at your disposal is beneficial (for example, when using iPhoto or another photo editing app).

When you work in Full Screen mode, it hides other active apps and allows you to concentrate more on the app you're currently working with. However, the other apps that are running will continue to do so in the background. You can then manually switch between active apps by pressing ⌘-Tab.

Figure 16.6 shows iPhoto running in an app window, and Figure 16.7 shows iPhoto running in Full Screen mode.

FIGURE 16.6

iPhoto running within a standard app window on a Mac Desktop.

FIGURE 16.7

iPhoto running in Full Screen mode on a Mac. Notice the menu bar and Dock are hidden.

OTHER DIFFERENCES

The following is a summary of some other commonly used features and functions that are different between Microsoft Windows and Mountain Lion:

■ Just like Microsoft Windows, Mountain Lion offers a wide range of keyboard shortcuts for commonly used commands within the operating system and when using specific apps. However, instead of pressing the Control (Ctrl) key on your PC's keyboard, on your Mac you press the ⌘ key along with the additional required keys for a shortcut. For example, the keyboard shortcut to print is ⌘-P, or the keyboard shortcut to quit an app is ⌘-Q.

> **⌇ NOTE** Instead of using the Alt key when running Windows in conjunction with a keyboard shortcut, or to insert a special character, on the Mac, press the Option key. Some keyboard shortcuts on the Mac will also utilize the Control and/or ⌘ key.

■ Instead of pressing the Backspace key to delete or the Delete key to forward delete, on a Mac you press the Delete key to backward delete and the Function (Fn) - Delete key to forward delete.

■ To find specific files, folders or content that's stored on your PC, you'd typically click the My Computer button and then navigate your way around the computer's file and folder hierarchy. On the Mac, open a Finder window to find, access, and open files, folders, or apps stored on your Mac (or on a storage device or another computer that's connected to your Mac). You can launch Finder from the Dock or by double-clicking a drive icon on your desktop. Figure 16.8 shows what the Finder icon on the Dock looks like.

Finder icon —

FIGURE 16.8

The Finder icon on the Dock.

> **✓ TIP**   Another way to quickly find something on your Mac using a keyword is to use the search option within Finder or the Mac's Spotlight Search feature. The equivalent feature in Windows is Windows Explorer. On your Mac, click the magnifying glass icon on the right side of the menu bar, next to the Notification Center icon. When the Spotlight Search field appears, enter any keyword, number, or text that will help you find related content that's stored on your Mac.

■ One way to launch applications on your PC is to access the Start menu or the taskbar. On the Mac, click the appropriate app icon on the Dock or your desktop, or use Launchpad. Remember, you can customize your Dock or what app icon aliases are displayed on the desktop by dragging the appropriate app icon from the Applications folder to the Dock or the desktop. You can then launch the app by clicking that app icon. You can also launch apps from the Applications folder or from whatever folder an app is stored in. To do this, double-click its app icon.

■ To access the contents of external drives or the optical disc connected to your PC, you typically use My Computer. On the Mac, these devices or drives are listed within the sidebar of the Finder window. They also appear as icons on your desktop. To customize what information appears within the sidebar of the Finder window and on your desktop, launch Finder and select Finder, Preferences from the menu bar. Then click the General tab to determine what items will appear on the desktop. Then click the Sidebar tab to determine what items will appear within the sidebar of the Finder window (shown in Figure 16.9).

FIGURE 16.9

Decide what information will be displayed within the sidebar of the Finder window.

- On the PC, certain keyboard keys serve specific functions. On your Mac, use the following equivalent keys.

Windows Key	Mac OS X Key Equivalent
Shift Key	Shift key (⇧)
Control Key	Control key (^)
Alt Key	Option key (⌥)
Windows Key	Command key (⌘)
Backspace Key	Delete key (⌫)

- If a program happens to crash or stop being responsive when using your PC, you typically have to press the Ctrl+Alt+Delete keys to reboot your entire computer. On a Mac, there is seldom a need to reboot your computer. Instead, you can force quit a specific application that becomes unresponsive and then relaunch just that app. Mountain Lion and any other apps you had running will continue running.

> **TIP** To force quit a specific unresponsive app on your Mac, press ⌘-Option-Esc to access the Force Quit Applications window (shown in Figure 16.10). Another way to access the Force Quit window is to select , Force Quit from the menu bar.

This window lists all apps currently running. A "Not Responding" or equivalent message will appear to the right of an unresponsive app. Highlight that app listing and click the Force Quit button. Or to Relaunch any other app, click the Relaunch button that otherwise appears near the lower-right corner of the Force Quit Applications window.

FIGURE 16.10

The Force Quit Applications window within Mountain Lion.

To eject a disc from an optical drive or eject an external drive connected to your Mac, you can either drag and drop (move) the icon that represents the disc or drive to the Trash icon along the Dock, or from within the sidebar of the Finder window click the Eject icon to the right of a drive's listing (shown in Figure 16.11). On most Macs (except for the MacBook Air), there's also an Eject key on the keyboard. It's located in the upper-right corner, next to the Volume Up function key.

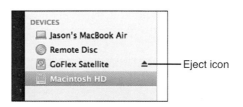

FIGURE 16.11

The eject icon appears next to a drive label.

> 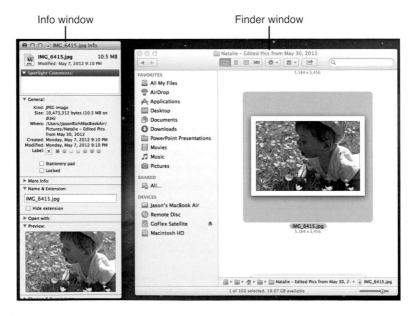**NOTE** Regardless of what app you're running on a Mac, running along the top of the screen will be the menu bar (unless you're in Full Screen mode). The contents on the left side of the menu bar are app specific, and the menu options change based on what app you're running and what features/functions are currently available to you. The icons on the right side of the menu bar relate more to Mac functions, and most are not app specific.

- Instead of using the Properties option in Windows to customize application, folder, or file options, on your Mac you'll use the options displayed within the Info window (shown in Figure 16.12). To access the Info window, select an item and choose the Get Info option from the File menu on the menu bar, or use the ⌘-I keyboard shortcut. You can also press the ⌘ button and click the mouse on an item to access the context menu (which is equivalent to a right-click).

FIGURE 16.12

The Info window allows you to access and customize information related to files, folders, or apps.

- When you want to discard items when running Windows, you place them in the Recycle Bin. On the Mac, the Trash icon serves the same function. You can find it on the right side of the Dock. To empty the Trash, click the Trash icon, and then use the Empty Trash command under the Finder pull-down menu on the menu bar. The keyboard shortcut to empty the Trash is Shift-⌘-Delete.

- To rename a file or folder stored on your PC, you use the Rename command from the File Tasks menu or right-click an item and use the Rename command. On your Mac, select and highlight the file, folder, or application icon or listing (within Finder or on your desktop, for example) and press the Enter key. You can then enter a new name for the item in the text box that appears.
- Windows offer a series of folders, such as My Documents and My Pictures, for storing specific types of files. On your Mac, within Finder, you'll find a separate Applications, Documents, Downloads, Movies, Music, and Pictures folder has been pre-created for you. You can then create subfolders within these main folders.

> **TIP**   On a Mac, to use Messenger to send and receive instant messages and communicate with other people who use the Messenger service, you can download the free Microsoft Messenger: Mac app (www.microsoft.com/mac/ messenger). It also comes bundled with Microsoft Office for Mac. If you use the Messages app (that comes preinstalled on your Mac), you can send/receive instant messages and communicate with iMessage, AIM, Yahoo!, and Google Talk users, but not Messenger users.
>
> See Chapter 5, "Communicating Effectively with Messages," to learn more about what this app can be used for and how to use it.

- To edit, view, and manage your digital photos on your PC, you might have used Microsoft Photo Editor or My Pictures. Or to edit and view your videos, you might have used Windows MovieMaker. On your Mac, the iPhoto app is used to view, edit, and manage your digital photos, and iMovie is used to edit and view your videos. You also have the option to use a wide range of other apps for these tasks.
- To customize the functionality of Windows and software running on your PC, you usually need to access Control Panel. On the Mac, customizations to Mountain Lion (as well as to some apps) are done by launching System Preferences. It's listed on your Dock, on the Launchpad, and is accessible from the Applications folder, for example. You can also access System Preferences from the Apple   pull-down menu that appears in the upper-left corner of the screen. Figure 16.13 shows what the System Preferences icon looks like on the Dock.

System Preferences window

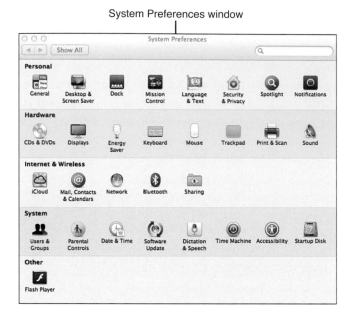

FIGURE 16.13

The System Preferences icon displayed on the Dock. The main System Preferences window is open on the desktop.

> ✔️ **TIP**   To make some app-specific customizations when running an app, select Preferences from the pull-down menu (which has the same name as the app you're running) just to the right of the   icon on the menu bar.

RUNNING MICROSOFT WINDOWS AND PC SOFTWARE ON YOUR MAC

So you've decided to make the switch to a Mac. Congratulations! Using apps that come preinstalled with Mountain Lion, as well as other apps available from the App Store or from individual third-party software developers, you'll discover that just about anything that your Window-based PC could do can also be done just as well, if not better, on a Mac.

In fact, many popular Windows PC applications also have Mac versions available. However, if you use custom software or specialized vertical market software created for a PC, a Mac equivalent might not be available. Or, you may discover that a popular PC-based game you enjoy playing doesn't yet have a Mac version.

In these rare cases when a Mac app isn't available to perform the same tasks as you perform on your PC (using your existing data), you always have the option of actually running Microsoft Windows on your Mac, and then installing and running Windows-based software.

The upside to this is that your Mac will perform exactly like your PC and run actual PC software. The downside is that you need to install both the Mountain Lion and Windows operating systems on your Mac (which takes up significant storage space).

If you want or need to run Microsoft Windows and Windows-based programs on your Mac, you have two options. For either option, you need to acquire a Microsoft Windows installation disc (or purchase and download Microsoft's operating system online). The OEM or backup version of Windows that came with a PC probably won't work. You'll need to use a standalone version of Microsoft Windows. You can find your options for Microsoft Windows 7 at http://windows.microsoft.com/en-US/windows/shop/windows-7.

USING BOOT CAMP

Mountain Lion comes with an app called Boot Camp. You'll find it by accessing the Applications folder and clicking the Utilities folder. Boot Camp allows you to install and then run Microsoft Windows on your Mac.

When you run Windows using Boot Camp, each time you turn on and boot your Mac, you need to decide whether you want to run Mountain Lion or Windows. If you choose Mountain Lion, your Mac will function as a Mac and give you access to all your Mac apps and related data. If you choose Windows, your Mac will function just like a PC, and your Windows-based software and data will be available to you.

The problem with this solution is that each time you want to switch between running Windows and Mac applications, you have to manually reboot your computer.

To install and run Windows on your Mac using Boot Camp, launch the Boot Camp app and follow the onscreen prompts. Once Windows is up and running on your Mac, you'll then need to install the individual Windows programs you want to use.

USING PARALLELS

Parallels is a third-party app for the Mac that makes installing and running Microsoft Windows and Windows-based software on a Mac mush easier. Plus, once Windows is running using Parallels, you can instantly switch between Mac and Windows applications (and even cut and paste content between apps running on different operating systems) without having to reboot.

Parallels Desktop 7 for Mac ($79.99, www.parallels.com) walks you through the Microsoft Windows installation process step by step, and even allows you to purchase (for an additional fee) a copy of Microsoft Windows from within the app's setup process. You'll then be able to seamlessly and simultaneously run both Mac and Windows apps on your Mac, side by side.

> **NOTE** Parallels Desktop 7 for Mac works with several versions of Microsoft Windows, including Microsoft Windows 7 and Microsoft Windows 8, as well as all Windows software that's compatible with these operating systems.

When you install Windows on your Mac using Parallels, it automatically syncs certain types of app-specific data, such as your contacts and scheduling information, between the two operating systems. Plus, your photos, documents, music, and web browser bookmarks will be synced on both operating systems.

Using this option to run Windows on your Mac also requires a significant amount of your Mac's internal storage space to store the Parallels app, the Microsoft Windows operating system and your Windows software. However, if you want or need to run Windows on your Mac, this is a viable option.

Index

B

S

Your purchase of *OS X Mountain Lion Tips and Tricks* includes access to a free online edition for 45 days through the **Safari Books Online** subscription service. Nearly every Que book is available online through **Safari Books Online**, along with thousands of books and videos from publishers such as Addison-Wesley Professional, Cisco Press, Exam Cram, IBM Press, O'Reilly Media, Prentice Hall, Sams, and VMware Press.

Safari Books Online is a digital library providing searchable, on-demand access to thousands of technology, digital media, and professional development books and videos from leading publishers. With one monthly or yearly subscription price, you get unlimited access to learning tools and information on topics including mobile app and software development, tips and tricks on using your favorite gadgets, networking, project management, graphic design, and much more.

Activate your FREE Online Edition at
informit.com/safarifree

STEP 1: Enter the coupon code: AKZZXYG.

STEP 2: New Safari users, complete the brief registration form.
Safari subscribers, just log in.

If you have difficulty registering on Safari or accessing the online edition,
please e-mail customer-service@safaribooksonline.com